*Promised Land*

NUMBER NINETEEN
Sam Rayburn Series on Rural Life
*Sponsored by Texas A&M University–Commerce*

M. Hunter Hayes, General Editor

# PROMISED LAND

*Solms, Castro & Sam Houston's Colonization Contracts*

JEFFERSON MORGENTHALER

Texas A&M University Press
*College Station*

Texas A&M University Press
College Station

Manufactured in the
United States of America

First edition

This paper meets the requirements
of ANSI/NISO Z39.48-1992
(Permanence of Paper).
Binding materials have been chosen for durability.

Library of Congress Cataloging-in-Publication Data

Morgenthaler, George Jefferson.
Promised land : Solms, Castro, and Sam Houston's colonization contracts / Jefferson Morgenthaler.
p. cm. — (Sam Rayburn series on rural life ; no. 19)
Includes bibliographical references and index.
ISBN-13: 978-1-60344-119-3 (cloth : alk. paper)
ISBN-10: 1-60344-119-0 (cloth : alk. paper) 1. Texas—Colonization—History—19th century. 2. Texas—Emigration and immigration—History—19th century. 3. Germany—Emigration and immigration—History—19th century. 4. France—Emigration and immigration—History—19th century. 5. Solms-Braunfels, Carl, Prinz zu, 1812–1875. 6. Castro, Henri, 1786–1865. 7. Texas—History—Republic, 1836–1846. 8. Adelsverein—History. I. Title. II. Series: Sam Rayburn series on rural life ; no. 19.
F390.M853 2009
325.76409'034—dc22

2009000523

For Jeanne Ann Buchanan:

*She is the reason.*

# Table of Contents

# *Series Editor's Foreword*

Since 1997 an abiding tenet of the Sam Rayburn Series on Rural Life has been to present books of meticulous research that illuminate life—predominantly in the East Texas region—not only as it once was but also as it is. Although the Rayburn Series continues to focus on a wide range of topics centering on the northeast section of the Lone Star State, at times we must stretch the geographical boundaries in order to accommodate pertinent works that examine the forces and individuals that have had an inexorable influence on the people who inhabit the region. Jefferson Morgenthaler's *Promised Land: Solms, Castro, and Sam Houston's Colonization Contracts* is such a book: one that charts the early political, economic, and personal struggles of those with personal and diplomatic interests in Texas while simultaneously reminding readers of the cultural diversity that continues to influence the state and each of its distinct regions.

Although East Texas might be viewed as a quilt stitched from varied social and ethnic fabrics, it likewise contains threads that hold together the entirety of the state. Morgenthaler points out that even as a republic, Texas's debt-ridden economy depended heavily on the cotton and cattle trades, both of which have markedly shaped both the state and region. Still, the republic's economic woes were so dire that they jeopardized Texas's security. While Morgenthaler deserves great credit for his achievement in tracing the mindset of the men responsible for colonizing Texas, as well as for presenting their very thoughts and actions, he also merits appreciation for astutely capturing numerous instances where romanticism and pragmatism collided—forging in the process settlements that would greatly affect Texas history.

Morgenthaler's choice of title is apt, an allusion to a paradox of sorts: a place where the material reality of land deeds meets immaterial aspirations. That this "promised land" served an array of underlying motives held by Europeans such as Solms and Castro and those whose names are perhaps less familiar, notably Saligny and Kennedy, offering them the hope of a personal value beyond sheer currency, indicates the complexities surrounding these settlements. Furthermore, Morgenthaler offers an important reminder that the past serves to elucidate—if not explicate—the present.

It is with sincere pleasure that I welcome Jefferson Morgenthaler and his fine book, *Promised Land,* to the Sam Rayburn Series on Rural Life. *Promised Land* makes a valuable addition to the Rayburn Series, joining others that together represent distinct portions of the region's and state's history and present. Sponsored by Texas A&M University–Commerce under the auspices of Texas A&M University Press at College Station, the Rayburn Series continues to gain many benefits from this partnership, one that would not be possible without the unparalleled efforts of its contributors.

M. Hunter Hayes
General Editor

# *Introduction*

Texian president Sam Houston issued colonization contracts for eleven parcels of land in 1842. The contracts were an element of his four-part plan to stabilize the republic. Houston wanted peace with Mexico, peace with the natives, financing for the republic, and an influx of productive settlers. Whether the fate of the republic was to be independence or annexation, these four accomplishments were key to stability.

Historians have treated the colonization contracts lightly and never adequately explored their causes and consequences. Typically, we mention that Europeans wanted to come to Texas for greater opportunity, which matched nicely with the Texian need for settlers. Then we look separately at the two most obvious results of the contracts: German colonists under the initial direction of Prince Carl of Solms-Braunfels established the cities of New Braunfels and Fredericksburg and the hamlet of Castell; French and German colonists under the direction of Henri Castro founded the Texas towns of Castroville and D'Hanis and the village of Quihi. Except for chronicling the struggles of the colonists, we seldom delve deeper. No one has examined all of the contracts in depth, in context.

On the German colonial side, the definitive treatment is Rudolph Biesele's 1930 *History of the German Settlements in Texas, 1831–1861*. It is a fine work, but it purposely focuses on German Texans, with markedly less consideration of surrounding issues in Texas or of the larger geopolitical issues that impacted Texas. In the course of a meticulous survey of German settlements across the state, colonial and otherwise, Biesele explored only the two colonization contracts that Solms dealt with under the auspices of a German nobles' society known as the Adelsverein. That limitation was consistent with the purpose of the work but left later historians with gaps to fill.

Henri Castro, of the French (and German) colonization, has been studied as another, separate aspect of the 1842 contracts. The most prominent resources dealing with the Castro colony are Julia Nott Waugh's 1934 *Castroville and Henry Castro, Empresario,* and Bobby D. Weaver's 1985 *Castro's Colony: Empresario Development in Texas, 1842–1865*. Waugh's work is a thorough local history, impressively sourced, but—like many local histories—it isolates its subject, taking a somewhat parochial view of a beloved town. Weaver was the first student of the colonization contracts who considered the larger picture. He touched on European involvement in the Republic of Texas, he understood that Castro's contract was part of a larger process, and he recognized the connection and competition between Castro and Solms. But his chosen topic was Castro and his colony, and subsequent historians are again left with substantial room for exploration.

It has been more than seventy-five years since Biesele and Waugh performed their research, and more than twenty since Weaver's. Much new information has surfaced in the interim and—even if that were not the case—there is a significant volume of undigested primary sources that, for whatever reason, weren't included within the scope of the earlier work.

The available information is more than adequate to assemble a full, rich, and compelling story, but the material has never before been analyzed and distilled as an integrated whole. For example, there are well-known primary resources in the Center for American History at the University of Texas (including Castro's Papers, Ferdinand Louis Huth's Papers, and the Solms-Braunfels Archives) and within the Texas State Library and Archives (the colonization papers and executive papers); those materials have been researched before but have never been melded together. Solms's report titled *Texas, 1844–45* has been translated, but only 750 copies were printed in English. Wolfram M. Von-Maszewski rendered an important annotated translation of Solms's Texas diary, and of the parallel diary of Alexander Bourgeois d'Orvanne, under the title *Voyage to North America, 1844–45,* but in its undigested form it is a book by a scholar for scholars.

Insights into the geopolitics surrounding the colonization contracts are best extracted from three formidable academic resources: the three-volume *Texan Diplomatic Correspondence* edited by George P. Garrison, *The French Legation in Texas* in two volumes translated by Nancy Nichols Barker, and the imposing *British Diplomatic Correspondence concerning the Republic of Texas* edited by Ephraim Douglass Adams. In all three cases, the researcher must pick through daunting haystacks to find helpful needles. And one must go further, into eight volumes of *The Writings of Sam Houston* edited by Amelia W. Williams and Eugene C. Barker and the seven-hundred-plus pages of Anson Jones's papers. Then, as every historian knows, it's time to delve into shelves of secondary sources.

And so, five years ago, when I began studying the history of the German settlement of the Texas Hill Country, I discovered that there was a great deal of work left to be done. I felt that some prior authors had established their perspective standing in New Braunfels or Castroville, looking outward at the

Germans and French who came there. Existing studies were largely bottom-up; no significant top-down work had been done.

Many historians have tried to get inside the head of Sam Houston, but none have explored how his colonization contracts fitted into his larger agenda. None have ever looked upon Texas colonization from the distance of London, Paris, or Mainz. None have explained how the contracts fit into an elaborate—and decidedly tense—international minuet over the future of what is now the western United States.

I mentioned earlier that Houston had a four-part plan to stabilize the republic: peace with Mexico, peace with the natives, financing for the republic, and an influx of productive settlers. The obvious purpose of the colonization contracts was to bring settlers to Texas. But there was more. Houston chose frontier lands for the contracts, placing settlers in a position to impede Mexicans and natives, thereby serving two more of his goals. Even more important, the contracts were meant to advance the financial search and the quest for peace, for all but one of the contracts were granted to people who wielded financial or diplomatic clout in Europe.

Europe was more important to Houston's plans than is generally understood. The lingering effects of the Panic of 1837 severely reduced the capacity of U.S. bankers. There was considerable sentiment in the United States for war with Mexico, not peace, and American diplomatic influence in Mexico was negligible. Rather than furthering stability, any involvement by the United States in Texas would reignite volatile questions of annexation versus independence.

Banking circumstances were better in Europe. England and France had invested heavily in Mexico and held considerable sway there. They had a common interest in seeing Mexico and Texas at peace and stable. They wanted a healthy Texas that could block U.S. expansion. Europe was teeming with underclasses that longed to begin new lives across the ocean—an obvious source of settlers.

Houston chose to use his colonization contracts to cement relations with influential Europeans and to foster ties with their governments. He wanted to promote good will among the nations that might deliver financing, peace with Mexico, and settlers for the frontier. He wanted to increase the republic's options by balancing the influence of the United States.

Thus the Texas side of the story—only a part of the picture—begins with diplomatic and financial efforts to preserve the fledgling republic at a time when it suffered a weak economy, potentially fatal political divisions, and a not entirely insubstantial military threat from Mexico. When well-connected Europeans appear in Texas, trailing wisps of financial promise, Sam Houston embraces them and offers them a partnership in the fragile enterprise that is the republic—proffering colonization contracts that can make the recipients wealthy, but only if Texas endures. He gives contracts to men with influence in France, England, Belgium, and Germany—the four most promising banking centers. Houston wants them to bring colonists, but it is even more important that these new empresarios further commercial relationships and common interests with their native lands.

French citizen Henri Castro, already on commission to locate financing for Texas, snatches a colonization contract from the grasp of the French charge d'affaires, incurring the lasting enmity of the French diplomatic corps. Nonetheless, he succeeds in locating a financial backer and begins soliciting colonists. Frenchman Alexander Bourgeois d'Orvanne, also commissioned to search for European financing, receives colonization authority and secures the backing of Solms's Adelsverein. But he flounders, and the Adelsverein shifts its backing to Henry Fisher, who holds a contract for a vast swath of Texas. Belgian diplomat Victor Pirson discards his contract because of an obvious conflict of interest. Suffering a similar conflict, British diplomat William Kennedy transfers his contract to investors, but no colony results.

And so the surviving contracts are soon reduced to two. One is held by Henri Castro. The other is held by the Adelsverein, represented by Prince Carl of Solms-Braunfels. Castro and Solms are very different men with very different purposes. To understand them (and to understand the exodus of Europeans to Texas) requires understanding post-Napoleonic Europe in the midst of a trying transition through the Enlightenment toward romanticism. Understanding Castro and Solms means understanding a bourgeois striver from a land of rising bourgeoisie and an entrenched noble from a reactionary, absolutist state.

Looking from the top down, Solms and Castro are the conclusion, not the genesis, of a story that can be divided into three periods.

First, there are the years before 1842 when Europe—and particularly the Germanic states—undergo dramatic changes that spur interest in emigration and in Texas as a destination. In those same years, while the United States digests Louisiana and eyes the West, Britain and France work unsuccessfully to achieve peace between Texas and Mexico, and Texas searches for European financing.

The second period begins in 1842, when Houston returns to the presidency of the republic. It is during that year that he uses the colonization contracts to advance European relations (and, of course, to bring settlers to Texas). The last, futile attempts at European financing transpire during 1842 and 1843, and the realities of colonization begin to take shape.

The third period is after 1843, as agitation for annexation to the United States begins to rise, as the British and French fret over the importance of an independent Texas (yet do little to ensure its survival), and as Texians become increasingly hostile to European interests. The colonization contracts lose their value for diplomacy and financing and become what they are on paper, nothing more. For the most part, the story becomes one of how Solms and Castro address their contracts and colonists, of how they differ and compete.

The narrative has a zoom-lens quality: beginning with broad international developments, it narrows its focus to the international relations of the republic, then to the loans and colonization contracts, then, as annexation intervenes, to the story of two remarkable individuals striving to make their colonies succeed. In this third, most focused period, Castro tends solely to the mechanics of populating his colony while Solms remains fixed on international intrigue, convinced that Texas retains value as a foil to U.S. expansion. Solms believes that a joint effort between Britain and Germany could preserve Mexico and the West. But most of the geopolitical jostling is in the past, and the story becomes one of the contrasting Castro and Solms, of dreams more than diplomacy. The two men are head-to-head competitors, ultimately struggling for the same lands and the same colonists. They sail on the same ships, meet in the same rooms, and consort with the same people.

There is a contest between the men, but it is a contest that fragments into distractions and departures. Texas, always mercurial, turns its back on colonization. The United States annexes; Texas consents. The Adelsverein collapses. Castro, inconstant and unreliable, runs aground. The two leaders' endings turn out to be as different as their origins. Ultimately, the winds of history sweep away an intense time of grand schemes and broken dreams, leaving only a few Texas towns and some bundles of papers to mark yet another moment when men defied impossibility.

*Promised Land*

CHAPTER ONE

# *Context*

In 1821, German writer J. Valentin Hecke penned *Travels through the United States of North America.* That account of a journey through the West was most complimentary to Texas. Here is how Hecke phrased his praise:

> If there is a land on the trans-Atlantic continent favorable as a colonial possession for Prussia, it is the province of Texas, the acquisition of which by purchase from Spain, to which it is neither of use nor political advantage, might be very easily made. . . . Although at present there is no, or very little, civilized population in that country, in a short time it would become a flourishing colony if Prussia would make use of the emigrants from Germany who, having become beggars through the expense of their voyage and lack of employment, suffer wretchedly in the United States. The Prussian government should furnish them free transportation to Texas on Prussian ships and either give them land gratuitously or grant them support, if only by advantaged payments.[1]

After Hecke penned his ideas, Spain had departed the continent, leaving Mexico poorer, weaker, and even less able to nurture and protect Texas. Then the Texians had asserted their independence from Mexico, making Texas' situation even more precarious.

The United States had pushed its legitimate territorial claims as far west as Louisiana, which France had won from Spain in the Napoleonic Wars then sold to the United States three years later. In the nineteenth century, the most valuable part of Louisiana was New Orleans and the right bank of the lower Mississippi River—and that is why the state of Louisiana is where it is today—but the territory was an immense blob that began at the Canadian border and tapered down to today's Louisiana. Bounded on the east by the Mississippi River, it extended to the Rocky Mountains on the west, overlapping parts of northeast Texas and its panhandle. These were the lands that would become Arkansas, Missouri, Iowa, the Dakotas, Oklahoma, Kansas, Wyoming, Montana, and parts of Texas, Minnesota, Colorado, and New Mexico.

Beyond Louisiana, what remained between today's Mexico and Canada boiled down to the Oregon territory (claimed by Britain and the United States), California and New Mexico (owned legitimately if impotently by Mexico), and Texas (which tenuously claimed independence from an adamantly opposed Mexico).

The 1840s fell within the period of Jacksonian democracy, the era that birthed the notion of "manifest destiny." It is mostly forgotten that the term originated not with Jackson, and not during his term as president, but with the journalist John L. O'Sullivan. In a July 1845 essay penned for his New York magazine, the United States Democratic Review, O'Sullivan wrote of "our manifest destiny to overspread the continent allotted by Providence for the free development of our yearly multiplying millions." In that particular essay, O'Sullivan was not arguing that the United States should advance to the Pacific. He wanted the United States to finalize the annexation of Texas.[2]

Within the United States there were two schools of thought about Texas. One believed that annexation was a bad idea because it would mean war with Mexico. The other believed that annexation was a good idea because it would mean war with Mexico.

For the United States, war with Mexico was an obvious and advantageous route to the Pacific Ocean. The Oregon Territory offered access to the Pacific, but with a fraction of the coastline of California and with Great Britain standing in the way. Conflict with Mexico might offer a bonus: pushing Mexico only two hundred miles south of the Rio Grande would change ownership of the rich silver mines of Chihuahua, Coahuila, and Durango.

The Republic of Texas claimed everything to the Rio Grande. Texians were acutely aware that the Rio Grande was not merely a southern border; upstream from El Paso the river curves to the north, reaching far into New Mexico. Santa Fe—and its rich mines—were inside the curve of the Rio Grande. Mexico argued—in a historically accurate way—that the boundaries of Spanish and Mexican Texas had never extended beyond the Nueces River, far to the north and east of the Rio Grande. If the United States annexed the Texian version of Texas, a Mexican conflagration would be virtually certain.

Mexico's army was not to be ignored, but Mexico was entangled in the internal power struggles that always seemed to swirl around Santa Anna. The nation was buried in debt to France and Britain—so much so that war with France had briefly broken out in 1838. Rebellions—first in northern Mexico, then in the Yucatan—sapped what strength it had. And Mexico had only the faintest whisper of a navy. It was so weak at sea that in 1843 Texas' two-ship comic-opera navy battled the Mexican fleet to a standstill, at least until Texas president Sam Houston declared his own navy to be pirates, prompting their return to Galveston to make amends.

Texas had always been at the farthest limits of Mexican military power. Even the Spanish had never been able to penetrate more than briefly beyond San Antonio. Missions and presidios farther north and farther east had failed. Between the settled portions of Texas and the centers of Mexico's population and economy lay vast swaths of unpopulated desert. Effectively, there were only two roads from central Mexico into central Texas. One crossed the Rio Grande at Guerrero (then also called Presidio), the other at Laredo. Both proceeded north to San Antonio, then headed east, into territory where Spain had failed to establish a permanent presence and where Mexico ventured only when challenged.[3]

On the Gulf, Galveston had been a Mexican port of entry since 1825. It was accessible by a coastal road and offered access to river valleys to the north, but Mexico so lacked the ability to defend Galveston that during the Texas rebellion it served as the home port for the first Texas navy. The Texas rebels captured Santa Anna at San Jacinto (within easy reach of Galveston) in part because Mexico lacked the infrastructure and money to project dominant force to that distance for any significant length of time. After Texas declared independence, Mexico's only material refutations of that status were the 1841 capture of a seriously misguided expedition to Santa Fe and two brief, symbolic captures of San Antonio in 1842.

Texas itself was in little better shape. At independence, its population was only about 35,000 Anglos and Tejanos. It had a debt of $1.25 million that ballooned to more than $8 million by the time Sam Houston began his second presidency in late 1841. Texas claimed more than 250 million acres of land, but it completely lacked cities, much less industry. Most of Texas was unsettled and in the firm control of Comanches and other aggressive natives. Everything along the Rio Grande was subject to constant Mexican threat. The miniscule Texas economy was almost entirely dependent upon cattle and cotton. Imports chronically exceeded exports, draining the supply of gold and silver. Outside of settlements at such places as Galveston, Houston, Velasco, Washington, Victoria, Goliad, Nacogdoches, and San Antonio—none of which had more than two or three thousand people, and some of which had a tenth of that—the economy was based on barter and credit, without currency or coin.

Texas was a land of speculation, and nothing was a greater subject of speculation than the land itself. Believing its supply of real estate to be virtually inexhaustible, and lacking any other collateral, Texas turned time and again to its land to raise money and to attract industrious settlers. Heads of families residing in Texas before the revolution were granted a certificate that could be used to claim a league and a labor (about 4,500 acres) of land, without any requirement that they ever occupy the tract. Subsequent grant programs gave certificates for up to 1,280 acres to a head of family but required the landowner to live in Texas for at least three years. Texas revolution veterans were treated the same as prerevolution residents. If a soldier was disabled or fought at San Jacinto, Matamoros, or Goliad, additional grants were available. More people sold their land grant certificates than converted them into land. Land speculators made a tidy business of buying up certificates for pennies and sending teams of armed surveyors beyond the frontier to locate and claim prime tracts.

At a time when public land in the United States sold for $1.25 per acre, Texas offered land scrip (certificates that could be used to claim Texas public lands) at fifty cents per acre. But the speculative traffic in scrip—and in counterfeit scrip—was more active than the actual sale of land. When an individual scrip holder did decide to buy land, he often found that the cost of locating, surveying, and obtaining title to a small tract was prohibitive—and that available land was too far away from settlements to be occupied or defended. Again, speculators stepped into the picture, agglomerating certificates and acquiring hundreds of thousands of acres of land with no intention of occupation. The value of land scrip—and of land—plummeted as speculation gyrated and counterfeiting increased.[4]

Sam Houston, the first elected president of the republic, was a realist who sought annexation to the United States at the beginning. But the initial overtures of Texas were rebuffed. Houston was prohibited by the Texas constitution from succeeding himself; Mirabeau B. Lamar became the second president. Lamar was intent upon the independence of Texas and opposed annexation. He ran up additional debt of almost $5 million pursuing aggressive policies toward the natives and the Mexican government.

Lamar may not have been the most thoughtful president, but he knew he had to increase the population and productivity of Texas for it to survive. Anglo-Americans had first settled in Texas in 1820 under Spanish land grants, but the greatest early influx came under later Mexican colonization laws that were meant to populate the frontier, defend it for Mexico, and generate income for the nation. The problems that had faced Mexico in the

1820s were not entirely unlike those that faced Texas in 1840, thus similar solutions came readily to mind.

In February 1841, the Texas Congress authorized the president to bring in settlers through a colonization contract with a group headed by William Peters, who commenced looking for financial backing in London. The Peters Colony was a business venture, uncomplicated by political considerations. It limped along for seven years and clouded North Texas land titles for another twenty.[5]

At about the same time that the Congress approved the Peters plan, it authorized six men, including Arthur Ikin, the Texian consul at London, to form the Texas Trading, Mining and Emigrating Company, purchase land in its name, and bring in emigrants to form a colony. The company was even authorized to raise a militia of three hundred men. The scheme did not turn out well. Ikin arranged to bring over a group of English settlers to occupy land that he purchased for $50,000 through John Woodward, Texian consul general at Boston. When the immigrants arrived and tried to take possession of their land, they discovered that their titles were fraudulent. The Texian government had to bail out Ikin, who had been defrauded by Woodward, and ended up making land grants to the immigrants. This small incident did nothing to dull the speculative interest in Texas land.[6]

When John Tyler became president of the United States upon the post-inaugural and pneumonial death of William Henry Harrison, the United States' mood about annexation changed. Tyler, like his principal political opponent, James Polk, favored annexation. But there were entrenched northern interests in the U.S. Congress that opposed admission of slave-holding Texas, and Texas under Lamar was not seeking to join the Union.

Houston returned to the Texas presidency in December 1841; his interest in a relationship with the United States was tempered by experience. He did not underestimate the obstacles that abolitionists would place before Texas statehood. A master of the possible, Houston recognized population, peace, and stability as essential to the prosperity of Texas. He knew that if war broke out again—whether with Mexico or anyone else—he could raise an army only by inviting in the rough, undisciplined, southern soldiers of fortune who had flooded Texas during the revolution and displayed a marked disinclination to submit to authority. It had taken years to flush the worst of them from the state after the revolution, and Houston—a man who lamented his own republic as a "mobocracy"—did not welcome the idea of their return.[7]

And so Houston embarked on a policy of fiscal restraint, careful diplomacy, a watchful engagement with the United States, and encouragement of organized settlement. He found himself sometimes frustrated by the decisions of the erratic and emotional Texas Congress. Some argue that his singular goal remained annexation, but his conduct of policy suggests an effort to balance the interests of Texas, play its suitors and enemies skillfully, and keep all options open. Houston meant to shepherd Texas to stability, in whatever form that might take.

Houston's task was made more difficult by Houston. He was a controversial and divisive figure. He was drunk and thoughtful, violent and peaceful, avaricious and generous, predatory and conciliatory, flamboyant and conservative.

But, as contradictory and inscrutable as Houston was, he was no fool. He understood that there were more than Texas, Mexico, and the United States involved in the minuet for possession of the West. There is an old expression to the effect that, if you dig yourself deep enough into debt, your banker becomes your partner; Houston knew that Mexico had achieved just that status with France and Britain, who found themselves with a large and risky stake in the Mexican economy. Beyond government-backed loans, French and British banks and citizens had made substantial investments in Mexico, investments that would be imperiled by war with Texas or the United States.

Despite Mexican chest thumping, most observers considered the independence of Texas a fait accompli; recognizing that reality, France and Britain had chosen neutrality between Texas and Mexico, but it was a meddling sort of neutrality that would not brook disruptive behavior by either side. Their policies recognized that a healthy Mexico could be a good continental counterweight to the aggressive United States, but there were also benefits to be had from a sustainable, independent Texas. Britain needed Texas cotton to feed its booming mills. Texas created price competition with the United States and offered relief from high U.S. tariffs. France felt that it could obtain trade concessions with Texas that it did not enjoy with the United States. And, from the outset, a duplicitously neutral France eyed the silver mines in Chihuahua and at Santa Fe, both within striking range of Texas.

Both countries strongly opposed U.S. expansion to the Pacific, which would completely upset the global balance of power. And both recognized that an independent Texas was, in any of several scenarios, the key to keeping California within Mexico's dominion. Texas could buffer manifest destiny's reach for Mexican territory to the west—or, in a less desirable outcome, could seize the territory for itself. So long as Texas remained independent, the United States was stymied and Mexico was protected.

Faced with European resistance to its ambitions, the United States calculated and recalculated its position. It made clear that it would tolerate no foreign intervention in the future of Texas—as if France and Britain were somehow more foreign to the Republic of Texas than was the United States. Annexation languished in a U.S. Congress that was more concerned about the balance between free and slave states than about geopolitics, and that was inclined to let matters simmer a while longer. A pause of twenty-five years in the nation's inexorable spread westward would, in a century or two, mean nothing.

Notably low-profile in this mix was Germany. Fragmented, introverted, and obsessed with Russia and France, Germany had never been a player in North American colonization. Even if it sensed opportunity in the complex political mix that centered on Texas, it was no longer the time to consider Hecke's plan of buying the whole place and turning it into a German colony.

Ultimately, it would be the United States that would determine the future of Texas, with France and England ineffectively proffering alternatives. Before that outcome was known, Houston would dangle colonization contracts before representatives of England, France, Germany, and Belgium. Among Houston's targets, it would turn out to be only France and Germany that would engage.

France was a center of liberal thinking. Dating back a century to the rationalist ideas of Rene Descartes, French philosophers and social theorists emphasized reason and rationalism in the workings of society and challenged the primacy of both church and state. It was French thought that spearheaded the Enlightenment. Jean-Jacques Rousseau—perhaps most famous for articulating the idea of a "social contract"—posited that social conditions, including the concept of private property, led to inequality and oppression. Claude Henri de Saint-Simon, Charles Fourier, and Étienne Cabet began the utopian movement that became socialism. It was Cabet who coined the word communisme, later adopted by Karl Marx. The thinkers of the French Enlightenment opened the door to the French Revolution of 1789, secularization of the state, the end of the feudal order, and a succession of other liberalizing movements.

Napoleon spent more than twenty years attempting to spread French liberalism, and French power, across Europe. His last attempt was in 1815, after escaping exile on the island of Elba. He was defeated and reexiled to the island of St. Helena in the South Atlantic. The Congress of Vienna convened to draw a new map of Europe. In the course of that realignment, the congress reduced more than three hundred small Germanic states to just thirty-nine and placed them in a German Confederation that included large parts of Austria and Prussia.

Recoiling from the excesses of the French Revolution, reeling from the Napoleonic Wars, resentful of years of French dominance and occupation, and influenced by the absolutism of post-Enlightenment thinkers such as Kant and Hegel, Germany after the Conference of Vienna undertook a restoration of the old order. The dominant figure in this process was Prince Klemens von Metternich, an astute diplomat and politician who led Emperor Francis's Austria and the German Confederation. Metternich was a realist, an absolutist, and an unshakeable conservative.[8]

Liberal intelligentsia and university students fostered ongoing resistance to the Metternichian absolute states. In those quarters, romantic ideals, nationalist aspirations, and concern for the rights of the individual thrived. The academic community remained under the influence of the French Enlightenment, tempered by post-Enlightenment romanticism; they proclaimed that republics, not princes, were the state of the future, and that the German heritage must be united in a single nation. Liberals voiced demands for parliamentary restraints on absolute monarchs, constitutional government, universal rights to private property, freedom of the press, extinction of the last elements of feudal law, and a unified German state. In response, Metternich imposed waves of repressive measures, which were met with demonstrations and riots.

Unrest in Germany during the 1830s and 1840s was not only a matter of politics and philosophy. The urban proletariat and the rural peasantry each independently chafed at their circumstance. Ironically, their troubles stemmed from economic and social modernization that proceeded alongside reactionary restoration of absolute governments. Restoration of the German monarchies did not mean restoration of pure absolutism and the feudal order; it meant restoration of at least partially enlightened absolutism within at least partially modernized states. Germany had been proceeding toward that condition, albeit more slowly than other European nations, since the eighteenth century.

As had always been the case, the goal of states large and small was simple: survival and, if possible, expansion. Since the Enlightenment, the process by which one state eclipsed another was, beneath the armies and battles, modernization—achievement of agricultural, industrial, social, and governmental efficiencies that increased nations' revenues and strengthened their armies. Agricultural reform. Industrialization. Professional bureaucracies. Capitalism. Deconstruction of the feudal order.

Learning from the French model, many German rulers realized that feudal social and legal structures reduced the competitiveness of the state. Peasants could be more productive when released from the strictures of serfdom. Crop yields increased when families worked their own land or paid rents in a set amount of cash rather than a burdensome percentage of the crop. Manufacturing blossomed when rigid guild rules, timetables, and quotas for apprentices, journeymen, and masters were relaxed. Permitting urban dwellers to seek their fortunes as they wished spawned new businesses. And better working and living conditions, along with better medical practice and access, made for a stronger, healthier, longer-lived rural peasantry more fit to work the fields and serve in the army.

In both reactionary Germany and liberal France, enlightened changes wrought for the common good often adversely affected one or another set of individuals. The landed nobles were obviously disinclined to accept changes in the legal and economic relationships between them and their serfs. Guild orders justifiably felt threatened by changes in artisans' rights. Dividing land—especially feudal common land—among peasants in need of money only set the stage for acquisitive nobles and upwardly mobile peasants to corner the supply of agricultural resources. As generations of small landowners passed, estates were divided among heirs into smaller and smaller parcels, soon becoming incapable of supporting a family.[9]

Increasing agricultural efficiency reduced the need for rural labor. Machines and factories displaced urban workers. Greater mobility allowed peasants to flood the cities and immigrant skilled workers to displace traditional artisans. Increases in lifespan caused populations to increase without concomitant job growth. Peasants and proles became paupers.

On both sides of the Rhine, modernization of agriculture and industry was essential to growth and strength, but it came at the expense of peasants and workers—classes that ironically suffered immensely by the removal of their chains. Pauperization became so extreme that the most affected states encouraged their poor to emigrate to other territories, shifting troubles elsewhere. Members of the confederation began restricting immigration and internal migration while encouraging emigration of the poor across the ocean to the fledgling United States.

It was a confounding time of conservatism and liberalism, the old order and the new, economic advancement and surging poverty, revolutions gone wrong and monarchs restored, enlightened rule and military might, romantic notions and hard-edged reality.

CHAPTER 2

# *France Meets Texas*

We can imagine Alphonse Dubois de Saligny fanning the aroma of the coffee to his nose. He had come to enjoy the tangy chicory, and he had especially come to enjoy New Orleans. He was spending a few days there, having traveled in the company of Sam Houston. Saligny—the French chargé d'affaires to Texas—remained in New Orleans while Houston continued on to Marion, Alabama, for his marriage to Margaret Lea.

Saligny was holding a letter from James Hamilton, a former governor of South Carolina now serving Texas president Mirabeau Lamar, charged with securing financing for the republic. Hamilton was an intelligent and cultured man, knowledgeable about Europe and Europeans. Saligny, who had met Hamilton in Paris and Austin, considered him "one of the warmest and most sincere friends of France."[1]

On that cool May morning in 1840, Saligny unfolded the missive that Hamilton had penned from Charleston on his way back to Europe. The letter made an interesting, bold proposal: if France could arrange a $5 million loan to Texas, the Texians would be only too glad to invest a sizeable portion of the money in capturing Santa Fe and turning over its silver mines to French management. Texas and France would split the earnings. After some consideration, Saligny recommended the venture to his foreign minister.

This was not the first time that Saligny had suggested backing Texian aggression against Mexico; In 1839, while France was still at war with Mexico over debt repayment, he had opined that, instead of landing French troops in Mexico, "an offensive by the Texians, supported by a few French arms and munitions supplied to them on credit, [would] be the better and safer way to bring them to terms."[2]

Once peace renewed between France and Mexico, however, the French adopted a policy of strict neutrality between Mexico and Texas. Nonetheless, Saligny inquired of his foreign minister, "I am well aware, Monsieur le Marechal, of the obligations incumbent on a nation toward a friendly people; and I also know that our particular position with regard to Mexico is somewhat delicate. But are there not circumstances in which the strictures of the laws of neutrality may be relaxed?"[3]

Saligny saw Texas as "an insurmountable barrier between the United States and Mexico." He believed that the Mexican republic was doomed and was certain "to be conquered by the Anglo-American race, but it will not go to add new stars to the federal flag." Texas—not the United States—would soon occupy as much of Mexico as it chose. Saligny calculated the chances of U.S. annexation as slight.[4]

Saligny had great faith in James Hamilton, saluting "the high repute in which he is held in the United States, the influence he exerts in the South, and the zeal with which from the first he took up the cause of Texas." At the outset, he was confident that Hamilton would succeed in his loan negotiations. But as spring turned to summer, then approached fall, Saligny became concerned. Hamilton had spent more time than Saligny liked talking to the English about loans, leaving him to wonder whether Hamilton had forgotten about the Santa Fe proposal.[5]

Hamilton's search for financing was not made easier in October, when Texas representative James Treat, after almost a year working under British mediation to negotiate peace with Mexico, was finally rejected. A formal state of war resumed, making a loan nearly impossible. The grim symbolism of Treat's death on the voyage home from Mexico had not escaped Saligny.[6]

Despite the state of war, Hamilton had managed to open negotiations with J. Laffitte & Co. for the $5 million loan. The French bankers would almost certainly insist on a French endorsement of Texas and might expect greater French involvement there before they committed funds. A well-connected Frenchman named Henri Castro had introduced Hamilton to the house of Laffitte and was facilitating the negotiations; Hamilton had appointed Castro an agent of the republic to sell lands and to foster the formation of colonization companies.[7]

In Texas, French chargé Saligny enjoyed the Austin spotlight and began to put down French roots. After staying a few days at Austin's primitive Bullock House inn, he had rented a somewhat better abode while he built a proper residence for the French legation. When finished, it would be a fine structure, one and one-half stories, with three dormer windows jutting above a covered porch. A mix of Greek Revival and Mississippi Valley French architecture, it was being built on a substantial foundation with a proper frame and milled siding, not the crude logs that characterized most structures in Austin. It would be the first suitable diplomatic residence in Texas, if only the nagging construction delays would cease.[8]

The French foreign ministry instructed Saligny to be circumspect about the Santa Fe adventure, calling it "extremely delicate. Since the agreement by which Texas would be obligated to share the produce of those mines with France would be contingent upon the conquest of the province where they are situated, this arrangement would fundamentally compromise our neutrality with regard to Mexico." But, the French foreign minister concluded, "I have nothing but praise for your idea of associating France and Texas in a joint venture to engage in the rich trade with Santa Fe, thereby forestalling the Americans, if the realization is practicable." Saligny had secured official approval of his scheme.[9]

In January 1841 he persuaded Congressman James Mayfield to introduce colonization legislation. Avoiding official French involvement, Saligny's Franco-Texian Bill named private citizens Jean Basterreche and Pierre Lassaulx as empresarios charged with bringing eight thousand French colonists to Texas. The colonists would build twenty forts within a three-million-acre grant scattered along the length of the Rio Grande—the western border that was claimed and coveted by Texas and hotly disputed by Mexico. The French and Texians would take Santa Fe, snatch the mines, and control commerce between there and Chihuahua. In return, the French colony would be exempt from import duties for twenty years, would have rights to all mines within the colonial lands (subject to a 15 percent Texas royalty), and would have exclusive trading privileges with northern Mexico.[10]

Passage of the bill would have a salutary impact on Texas' relationship with France. It was precisely what was needed to pave the way for Hamilton's $5 million loan. With eight thousand Frenchmen planted in Texas, with French domination of a critical Mexican trade route, France would quickly extend even greater support to Texas, and the European financial community would take an entirely new view of its prospects—especially once the republic had cash flow from French-operated mines in newly fortified Far-West Texas.

Although the colonization contract was to be given to Basterreche and Lassaulx, no one in Austin or Paris misunderstood the interest of the French government in the project. It was a lightly camouflaged effort to prevent annexation of Texas and maneuver armed, fortified French communities between the United States and Texas to the east and Mexico and California to the west. To ensure France's ability to secure the new bulwarks, the bill provided that no other colonization was to be permitted in western Texas for twenty years. But some Texians harbored doubts about the wisdom of conceding such a position of strength to the French.

James Mayfield repeatedly argued for the bill on the floor of the house, but an unusual problem emerged: Sam Houston agreed with Mayfield, supporting the measure. Mayfield was a member of the anti-Houston camp and, as politics worked then and now, the two factions were not supposed to agree on anything. The division between the two groups was not a matter of arcane policy differences. It was more of a virulent, vitriolic, libelous, elbow-jabbing, fist-swinging barroom brawl.

The Texas Congress had been in session for two months, mired in partisan bickering between the Lamar-Burnet camp and Houston's followers. Finally, the Franco-Texian Bill worked its way through the House of Representatives and reached the Senate, but not without James Mayfield turning on his own bill in denunciation. Mayfield claimed that he had come to realize that the bill was "the result of a plot contrived by His Majesty the King of the French and General Houston through the intermediacy of the French chargé d'affaires designed to deliver up Texas to France, who would make it into a kingdom for one of the sons of the King." To the shocked Saligny, it was obvious that Mayfield's change of heart had only to do with opposition to anything supported by Houston.[11]

Factionalism raged. Saligny heard accusations that he somehow had a personal financial interest in the colonies. Acting president Burnet threatened to veto the bill should it pass.

On February 3, the Senate tabled the bill, then adjourned. To add insult to injury, two weeks later Burnet rewarded James Mayfield with the office of secretary of state. Saligny was now obliged to conduct his nation's affairs with a turncoat who had undermined his project, his credibility, and surely the French foreign minister's view of his effectiveness.

Saligny sat in his small rented house, mulling this frustrating turn of events. It did not reflect well on him. The dapper, demanding, precise, and sometimes petulant Frenchman had never complained to Paris, but the conditions in the Texian capital, and the condition of the Texians, had never been to his liking. This latest frustration only confirmed his perception of the locals as shortsighted, rough, aggressive, shallow rabble who descended quickly into contentious rivalries at the expense of the interests of their state.

Despite his humble origins, Saligny felt himself above such senseless pushing and shoving. Born Jean Pierre Isidore Alphonse Dubois in 1809, he was the son of a Caen tax collector. He had adopted the noble-sounding surname "de Saligny" precisely to illustrate his commitment to the genteel and sophisticated world of diplomacy. He was proud and sensitive. This was his first important post; until the previous year he had served as secretary to the French plenipotentiary in Washington, D.C. He accepted that he would have to work his way up the diplomatic ladder, but he still chafed at being assigned to Austin, so far from civilization that even Sam Houston openly doubted that it could be defended against Comanches or the Mexican army.[12]

There had been no Austin a year earlier. When the Congress finally decided on a permanent site for a capital, surveyors and carpenters headed to the Colorado River to hack a town out of the woods. The streets were horse-trampled mud. The capitol itself was nothing more than a hastily built, still-unfinished one-story wood-frame building. The best hotel in town was the pitiful Bullock House, a log lodge where Saligny had been obliged to stay for a few nights. The proprietor of the inn, Richard Bullock, was a crude bully by Saligny's measure. There had been a dispute over Bullock's charges for lodging and services.

Saligny glanced out the window. The garden fence was intact. That was good. Bullock allowed his pigs to run loose in the muddy streets of Austin, and they had repeatedly broken down the fence to eat vegetables and flowers. On one occasion, Saligny had returned home to find the swine inside the house, happily munching his bed linens.

Saligny regretted it, but there had been no choice: he directed his servant, Eugene Pluyette, to exterminate the half-wild pigs if they approached his property. Pluyette did well, sending more than a dozen of the offenders to an unhappy end. Bullock would be angry, but Bullock was no friend of Saligny and, between Saligny's diplomatic immunity and his connections at the highest levels, there was nothing that Bullock could do, except keep his livestock in their pens. No one would trifle with the representative of the king of France.

These may have been Saligny's thoughts as Eugene Pluyette came through the door, bloody and beaten.

Walking down the road, Pluyette had been spotted by Richard Bullock. Bullock believed—correctly—that Pluyette had killed a number of his pigs. Intent on engaging in battle, Bullock first softened up his target with bombardment—that is, he threw stones at Pluyette. Then, while "making use of all kinds of menaces and atrocious imprecations" (as Saligny later put it), he grabbed a stick, closed in, and commenced thrashing Pluyette. The Frenchman managed to escape, but Bullock followed and jumped him again. Extricating himself, Pluyette dashed home.

Saligny wrote a letter protesting the attack, which he saw as an insult to the French diplomatic mission. He claimed injury under international law. He demanded redress. Of course, the protests, claims, and demands were submitted to Saligny's new enemy, Texas secretary of state James Mayfield. Rather than visiting the French chargé to discuss his concerns, Mayfield replied the next day with a long, formal, floral letter that in substance said little more than that the district attorney would look into it.

Saligny did not want justice from the district attorney. He wanted Bullock's head, and he likely wanted Mayfield's, too. In a letter the next day, he couched his desires in terms of the necessity of redress under international law, not municipal ordinances.

From there matters deteriorated into daily letters, disputes over diplomatic minutiae, quarrels over passport etiquette, and refusals to submit to Texas jurisdiction. Letters became longer and insults more apparent. Saligny began using phrases such as "slanderous libel" and "tribe of savages." On March 31, Saligny advised Mayfield that he was suspending all relations with Texas. He withdrew to Houston, then Galveston. In May, Mayfield asked the Texas representative at the court of France to request that Saligny be instructed to leave Texas. By June 1841, Saligny was back in New Orleans.[13]

In France, against steep odds, James Hamilton and Henri Castro were still trying to place the $5 million loan. But the project had stalled. That may have had something to do with the fact that Saligny's brother-in-law served as the French minister of finance. Hamilton needed France. If Hamilton and Castro could obtain a guarantee from the French government, the loan that they were trying to obtain from Laffitte & Co. would be at a most favorable rate and Laffitte would have no difficulty finding the necessary investors. Otherwise, it would "approximate more nearly to the credit of the Government of Texas," and subscribers might be scarce. To seek the guarantee, Hamilton had to negotiate with Francois Guizot, Saligny's immediate superior and reliable supporter. It would be awkward.[14]

In May 1841, Hamilton was still upbeat about the Laffitte loan, but he was traveling from London to Paris to "set all things right." In July, while Hamilton was again in London, he saw an article in a Paris newspaper to the effect that a squadron of French brigs was set to sail for Texas and settle Saligny's Pig War. He rushed to Paris, where he happily discovered that the Texas chargé d'affaires, George McIntosh, had calmed the waters at the foreign ministry, removing any risk of a French demonstration of naval might.

Hamilton and Castro pushed forward on the Laffitte loan, expecting that the bankers could find enough subscribers by September. But Franco-Texian relations were still strained; in that month McIntosh formally requested the recall of Saligny. France refused. Ironically, in that same month the Texas department of state concluded that it was so impecunious that it could not pay McIntosh's expenses without the Laffitte loan. Hamilton continued to work with the French but broadened his efforts with the English, Dutch, and Belgians.

September brought more bad news. In June, President Lamar had dispatched fifty civilian traders and 270 armed escorts to Santa Fe. Lamar wanted to demonstrate that Texas could exert its will to the far western border that it claimed, and he believed that the citizens of Santa Fe could be persuaded to join the Texas cause. Unfortunately, Lamar had signaled his move more than a year earlier. He had published an open letter to the citizens of Santa Fe, advising them that the United States and France had recognized Texas and alerting them that he would send a commission to express the republic's best wishes. As the Santa Fe expedition neared its destination, having struggled across hundreds of miles of desert without any clear sense of direction, its members found that New Mexico governor Manuel Armijo had arranged for detachments of Mexican soldiers to greet them. The Texians surrendered without a fight and were marched to prison in Mexico.

The Texian Santa Fe expedition did nothing to raise the republic's stature in Europe. By the end of the year the Laffitte loan had disintegrated and Hamilton was trying to locate funds in Belgium.

In December 1841, Sam Houston succeeded David Burnet as president of Texas. The republic was in chaos. The Franco-Texian Bill had collapsed, along with French relations. Saligny was still in New Orleans, fuming. The Santa Fe expedition was in Mexican prisons. Lamar and Burnet had run up huge debts attacking Indians and menacing Mexico. Castro had not been able to cement a deal with Laffitte & Co. Hamilton's loan efforts looked futile. To make matters worse, one of the Texas Congress's first acts in 1842 was to revoke the authorization for the $5 million loan, ensuring that Houston would face a financial crisis. Defrocked, James Hamilton sailed for Texas with Henry Castro. They had to pay their own passage, because Texas lacked the necessary funds.[15]

CHAPTER 3

# *The Colonization Contracts*

As Sam Houston went about trying to clean up the mess left him, Saligny—still ensconced in New Orleans—was certain that reconciliation with the French was high on the agenda. He was pleased to report to his foreign minister that the Franco-Texian Bill had been reintroduced in the Texas House of Representatives. But the measure was quickly voted down because Basterreche and Lassaulx had long since returned to France.

On January 16, Saligny received two welcome visitors: James Hamilton and Henri Castro, who were on their way to Texas from Europe, where they had worked together on the Laffitte & Co. financing. Castro, it turned out, had been authorized to represent Basterreche and Lassaulx on the Franco-Texian Bill. Or so Saligny pronounced; the timing appears most fortuitous. Castro continued on his way to Austin with letters of introduction from Saligny, and Saligny was hopeful.

Having left the table before the game was over, Saligny had no alternative but to trust Castro as his proxy in Austin, even though he knew little of the man.

Born in 1786, at Saint-Esprit in the department of Landes, France, Castro was a descendant of Portuguese Jews who had fled the Spanish Inquisition. The Castros were affluent but of course not noble, though they could trace their roots to Juan de Castro, the fourth viceroy of the Portuguese Indies, and to his father, the civil governor of Lisbon. Henri Castro served in Napoleon's army, entering Spain in the emperor's guard of honor and later battling to defend Paris from invading forces in the last struggles of 1814.

In 1827, perhaps because he had married an Italian woman, perhaps because he traveled in the right circles, he was appointed vice-consul for the Kingdom of Naples at the port of Providence, Rhode Island. He promptly adopted American citizenship. Later, he represented French foreign minister Francois Guizot's personal commercial interests in Louisiana. After returning to France in 1838, he became associated with the prominent French banking house of J. Laffitte & Co., a connection that he had used to seek the $5 million loan.[1]

Castro's situation would not have been possible without the liberalization of France. Born a Jew and far removed from the advantages of nobility, his ability to climb the social and economic ladder would have been severely constrained in other societies. Fortunately for him, opportunities in Texas were even more available than in the most liberal quarters of France. He had no difficulty linking to Hamilton, no difficulty escorting Hamilton through the halls of French finance, and no difficulty forging a sudden relationship with Alphonse Dubois de Saligny.

By mid-February, Saligny learned that Castro had been well received in Austin, though the legislative session had been too far along to allow passage of the Franco-Texian Bill. (In fact, the Texas Congress was quarrelling constantly with President Houston and remained hostile to France; the Franco-Texian Bill was an unlikely candidate for passage, regardless of timing.) Saligny nonetheless had some good news about Castro for his foreign minister: "Acting on the advice that I had given him, he hopes to be able to achieve the same end by another means and to obtain from the government a concession that will be the complete equivalent of the project presented last year by Messrs. Basterreche and de Lassaulx."

Saligny did report one disturbing development. An Englishman named William Kennedy was in Austin. Though Kennedy "has no official status, he is performing some kind of mission for the British government whose purpose is unknown." Kennedy, who had been to Texas before, had recently published a book titled *The Rise, Progress and Prospects of the Republic of Texas.* Saligny described it as "of little merit, as it is merely a compilation of unreliable recommendations." As yet, there was no official British representative in Texas; Great Britain was withholding that move until a set of three treaties had been ratified by a reluctant Texas Senate. Kennedy was the closest to an official visitor as was appropriate under the circumstances.[2]

William Kennedy was then a forty-four-year-old Irishman. Born in Dublin, schooled as a journalist, he moved to London, where he worked on literary projects and served as a secretary. In 1838 he traveled to Canada as secretary to the Earl of Durham, who was researching British policy considerations in the commonwealth. Kennedy spent the next year crossing the United States and its frontier, gathering material for the book that Saligny so disparaged. In late 1841 he approached British foreign minister George Hamilton Gordon, the fourth Earl of Aberdeen, to offer his services as an informal British representative in Texas. He cautioned Lord Aberdeen that Houston's election to his second presidency might lead to passage of the "mischievous" Franco-Texian Bill. His repeated applications to Aberdeen finally resulted in approval for an unofficial visit to Texas. He left London and reached Galveston on January 9, 1842, just as new Texas president Sam Houston was settling into power.[3]

It took no time for Kennedy to be swept up in Texas factionalism. On January 28 he advised Aberdeen that James Hamilton's influence was completely spent, and that he would have no further diplomatic role. Unbeknownst to Kennedy, a week earlier Hamilton had written Aberdeen from Galveston, calling Kennedy "utterly unworthy of Your Lordship's confidence." In a second missive to the British foreign minister, Hamilton complained of Kennedy's "perfidy and ingratitude to myself (lest I should supplant him in influence with the people of Texas)." Hamilton was a creature of the aggressive, expansive Lamar mindset and found himself sidelined by the rise of the more moderate Houston. Kennedy's arrival—and his important if unofficial relationship with the foreign office—was pushing Hamilton farther into the periphery of power, rendering him unnecessary in the relationship between Texas and England. He wanted to bring Kennedy down.[4]

Kennedy's goal in Austin was amorphous. He was to survey the landscape and report back to Aberdeen. Lord Aberdeen's goal was, however, perfectly clear: to interpose British interests between Texas and the United States, preventing annexation, and to soothe hostilities between Texas and Mexico.

Castro represented no one except himself in Austin. He was following up with his work on the Laffitte loan, seeing what other opportunities might exist. His relationship with Hamilton was no longer of any use; he needed to forge new alliances.

Austin was a small town. It did not take long for Castro and Kennedy to get to know each other. Castro settled into the newly finished French legation that Saligny had built but never occupied. There he hosted grand dinners for everyone of influence in the capital. President Sam Houston and Secretary of State Anson Jones graced his table, along with the convivial Irishman Kennedy. Candlelight flickered, French wine flowed, and alliances formed. Talk was of Mexico and the United States, of England and France, of peace and war, of loans and land and colonies and silver and Santa Fe.

A series of events occurred rapidly in February 1842. On the third, Texas named Castro, Texas consul general to France, and on that same day it named Kennedy, Texas consul general to England. On the fifth, the Congress amended the colonization authority given the president in connection with the Peters Colony, making it a general power to bestow more land grants on similar terms. The law had no sooner passed than Kennedy and Castro jointly applied for a land grant on the Nueces River and a second grant on the lower Rio Grande.[5]

On February 15, President Houston inked colonization contracts for Kennedy and Castro. Rather than make a joint grant, he made one contract with each of them—one for Britain, one for France. Kennedy and Castro each named a partner, because Houston had congressional authority to grant contracts only to "companies," not individuals. Castro chose Jean Jassaud, an associate from J. Laffitte & Co. Kennedy named William Pringle, his lawyer in London. Neither Jassaud nor Pringle were in Texas and neither knew that he had become an empresario.[6]

Each of the two contracts embraced three tracts of land. Houston divided a stretch of the Rio Grande into four parts and gave each two. Then he split between them a block of land along the Frio and Nueces rivers, southwest of San Antonio. Each colonization contract required that the empresarios settle six hundred families on the lands and granted them the right to increase that number to one thousand. The contractors had three years to homestead the families, but they had to bring at least one-third of them to Texas within a year.

The empresarios would receive ten sections of land (6,400 acres) for every one hundred families settled on their land and five sections for each one hundred single male settlers over the age of seventeen. Each colonist family was entitled to 320 acres of land, and each bachelor colonist 160 acres. The empresario could assess settlers up to one-half of their lands as compensation for expenses incurred.[7]

Looking at the locations of Castro's and Kennedy's grants on a map, it is clear that the empresarios did not do the choosing by themselves. The colonies were where Texas needed them most, not necessarily where conditions for settlement were best. The two interior grants straddled the road from Laredo to San Antonio and bordered the road from Guerrero, potentially impeding any Mexican invasion. The four grants along the Rio Grande formed a barrier to cross-border aggression from Tamaulipas and Coahuila. All of the grants were beyond the limits of actual Texian dominion. The interior Castro grant above the Frio had agricultural potential, but most of Kennedy's interior grant below the Frio was useful only for grazing. From the northern edge of Castro's interior grant to the southern reaches of Kennedy's, the land changed from rolling, wooded hills to challenging plains of tall grass and mesquite.

The four Kennedy-Castro tracts on the Rio Grande were within the limits claimed by the Republic of Texas, but Texas had never controlled those regions. In 1840, the people of Northern Mexico had declared themselves the independent Republic of the Rio Grande. Their new republic included Mexican lands west of the Nueces (historically part of Tamaulipas and Coa-

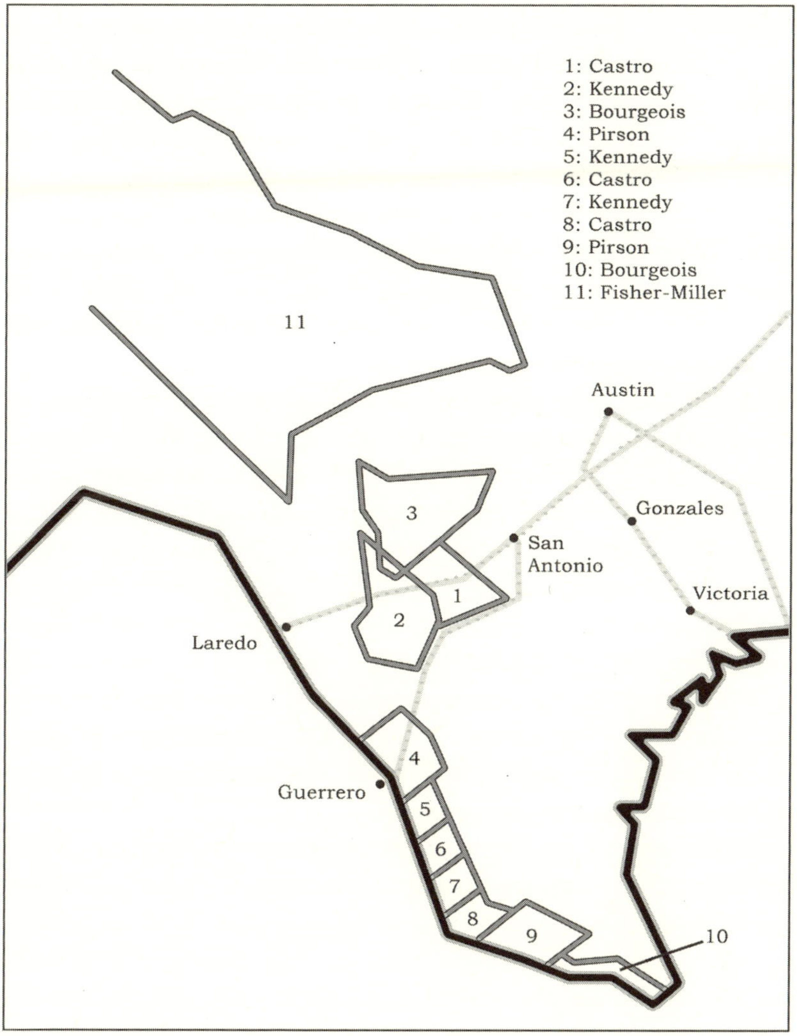


huila, not Texas), thus it overlapped the lands claimed by Texas and the lands granted to Kennedy and Castro. The breakaway states rebelled against (and were put down by) Mexico, not Texas. In fact, their leaders were welcomed in Austin and Houston, despite the territorial conflict. After the rebellion was suppressed, the region settled back into the Mexican fold; Laredo and Guerrero became Santa Anna's secure staging points for invasions of Texas.

Though the colonization lands were remote, the contracts were still potentially lucrative, especially if Texas could achieve peace with Mexico. Sam Houston did not in the least mind dangling a fortune before the eyes of Kennedy and Castro, because the contracts could prove to be remedies for any number of Houston's problems. He had convinced influential men to represent Texas as consuls to their own countries—the two European countries most important to Texas financing, settlement, and independence. He had issued colonization contracts for lands in defensive positions beyond the present limits of settlement. New settlers, new money, new trade, new agriculture, and new industry would be coming to Texas. The mines of New Mexico were still open to Texas (though Houston was much less inclined than Lamar had been to assert the claim loudly). And all of this had been achieved by committing only the most abundant and inexpensive consideration in Texas—land. Houston welcomed more transactions of this sort.

Kennedy and Castro left Austin, apparently intent on recruiting colonists. Castro paused a few weeks in New Orleans on his way to France, checking in promptly with Saligny, who immediately penned a letter to the French foreign minister. "This contract is much less advantageous for Texas than the Franco-Texian Bill would have been," he reported, "but on the other hand it is much more favorable for the grantees. Still, if it goes into effect it would undoubtedly tend to increase our influence and develop our economic interests in the young republic."[8]

It is important to savor those words for a moment and to recall what Saligny meant to accomplish with the Franco-Texian Bill. Castro's lands—even his Rio Grande lands—were not on the western stretch of the river that embraced Santa Fe. The Castro contract had no provision for mines or forts. It was perhaps two million acres, less than what Saligny intended. It did not provide any privileged trade or tariffs. It may have been a windfall for Castro, but it did virtually nothing for France. And it certainly did nothing for Saligny.

In fact, it was worse than Saligny knew. He believed, and perhaps Castro led him to believe, that the names of Basterreche and Lassaulx were on the contract alongside Castro's. They were not. Castro had nabbed a land grant for himself. He had pulled the rug out from under Saligny. He was headed back to France with his prize while Saligny stewed in New Orleans.

Saligny would have his revenge. By the sheerest coincidence Saligny had, in the ten days since his last report about Castro's work in Austin, discovered that Castro was a scoundrel. Advising his foreign minister of that, he offered no specifics except that information "received from several reliable sources on the earlier career of this individual both in Europe and in New York, where he lived for a long time, is scarcely to his credit." Castro had not, Saligny complained, "made use of [the letters of recommendation] and the hospitality that I offered him at the mansion of the Legation with the discretion that I had the right to expect of him under the present circumstances, especially considering the still delicate position of the two governments in regard to their *official* relations with each other."[9]

As is often the case with Saligny, it is worth taking a moment to parse his words. Saligny's complaint was that Castro used the letters and the legation to benefit Castro, not Saligny or France, and that Castro had made friendships, alliances, and business deals there even though Saligny remained behind in New Orleans, fuming that the new Texas government hadn't yet called on him. Saligny was taking it personally.

Saligny also explained Kennedy's work in Austin in his own idiosyncratic way. According to Saligny, Kennedy "has moved heaven and earth in his attempts to combat the good will of the Austin cabinet toward France." Houston had no friendship for England but "he nonetheless believed it prudent under the circumstances to avoid wounding Great Britain by a too marked favoritism toward France. Therefore, he is granting to Mr. Kennedy some six or seven thousand acres of land on the same terms as those accorded to Mr. Castro." The acreage figure was off by about two million; Kennedy's grant was in fact more generous than Castro's.[10]

Saligny didn't realize it—or at least he never admitted it—but he had never been on the inside track in Austin. Castro and Kennedy had gotten inside in a matter of weeks. Saligny still sat on the sidelines, sulking, posturing, and uninformed, waiting for Texas to pay him some attention.

Surprisingly, Saligny would finally receive that attention in no small part because of Henri Castro. On March 2, Texas secretary of state Anson Jones wrote a note to Saligny, stating President Houston's desire "that the unfortunate difficulties existing between Texas and France should be immediately arranged to the satisfaction of both parties. . . . For the more speedy attainment of this important object, His Excellency [Houston] has instructed me to say that he would be most happy to see you again at your post, near this Government."[11]

The note was hand-delivered to Saligny on March 15 by the new Texas chargé d'affaires to England and France, Ashbel Smith, and the new consul general to France, Henri Castro (who was still lingering in New Orleans). Smith explained that he regretted the delay in approaching Saligny, but the president had felt it inappropriate to do so until the Texas Congress had adjourned. In reporting back to Jones, Smith stated that Saligny seemed soothed and would surely be traveling to Texas soon. Smith was correct; Saligny promptly advised his foreign minister that he would be returning to Texas.[12]

Given Castro's involvement in seeking his return, Saligny must have been gritting his teeth as he prepared to travel to Austin. On the other hand, he was probably looking forward to a grand reception from a contrite government.

Sam Houston, however, was preoccupied with other matters. Ten days earlier, Mexican general Rafael Vásquez had raided Victoria, Goliad, and Refugio, then confronted San Antonio. Outnumbered, the Texian defenders had fled. Vásquez's troops raised the Mexican flag in Alamo Square, declared Mexican law to be in force, then sacked the town. After two days, Vásquez decided that he had made his point and returned to Mexico.

This concrete demonstration of Texas' weakness was exactly what Houston did not need. It could only make financing and colonization less likely, and it agitated the bellicose Lamar-Burnet wing, changing the shaky republic's focus from stabilization to revenge. Houston was in the midst of coaxing the French into reengagement and was trying to broaden European exposure and relationships. He needed financing; war with Mexico would both exacerbate the need and lessen its likelihood.

The president declared a national emergency on March 9 and ordered the state records and archives moved to Houston, where they could be protected. The citizens of Austin, sensing a ruse to relocate the capital, refused to permit the records to leave.

Texas had no significant standing army. It could not afford one. It was obliged to depend upon volunteers—the rough adventurers Houston dreaded. The rowdy volunteers and the aggressive tendencies of the Lamar-Burnet camp would inevitably feed on each other, spinning Texas beyond Houston's control. But it was mandatory that Houston respond aggressively; his tactics at San Jacinto had already attracted charges of cowardice, and the bellicose elements of the Congress had to be at least partially mollified. Politics aside, there was the fundamental matter of protecting the republic from Mexican invasion and conquest. Vásquez's brief foray might have been only a feeler for a larger campaign; if so, the Mexicans must have come away encouraged.

Houston called out the militia, which assembled at San Antonio, recently abandoned by Vásquez. He appealed to the citizens of the United States for money and volunteers and dispatched an officer to Corpus Christi to organize volunteer forces.

Because Texas lacked the money to mount an army, most of Houston's war preparations were no more than window dressing; he ended up vetoing a bill to finance an invasion of Mexico and dismissed the volunteers gathering in Corpus Christi, who had managed only one quick skirmish with the Mexicans. Houston's most aggressive move was to declare a blockade of the east coast of Mexico in March. But the Texas navy had only three ships, one of which was being refitted in New Orleans. While there, its crew mutinied. The other two Texas ships—a sloop-of-war and a schooner—had just reluctantly returned from an excursion to aid Mexican rebels in Yucatan and were not ready to sail. Houston announced that the blockade would not be implemented until September, and he knew that without financing it would have to be prosecuted with privateers—legalized pirates blockading for plunder. Houston did not want to go that route. It was, as the French foreign minister observed, a paper blockade. By June, Texas, without army, navy, or active militia, would revert to an undefended state.[13]

At the same time that he dealt with the sacking of San Antonio, Houston was trying to mend fences with Saligny (via the visit by Smith and Castro) and entertaining Victor Pirson, a member of the Belgian diplomatic corps who was in Texas. Pirson had been sent to inspect the republic and advise his government whether to guarantee Hamilton's $5 million loan. We can imagine Houston leaving a room filled with shouts of war and cries for revenge, crossing the hallway and sitting down for a quiet diplomatic discussion about Belgium's bright business and financial prospects in Texas. It must have required unrelenting composure, penetrating persuasion, and not a little sleight of hand.

When the Congress had canceled the authorization for the $5 million loan in January, Pirson's purpose had been mooted, but he traveled the republic and met with its officials nonetheless. He had journeyed from Washington, D.C., to New Orleans in the company of Henri Castro (Castro was returning from France with James Hamilton after failing to secure the $5 million loan from Laffitte & Co.) and met with Saligny there. He reached Austin in February, while Castro and Kennedy were arranging colonization contracts for themselves.

Texas was not in the habit of letting an important visitor leave without a colonization contract in their pocket. Secretary of State Jones offered Pirson a contract in late February, which he accepted on March 9, the day before Houston declared a national emergency (and a few days before Castro and Smith delivered Jones's conciliatory letter to Saligny in New Orleans). Pirson's lands were in two blocks, one just upstream of Kennedy's and Castro's Rio Grande lands and one just downstream. His upstream block was opposite Guerrero, where General Vásquez was at the moment counting his plunder. The block was a dubious prize.[14]

Saligny and Pirson weren't the only Europeans visiting the Texas capital in February and March. At about the time that Anson Jones offered a colonization contract to Pirson, he also offered one to two Germans, Burchard Miller (Burkardt Mueller) and Henry Fisher (Heinrich Fischer), but they didn't get their arrangement firmed up until June. Fisher had been in Texas since at least 1838, serving as consul at Houston for the Hanseatic League, an ancient mercantile association formed by maritime cities on the Baltic and in northern Germany. James Hamilton had sought his $5 million among the league, without success, but the league members still held great promise as trading partners, investors, and lenders. Fisher had long been interested in Texas colonization; he was a founder of the San Saba Colonization Company, which had failed in an early attempt at private German colonies in Texas.

Not much is known about Burchard Miller; he appears to be the sort of second-chair partner that appeared in several of the Texas colonization contracts. Fisher and Miller were joined in the application for a contract by Joseph Baker, a prominent and respected newspaperman and public official, but the final colonization contract named only Fisher and Miller as empresarios.

Castro, Kennedy, Pirson, Fisher—Houston was forming indirect relationships, in the form of colonization contracts, with France, England, Belgium, and Germany, all the while fretting about an invasion from the south. The risk of invasion made these relationships all the more important. Texas had no money and no credit. It could not afford to feed and house even a small military force, much less supply ammunition, cannon and other weapons, horses, and equipment for an extended campaign. The options were to defend the republic with a mob of volunteer rabble, secure foreign financing for defense, or wait and hope. Foreign financing was the most difficult option but the most desirable.

Still reeling from the Panic of 1837, the United States was experiencing financial difficulties of its own, making a European partnership especially attractive. England and France were the most likely protectors. They both averred neutrality between Texas and Mexico, but outside Switzerland, neutrality comes and goes. Since Mexico had been the recent aggressor, spending perfectly good pesos to invade Texas instead of using them to repay European debt, France or England might be persuaded to move off center.

In hindsight, the Franco-Texian Bill was looking attractive to Houston. Frenchmen might already be building forts along the Rio Grande, if only Saligny hadn't made such a mess of things.

In April 1842, with Castro on his way to France, Saligny resumed his campaign of character assassination, informing the French foreign minister that "Mr. Castro lived in New York for several years. There he acquired a most deplorable reputation through certain financial operations, or rather through his shameful manipulations of the stock exchange. In 1833 or 1834 he was obliged to flee to avoid prosecution for having set fire to a bank (I do not remember the name of that establishment), of which he was president or director, and, I am assured, after having previously emptied its coffers of all valuables."[15]

Saligny again complained that Castro had hosted dinners in Austin at, and at the expense of, the legation (tellingly, Saligny described the parties as having occurred at "my house" and "my expense"), to which Castro invited "not only the President, his cabinet, and the members of Congress favorable to France, but also two or three individuals who for nearly a year have been continuously conspicuous for the impudence of their invectives against France and her representative." To hear Saligny tell it, Castro secured his role as Texas consul general to France "by dint of base and sycophantic toadyism" and by denigrating the king and his government at every opportunity. Saligny let his foreign minister know that it would be "an atrocious scandal" if the French government recognized Castro as Texas consul.[16]

President Houston, who wanted a good relationship with France, was having a hard time of it. Even though Saligny was back in Texas, he was tarnished goods and his Franco-Texian ambitions remained controversial. Castro, formerly Saligny's anointed one, was under attack, leaving a diplomatic vacuum. Houston was again in need of a solidly connected Frenchman.

Alexander Bourgeois d'Orvanne reached Houston in May, sent by the French minister of commerce. Bourgeois, the former mayor of Clichy-la-Garenne, most recently an immigration agent, was spending the spring traveling Texas, studying the needs and resources of each locality, preparing a report to submit to the minister upon his return to France.[17]

As was customary, Bourgeois checked in with chargé d'affaires Saligny, who was ensconced in Houston. Sam Houston's declaration of emergency had made it unnecessary for Saligny to return to Austin. Upon leaving New Orleans, Saligny had first taken a ship to Galveston, which he found in the grip of war fever. Before he could make plans to travel farther, President Houston appeared in Galveston, followed by a coterie of generals and ministers. Saligny basked in cordiality afforded him and his renewed relationship with Texas. A month after arriving in Galveston, he took a steamer to Houston, where the Texas government was temporarily seated.[18]

Also in Houston, and also making contact with Saligny, was Armand Ducos, who had traveled to Texas to assert a claim to a Mexican land grant. Though he was traveling on private business, Ducos—a former subprefect of Civray—had been endorsed by French minister of finance Jean Pierre Lacave-Lapagne.[19]

Bourgeois and Ducos both wanted to visit Austin, so Saligny offered to escort them there. But Saligny fell ill in the tiny German Texian settlement of Industry, less than halfway into the journey. Too weak to travel on horseback, Saligny stayed behind while the other Frenchmen went on to the capital.[20]

Bourgeois was surprised by Austin. It was more remote, more vulnerable to attack, than he had conceived. The best he could observe was that "the establishment of the government in the middle of a desert occupied by Indians attracted to it a hardy population strong enough to overawe the savage tribes and to force them to withdraw further into the interior."[21]

He planned to research the government archives and records in Austin, but Austinites were holding the records hostage, refusing to allow their transport to Houston. Under the circumstances, access to the archives was impossible. Bourgeois saw little purpose in lingering in Austin and so returned to Houston.

Saligny was still ill, having been carried from Industry back to Houston in a wagon. By June 1 he was out of bed, meeting with Bourgeois and Ducos. Saligny made introductions for them among the Texas government, and it wasn't long before conversations naturally turned to colonization and financing. Bourgeois and Ducos were exactly the kind of people Sam Houston was looking for.

By June 3, 1842, Bourgeois and Ducos were holding a colonization contract for over a million acres of land on the Medina River, in prime territory just above the Castro and Kennedy tracts. The terms were similar to those extended Kennedy and Castro, calling for a minimum of 1,200 colonists (one-third of them to be settled within eighteen months) and reserving half the lands, in a checkerboard pattern, to the republic. The tract was, as would be expected, beyond the limits of present settlement, but much of it was above the Balcones Escarpment, which meant that it was within the beautiful and temperate Texas Hill Country. There, limestone hills covered in oak and cedar descended into broad valleys coursed by clear, cool spring-fed streams lined with cypress trees.[22]

Their tracts were better than Castro's, Kennedy's, or Pirson's, but—like the other instant empresarios—Bourgeois and Ducos had never actually set foot on them. Everyone involved in the transaction was working from secondhand information. Even Sam Houston and the other Texian officials were so ignorant of the actual geography west of San Antonio that no one realized that the Bourgeois-Ducos grant overlapped the Kennedy grant by a few miles.[23]

Fisher and Miller finalized their contract within a few days of Bourgeois and Ducos inking theirs. The Fisher-Miller grant was truly immense, but it is impossible to say precisely how immense; reflecting geographic ignorance shared by the grantors and the grantees, the grant borders, as described in the contract, did not meet on the west. This grant was the most distant of all, lying above the Llano River, more than one hundred miles northwest of San Antonio. It was deep into Comanche country, which may explain why the empresarios were required to settle only six hundred families within eighteen months.[24]

A month later, Bourgeois and Ducos obtained a second grant, along the Rio Grande, south of the Kennedy-Castro-Pirson string of grants. The Bourgeois-Ducos Rio Grande grant was only ten miles wide, but it extended to the mouth of the Rio Grande at the Gulf of Mexico. Its commercial and navigational value was as manifest as the resistance that Mexico would present to its occupation.[25]

And Bourgeois secured a lagniappe on his own. Sam Houston had discovered that, although the Congress had revoked the authorization for the $5 million loan, there remained on the books a forgotten authorization for a $1 million loan. He signed a contract with Bourgeois to seek the $1 million in France and authorized Secretary of State Jones to work with Bourgeois on the project. Texas could use the money, especially with Mexico threatening. Bourgeois was incentivized with a 10 percent commission.[26]

Bourgeois and Ducos had been aided in their endeavors by Saligny, who took no offense at their colonization opportunity, despite the outrage he had felt over Castro's contract. The circumstances were different, of course: Bourgeois and Ducos were not diminishing the likelihood that the Franco-Texian Bill could be revived. In fact, Saligny was making parallel progress on his own plans: two-plus months earlier, when he had gone to wish Houston bon voyage on his May steamer trip from Galveston to Houston, the president had pulled Saligny aside to discuss the Franco-Texian Bill and more. Houston suggested that the bill might be introduced again, but—according to Saligny—Saligny responded that it was up to Basterreche and Lassaulx, and that he personally had no further interest in the matter.

But Houston pressed on. Lowering his voice, he said, "Even passage of the Franco-Texian Bill would not be enough. France has need of colonies. Why does not she look around for some close to us? It would be very easy to find something among the Mexican possessions to suit her taste."[27]

Houston paused to gauge his words' effect on Saligny, who replied, "I do not know if it would be to the interests of France to increase the number of her colonies. She has one in Africa that is of the greatest importance to her and where she is working to lay the foundations of a glorious and lasting society. Furthermore, you know that for the last ten years she has proven to the entire world that she is completely dedicated to the peaceful development of her own immense national resources and has renounced all idea of aggrandizement or conquest. Finally, I do not see by what right, under what pretext, or by what means she could seize some part of the Mexican territory."

(Remember, this is Saligny's own version of the conversation, as he related it to his superior. It tells us as much about Saligny and his interest in French colonization as it does about the exchange itself.)

"Oh! If that is all that is troubling you," interrupted the president, "nothing would be easier to arrange. We would take care of that. If Texas were to seize a portion of the territory of Mexico by force of arms, and, after holding it for a time, then choose to cede it to France, I, for my part, do not see who could stand in the way."

At that moment the ship's bell signaled departure. Houston jumped hastily on board with the words, "Goodbye, Mr. de Saligny. We shall talk of this another time. I hope to have the pleasure of seeing you again."

It is difficult to reconcile this conversation, even if toned down somewhat, with Houston's aversion to invading Mexico. But Houston was politically obliged to maintain an aggressive posture toward Mexico, even as he avoided further conflict. It was during this period that Houston was pretending a blockade of Mexico and training volunteers at Corpus Christi. And the conversation is entirely consistent with Houston's willingness to attract France's attention by dangling whatever treasure he thought the French might most want. Saligny wanted the Franco-Texian Bill, and Houston (who certainly realized its political difficulty) was signaling his inclination to go even further.

Saligny's other passion was Richard Bullock, and he continued to bring that matter up with Houston and his secretary of state, Anson Jones. Saligny got—or at least gave his superiors—the impression that Texians blamed Bullock for the failure of the French loan; of course, they blamed Saligny himself. In any event, a higher power ended up writing the last chapter of the Pig War: Richard Bullock died within six weeks.

By the time that Saligny escorted Bourgeois and Ducos toward Austin, only to take sick en route, he was becoming enmeshed in a plot by George Washington Hockley, who was the Texas secretary of war, and several others—reportedly even Houston—to conquer the island of Cozumel off Mexico's Yucatan Peninsula. This, concluded Saligny, was what Houston had been hinting at. Hockley was seeking French financing for the campaign, with the understanding that Texas would turn the island over to France at the end of the adventure.[28]

Saligny liked the idea, seeing many advantages from possession of Cozumel. But the illness he contracted in Industry was one of a series of malaises that only worsened. As his health failed, he lost the ability to pursue the Cozumel scheme. He pleaded with Paris for a leave of absence. The French foreign minister advised him that he could return to France; the Viscount of Cramayel would assume his post. Saligny departed.[29]

In June, Bourgeois d'Orvanne and Texas secretary of state Anson Jones went to New Orleans in search of the $1 million loan. Negotiations there were inconclusive, and Bourgeois sailed for Europe in early July. On board the *Britannia,* Bourgeois composed his report to the French minister of commerce. His conclusions included that France should "facilitate solution of the Mexico-Texian question," prevent the annexation of Texas by the United States, sponsor French emigration to Texas, and "facilitate, insofar as the interest of the state permits, the project of diverting the Santa Fe trade."[30]

Bourgeois appears to have adopted Saligny's interest in Santa Fe, and his report was flattering to the chargé d'affaires. But Bourgeois was not above advancing his own personal interests. He suggested to the minister of commerce that France could "profit by the concessions made to French companies and provide our French emigrants a powerful protection by procuring a few strategic military posts. The concession of Point Isabel, which extends to the mouth of the Rio Grande and commands the river, is worthy of consideration."[31]

The Point Isabel concession: that would be the concession that Bourgeois had in his pocket as he wrote his report.

CHAPTER 4

# *Shifting Diplomatic Winds*

Ashbel Smith, the new Texas chargé d'affaires to Britain and France, had crossed the Atlantic in the spring of 1842 to assume his post while Sam Houston grappled with Mexico and issued more colonization contracts. Only thirty-seven, the lean, angular Smith would prove himself to be the most skilled diplomat ever to serve Texas. Born in Connecticut, he earned bachelor's, master's, and medical doctor's degrees from Yale. He studied medicine in Paris for a year and ministered to victims of the Paris cholera epidemic of 1832. At times a politician and a newspaper editor, he was Sam Houston's double-bed, log-cabin roommate during the early years of the republic. Acting as an emissary for Houston, Smith negotiated peace with the Comanches and other tribes in 1838.

His education and his travels left him comfortable in London and Paris, the two European capitals that were most important to Texas. When he sailed for Europe as the chargé from Texas, he had a full diplomatic plate. His first priority was securing ratification of the three treaties that England required before sending a diplomatic representative to Texas. Second was the matter of English and French involvement with Mexico, and their ability to bring about peace. Third was Texas' desperate need for financing; Alexander Bourgeois d'Orvanne required Smith's support in his quest for a $1 million loan. Then there were the colonization contracts held by Kennedy, Castro, and Pirson; facilitating European emigration to Texas was an important element in his portfolio.

Smith arrived in London on May 10 in the company of Henri Castro, newly appointed colonial empresario and consul general to France. They had been traveling together since New Orleans, where they had calmed the waters with Saligny. Castro, who had worked with James Hamilton on the $5 million loan, had helpfully introduced Smith to several bankers in New Orleans. When Smith reported back to Anson Jones about his meetings there, he wrote, "Before closing this letter it may not be deemed amiss to state that Henri Castro, Consul General to France, has taken an active and judicious interest in the affairs of Texas here." One of Smith's first acts was to send Castro to departing Texas chargé George McIntosh with a letter asking McIntosh to assist Castro in registering himself with France as the new consul general. Smith also sent scrip for 9,600 acres of Texas land with Castro and asked McIntosh to try to dispose of the certificates to raise money. McIntosh was surely eager to do so, for he had been without funding since Hamilton and Castro sailed back to Texas without obtaining Lamar's $5 million loan. But he doubted that there was any market for the scrip and despaired at the financial outlook.[1]

In London, Smith immediately set about negotiating the final details of the three treaties with British foreign minister Lord Aberdeen. He managed to bring the matter to a successful conclusion on June 27, opening the way for Britain to send official representatives to Texas.[2]

For chargé d'affaires to Texas, Aberdeen selected Charles Elliot, a British knight and navy captain who entered the colonial service in 1828. Rising in the ranks of the foreign office, in 1835 he became trade superintendent and plenipotentiary at Guangzhou (Canton), China.[3]

British merchants in China profited handsomely by illegally importing opium made from poppies grown on British plantations in India. In Guangzhou, the British traded the opium for Chinese tea and manufactured goods—and for copious amounts of Chinese silver. Disturbed by addiction and the outflow of bullion, in 1836 the Chinese banned opium; China's imperial commissioner at Guangzhou, Lin Zexu, began closing down opium dens, prosecuting corrupt officials, and clamping down on British trade.

The confrontation escalated into a series of expulsions, blockades, attacks, negotiations, and betrayals known as the First Opium War. Elliot, the queen's man on the ground, was widely seen on both sides as weak and ineffective. The war had been one of repeated diplomatic failures followed by military intervention. It is possible that Elliot never felt committed to the cause of the opium trade. Whatever his feelings, the outcome was that he was recalled, censured, and replaced.

Elliot's career was indelibly stained, but—given his lifetime of loyal service to the queen—he was not ejected from the diplomatic corps. Instead, in May 1842 he was posted to Texas, a not entirely desirable station.

Elliot's instructions were to assist in bringing about an amicable and early peace with Mexico while maintaining the strictest neutrality and without "using any language which may, in the remotest manner, lead to a hope that we may ever be disposed to take any part in [Texas'] contest with Mexico."[4]

Aberdeen's choice of Elliot as chargé to Texas is a clear indication of where Texas ranked among British priorities. That circumstance is difficult to explain, given that the British foreign office entirely understood the importance of an independent Texas in maintaining a diverse North America and understood the forces that might allow or deny that outcome.[5]

Texas was likely not Elliot's first choice. But another British subject had actively lobbied for a post in Texas. William Kennedy had gotten a colonization contract and returned to London as the Texas consul general to Great Britain. But Kennedy, who had gone to Texas as an informal British representative, was not deceived about the differences between a consular title from Texas and one from Her Majesty Queen Victoria. One of the critical differences was that the queen could afford to make payroll.

On June 7, 1842, Kennedy paid a visit to the foreign office and from its waiting room submitted a note asking to be interviewed for an appointment to the British consulship at Galveston. Then he politely advised Ashbel Smith, the Texas representative in London, that Texas should commence looking for another consul. Kennedy had good connections in the United States and Texas, and he demonstrated them to Lord Aberdeen in a series of letters covering war preparations in Texas and incitement coming from the United States.[6]

It took until August, but Kennedy finally secured his commission. Realizing that his colonization contract might present a conflict of interest, and recognizing that he lacked the funds to execute it in any case, he advised the foreign office that he would find capitalists interested in buying out his position. Kennedy certainly recognized the difficulty of colonization; a few days before learning of his appointment, while still positioned to profit from his contract, he had advised an association of unemployed workmen in Scotland not to consider emigration to Texas because of "the present doubtful state of the relations between Mexico and Texas." By the time Kennedy sailed for Texas in November, he probably felt his concerns entirely justified—and his contract worthless—in the aftermath of Mexican general Adrián Woll's September march across his tract on the way to take San Antonio a second time.[7]

While Smith was cementing relations with Great Britain, McIntosh accompanied Castro to Paris. Diplomatic protocol required Castro to present his commission to the French foreign ministry and for the French to issue an exequatur recognizing his office. In Paris, departing Texas consul Theodore Barbey warned McIntosh that Sam Houston had already revoked Castro's credentials. But Barbey was overtly interested in keeping the consulship for himself. For that reason, and having no information to confirm

Barbey's claim, McIntosh disregarded the rumor; although there did seem to be a delay in the issuance of Castro's exequatur, he attributed it to French preoccupation with upcoming elections.[8]

But in Texas, Alphonse Dubois de Saligny had continued his attacks on Castro's character, prompting Secretary of State Jones to write Smith on June 7, authorizing him to remove Castro from his office, should facts so warrant, and cautioning Smith to be on the alert for any attempt by Castro to use his colonization contract improperly.[9]

When Ashbel Smith finally had the opportunity to sit down with French foreign minister Francois Guizot on August 15, he heard firsthand about French objections to Castro's appointment. Taking into account the warning from Anson Jones, Smith immediately advised Guizot that Castro's commission would be withdrawn. And, so, he told Jones, "the Consular Office in Paris again becomes vacant."

It was yet another blow to relations between Texas and France, and it came just as the French were considering the idea of a joint mediation by France, England, and the United States of the conflict between Texas and Mexico. Guizot told Smith that France was favorable to the idea of a triple mediation, and discharging Castro was meant to keep Guizot in that mood, but the bad blood between Saligny and Castro had taken its toll.[10]

Smith, like many others, saw peace with Mexico as the key to progress on other fronts. The blockade was doing nothing to ingratiate Texas with England or France; peace would solve that. Neither Castro nor any other empresario was likely to attract colonists to Texas while there remained a risk of Mexican invasion. And, as had been the case with Hamilton and Castro before him, Bourgeois's effort to obtain financing for Texas was unlikely to succeed unless hostilities ceased.[11]

The British began mediating with the Mexicans in July, as mandated by the treaties that accompanied British recognition of Texas. When he first directed his minister at Mexico to broach the subject of mediation, Lord Aberdeen's message seemed perfunctory. But within two weeks his mood changed, and he issued a second, more urgent, direction. Aberdeen was worried that continued Mexican hostility toward Texas would make Texas amenable to annexation by the United States; he wanted to press upon the Mexicans the calamities that could ensue if the United States became their neighbors. But the relationship between Texas and England was still mixed. England was—over loud Texian objections—allowing the export of two ironclad military steamships to Mexico, at a time when Texas was—to the immense annoyance of the British—claiming a blockade of the Mexican coast.[12]

Whether England sincerely wanted to help Texas or not, the truth on the ground in Mexico was that any politician who brooked Texas independence was certain to be ousted. By August 30, Mexico had firmly and finally rejected any mediation by England. The triple mediation—sometimes phrased a triple "interposition"—seemed to be the next step, and Texas and France endorsed the idea. But England was reluctant. On September 10, British chargé Elliot made it plain that the blockade made them less than eager to mediate further. On September 21, London announced that since no real blockade had materialized the British were declaring it "to be null, and of no effect." Unbeknownst to them, they had already won that argument: Sam Houston capitulated and revoked the blockade on September 12, creating the possibility of better relations with England and France.[13]

Nonetheless, on October 15, Lord Aberdeen formally declined to participate in a triple interposition. He pointed out that England—which enjoyed good relations with Mexico—had already tried to bring Mexico to the bargaining table more than once that year, and all efforts had failed. No other nation was likely to prove more effective—particularly not the United States, whose relationship with Mexico was prickly in the extreme. Aberdeen saw merit in continued individual efforts by England and France to achieve peace, but he dismissed any joint project.[14]

England and France both instructed their representatives in Mexico to press for recognition of Texas independence, but little occurred. The British chargé in Mexico City politely scorned the instructions, calling any further entreaties futile. He was soon promoted to the ministry at Washington, D.C., and his post in Mexico was filled by a temporary replacement, reducing English influence there.

Meanwhile, Henri Castro, rejected as consul general to France, rented luxurious quarters on the Rue de Lafitte in Paris and went about the business of securing colonists. He organized the Société de Colonisation Européе-Américain au Texas and opened offices on Rue de la Beaume. But it was at his apartment on the Rue de Lafitte that he preferred to receive potential colonists such as Auguste Frétellière: "We were kept waiting in the antechamber rather a long time. (The custom is fairly general in France, since it gives importance to the personage on whom one is calling.) Finally a butler, conventionally dressed, came to show us into the drawing room. The apartment was magnificent, Brussels carpet, a tête-à-tête and arm-chairs upholstered in crimson satin; a Saint Gobain mirror with an ornate frame; and a series of paintings which depicted scenes in America and Indian life. It was marvelous."[15]

Castro was not without personal financial means, and he was backed by Ludwig Huth, a wine merchant and insurer. His organization was small but effective; by the end of October, Ashbel Smith reported that "Mr. Castro is in Havre, at this time, superintending the embarkation of some emigrants for Texas." He informed Anson Jones that they appeared to be "persons of respectability and means; and that we have good reason to believe they will be a valuable accession to our population and deserving the fostering care and protection of our Government."[16]

It was true: Henri Castro had booked passage for 114 colonists on the *Ebro,* sailing November 2 for Galveston, and more ships were to follow soon. His arrangement with the colonists was this: He would permit them to colonize his grant, which would entitle each head of a family to 640 acres of land and each single male 320 acres. In return, the colonists would convey to Castro one-half of the land that they received, retaining 320 or 160 acres. In a printed *avis au immigrants,* the colonists found advice and instructions on expenses, provisions, lodging, customs, and so forth. The colonists were expected to be self-reliant; they had to pay their own passage ($32) and provide for all of their own needs. To give them an added incentive to carry out their agreement (and not drift away when they reached Texas) Castro required each colonist to make a deposit of one hundred francs ($20), refundable when they reached the land grant.[17]

Castro asked Smith to seek Texas government assistance for his colonists, because they were going to be strangers in a strange land and because Castro was not going to be in Galveston to meet them. He would still be in Europe, recruiting more colonists. And Castro was acutely aware of another problem that might arise: given that the grant lands might be vulnerable to Mexican raids, and therefore uninhabitable, he asked Texas to appropriate another tract for the first immigrants and requested an extension of twelve months (beyond August 15, 1843) in which to deliver the required two hundred families or single men to Texas. Smith was sympathetic: "They appear to be a desirable class of persons; and from his sending them at the present time, it is fair to presume that under more favorable circumstances he will be able to introduce a large number of colonists who would be valuable citizens." Castro assured Smith that the colonists were "industrious farmers from the *country* who possess moderate means." And, Smith reported, "So far as I am able to judge, Mr. Castro has labored to execute the terms of his contract with promptness, energy and good faith. I strongly incline to the opinion that the 'objections' which rendered it proper for me to withdraw his 'Commission' from the Foreign Office were chiefly of a political nature."[18]

Castro, ever the promoter, had pulled some fine French wool over Smith's eyes. Texas had instructed him to send only colonists qualified to tame the wilderness, fully equipped with food, tools, equipment, and funds to last them not less than six months. Sam Houston himself had warned that colonists must arrive "prepared, and, with the arms and munitions of war, bring six months provisions and clothing." And Castro described his colonists in just that way to Ashbel Smith. But Smith was in Paris, and Castro had found most of his colonists far to the east, in Alsace and Lorraine. Many were more German than French. They were impoverished peasants fleeing the shock of feudal breakdown, industrial revolution, and social instability. Though most of the colonists on the *Ebro* were farmers, that was not true of subsequent ships; over all, at least half of the heads of household did not claim agricultural skills. As for their financial means, one historian reports that of the first ninety-six households sailing for Castro's colony, eleven reported owning no property at all and seventeen had $100 or less. Another third of them had less than $500 to carry their families to Texas and build a new life.[19]

As might have been expected in the circumstance of central Europe, Castro had been able to recruit only a mix of paupers and working-class families, with a few petit bourgeoisie and political refugees thrown in. It was no wonder that a $20 deposit was enough to ensure that they would colonize as promised. And it was dead certain that they were going to need help from someone—Texas or Castro or someone else—when they landed in Texas.

But Castro had no infrastructure on the ground in Texas other than a few Galveston merchants who had agreed to meet the colonists, sell them goods, and point them in the right direction. For leadership, he appointed two of the emigrants—nineteen-year-old Albert Laude and twenty-three-year-old Francois Phene—as directors of colonization. At Castro's request, Ashbel Smith wrote the young men a letter of introduction to Anson Jones: "I have not the pleasure of a personal acquaintance with these gentlemen; I am however assured by Mr. Castro that they are worthy of every attention and of confidence." In fact, they were two naïfs with no idea of what lay ahead.[20]

Thus began Castro's colonization. By February 1843 he had sent 256 people—ninety-six families and two bachelors—on their way to Galveston. With the hot summer months looming, he then ceased departures, but by April he had signed another seventy-six colonial contracts binding families and bachelors (240 people in all) to sail in the fall. Castro was well on his way to filling his quota of colonists.

One factor that motivated Castro to proceed expeditiously was his late discovery that Texas had granted a colonization contract to Bourgeois and Ducos. Frenchmen both, they would surely end up recruiting from the same pool of potential colonists that Castro was working. Castro complained directly to Secretary of State Jones that the Bourgeois contract was an infringement of his rights and calculated to prejudice the success of his own colony, but Jones rejected his complaint: "Mr. Castro was never assured, as he seems to think, by this government, that he was to have the monopoly of colonizing in this country, with French emigrants."[21]

Castro needn't have worried; Bourgeois was more interested in earning a 10 percent commission for securing the $1 million loan. That is where he spent his time. But circumstances in Texas made finding money even more difficult than finding colonists. In December, he wrote Jones from his exclusive flat at 5 Rue Faubourg St. Honoré. His letter displays optimism that the loan can be placed but complains at the outset that "the Mexican invasion has completely discouraged capitalists and I will not venture to hope for their cooperation." As much harm as the invasion did, the bigger issue in his mind seemed to be the "unfavorable impression produced in France by the failure of Gen. Hamilton's negotiations. This unfortunate affair has destroyed all confidence and places the republic in a very bad credit." Bourgeois recommended offering trade advantages to the government of France if it would guarantee the loan, or to the lenders if no government guarantee was forthcoming. Ashbel Smith endorsed his recommendations in a separate letter a few days later.[22]

Communication between Texas and France was insufferably slow. Only a day before Bourgeois wrote his letter, Anson Jones was writing a reply to a letter Bourgeois had written four months earlier. The topic was the same, and—a full step behind events—Jones authorized Ashbel Smith to meet with Bourgeois to discuss changing the terms of the loan. It was February 26 before Jones replied to the Smith-Bourgeois recommendations of late December. He saw merit in their recommendations, but his two emphatic messages were these: first, "I have only time at present to say in reply that the Loan of One Million of Dollars is a matter of pressing importance to Texas at this moment"; and second, "We are tired of futile and unsuccessful efforts to obtain money by means of a loan and no other or further ones will be made unless predicated upon something like positive certainty."[23]

And then Jones made an observation that, in light of other events, was ironic—no, it was inexplicable. He acknowledged that "the principal reliance which the President has for obtaining a loan of money for this country in the dilapidated condition which the late administration left it is through the friendly influence of the French Government. If Texas can offer her such inducements as will incline her to use this influence effectively it is believed the object may be accomplished. . . . The introduction of her wines, etc, into Texas free of duty would also be an object of considerable national importance." Why was this inexplicable? Because Lamar, during his administration, had already granted duty-free status to French wines. But Sam Houston, just a month before Smith wrote his letter, had revoked the exemption. And when the French found out, they were not amused.[24]

CHAPTER 5

# *The Nobles and the Pilgrims*

In April 1842, more than a year before Castro began seeking colonists in France, the Duke of Nassau had hosted a gathering at the palace in Biebrich, where his ancestors had resided for more than a century. The magnificent baroque complex was tinted rose and white and reigned over a swath of gardens just steps from the Rhine. Though smaller, it possessed the intimidating beauty of the palace at Versailles.[1]

Biebrich was a nascent industrial center across the Rhine from the ancient walled city-state of Mainz. Its entrepreneurs were learning to manufacture concrete and chemicals, but—situated within the grape-growing Rheingau—it was best known for production of sekt, the German sparkling wine.

The meeting had been the idea of Count Carl of Castell, an officer in the Austrian emperor's army who was then posted to the garrison at Biebrich. Prince Carl of Solms-Braunfels, who was posted to the same garrison and attended the meeting, described the session this way:

> In the year of our Lord One Thousand Eight Hundred and Forty-two, an association of Princes, Counts and Gentlemen was formed in Germany, who, mindful of the increasing excess of population and the poverty growing therefrom, particularly among the lower classes of people, made it their object to redress this evil by regulating the already considerable emigration. The number of members was at that time twenty-one:
>
> His Highness, the Duke of Nassau
> His Highness, the Prince of Leiningen (President)
> His Highness, the Prince Moritz of Nassau
> His Highness, the reigning Prince of Schwartzburg Rudolstadt
> His Highness, the reigning Prince of Solms-Braunfels

His Highness, the reigning Prince of Wied
His Highness, the Prince Colloredo
His Highness, the Prince Alexander of Solms-Braunfels
His Highness, the Prince Carl of Solms-Braunfels
The Illustrious Count of Castell (Vice-President)
The Illustrious Count of Colloredo
The Illustrious Count August of New Lieningen-Westerburg
The Illustrious Count Christian of New Lieningen-Westerburg
The Illustrious Count Friedrick of Alt Leiningen
The Illustrious Count Victor of Alt Leiningen
The Illustrious widowed Countess of Isenburg-Meerholz
The Illustrious Count Edmund of Hatzfeld
The Illustrious Count Clemens of Boos-Waldeck
The Illustrious Count Joseph of Boos-Waldeck
The Illustrious Count Anton of Boos-Waldeck
The Illustrious Count Renesse.[2]

"Regulating" emigration is an odd and abstract goal. It doesn't translate well from the German. The association meant to facilitate and guide emigration. It was undeniably idealistic, but its goals were not as eleemosynary as Solms's description indicates. Profit, prestige, and power were in play.

With the widowed Countess of Isenburg-Meerholz in attendance, the meeting was certainly formal, a gathering of nobles addressing a serious circumstance. After a discussion of the causes and consequences of emigration, the association formulated a plan of action. They collected subscriptions for funding, then voted to send two of their number to Texas.

As far back as 1821, when German emigration was a relative trickle, Texas had been on the minds of the adventurous. Writers such as Scherpf, Duden, and Hecke had published widely read reports on the condition of—and abundant opportunity within—what was then a distant frontier state of the new nation of Mexico. When Texas declared independence from Mexico fifteen years later, the lure of romance, freedom, opportunity, and adventure only increased. In 1841, the year before the nobles gathered at Biebrich, Carl Anton Postl, using the pseudonym Charles Sealsfield, published a heroic novel titled *The Cabin Book* that portrayed Texas as the world's hope for the future. It proved immensely popular—so much so that it would soon be translated and published in New York.

Also in 1841, William Kennedy had published his *Rise, Progress and Prospects of the Republic of Texas.* Kennedy's book, almost entirely favorable to the republic, garnered widespread notice throughout Europe.

At their Biebrich posting, Prince Carl of Solms and Count Carl of Castell read Scherpf, Sealsfield, and Kennedy, as many of the other nobles in the association surely did. We can postulate that Solms, Castell, and the association's other members, among them several present and former military officers, also read Hecke, who had proposed that Prussia purchase Texas from Spain in 1821.

Buying Texas was no longer practicable, but a small group of German nobles possessed of wealth, education, and military experience might look at Texas on the one hand and Germany on the other and conclude that some interesting possibilities existed. It would not escape the nobles' notice that they were in the position to land five, ten, or fifty thousand German emigrants in Texas and to settle them onto some inexpensive Texas land, even if it were deep into the frontier. The emigrants would be organized and armed, to protect themselves from native depredations. They would stick together within a colony, forming their own communities instead of dispersing into existing towns. And something might happen.

Take over Texas? No, of course not. But just as Texas occupied a political, military, and physical blocking position between the United States and the Pacific, so might a strong German colony—perhaps a strong, independent, militarized German colony; perhaps a colony supported overtly or covertly by Mexico, France, or Great Britain—be able to maneuver into a blocking position of its own. At a minimum, as a worst-case scenario, a German colony could prove to be a strong trading partner for the homeland and might foster some very profitable investments for its sponsors.

As the Biebrich meeting broke up in April 1842, it was too early to tell whether something along those lines might be possible. But the situation in Texas looked for all the world like a pack of coyotes slowing circling a deer carcass, waiting for one to make the first move. Some of the coyotes were hungry but weak. Others were strong but hesitant. There might be alliances to be made. There might be a chance to dart in and grab some of the spoils. And the whole effort could have a legitimate and most un-coyote-like humanitarian purpose. It was certainly worth looking into, worth sending two nobles to assess the situation.

The chosen two were Count Ludwig Joseph von Boos-Waldeck and Count Victor August of Leiningen. Boos-Waldeck was forty-three years old when he left Germany for Texas. Leiningen was just twenty-one. Their positions reflected their age: Boos-Waldeck was a major in the Prussian army and an aide-de-camp to Duke Adolf of Nassau; Leiningen was a lieutenant in the Austrian army.

They sailed from Havre on the bark *Lorena* on June 10, 1842. It took more than a month to cross the Atlantic; they arrived in New York on

July 18. There they spent two weeks learning what they could about Texas. Fortunately, G. A. Scherpf—who had written a popular book about Texas the previous year—was then residing in New York, and they were able to consult him repeatedly. After stocking up on books, maps, and advice, they embarked August 2 on the schooner *Tarry-not* and arrived at Velasco, Texas, on the twenty-seventh.[3]

Velasco was a port south of Galveston, four miles upstream from the mouth of the Brazos River. It was where the first of Stephen F. Austin's colonists had stepped ashore in 1821, and it served briefly as the capital of Texas after the battle of San Jacinto. Velasco was by 1842 a small but bustling town. Boos-Waldeck and Leiningen lingered only three days before sailing for Galveston, the most prominent Texas port.

They managed to sail into Galveston Bay just ahead of a tropical storm. The weather became violent, slashing the sand-spit town, pushing waves ashore. The storm's surge swamped the lower regions; citizens navigated the marketplace in rowboats. The wooden Episcopal church—with the only steeple in town—was severely damaged. When the winds let up, the mosquitoes swept in. A mourner at a funeral reported "some three feet of water at bottom [of the grave] owing to the present high tide."[4]

On September 9, with the weather still foul, the two Germans took the steamer to Houston, where they introduced themselves to President Houston. They briefed the president on the details of their mission to Texas, and he exuded hospitality and interest, even though he almost certainly had bigger matters on his mind. The treaties with England had only been ratified in June, Charles Elliot had been in Texas for only two weeks, and William Kennedy was yet to arrive. Houston had called a special session of the Congress in June to deal with the Mexican threat in the wake of General Vásquez's sacking of San Antonio. Mexico had firmly rejected England's mediation for peace in August, and talk of a triple intervention was in the air. While Boos-Waldeck and Leiningen were in Houston, President Houston signed the order revoking his paper blockade. Most urgent of all, word was filtering in from San Antonio that General Woll was advancing on the city.[5]

The heat was oppressive, so much so that the two concluded that traveling on horseback in the summer would be dangerous for their health. They elected to remain in Galveston, where at least there was an offshore breeze, until October 15. "However," Boos-Waldeck concluded, "we may regard this time as well applied, and indeed as very useful preparation, because we found the opportunity to get to know people and conditions, which in turn enabled us to accomplish our goals with greater certainty."[6]

One of the people they got to know was Morgan Smith, who, with his partner John Adriance, had just founded a plantation at Columbia, a few miles west of the Brazos River, about thirty miles from the coast. Columbia had been established in 1826 by Josiah Hughes Bell, a member of Stephen F. Austin's "Old Three Hundred." Sam Houston was familiar with Columbia; it was the capital of Texas for a few months in 1836, and it was there that Houston was first inaugurated as president.

When Boos-Waldeck and Leiningen sallied forth from Galveston in mid-October 1842, Columbia was their first stop, for they had become close to Smith—so close that Smith would name his plantation Waldeck, a name it bears to this day. There they met a number of new acquaintances, among them Anson Jones, the secretary of state. In Columbia they hired a guide before departing on the twenty-ninth. They traveled with Jones for a few days until their paths divided. Jones was headed for the hamlet of Washington; the two Germans were bound for Mill Creek.

Mill Creek was an understandable destination. It was one of several settlements in a German-speaking region on the Brazos River. Boos-Waldeck and Leiningen encountered their first German town at San Felipe de Austin, about forty-five miles southeast of Mill Creek. A few Germans had come with Stephen F. Austin in the early 1820s (only five had received grants within his colony); others had emigrated during the German upheavals of that decade and the next two. Germans naturally gravitated together, and the countryside along Mill Creek and Cummins Creek became a notable ethnic enclave within Austin's colony.

The center of the German community was a town called Industry, after the industrious habits of the Germans (it was where Saligny had fallen ill on his trip to Austin with Bourgeois and Ducos). Industry had been founded by Friedrich Ernst, the former chief gardener for the grand duke of Oldenburg. In company with Charles Fordtran, Ernst had arrived in 1831 by way of New York, New Orleans, Harrisburg, and San Felipe de Austin. He purchased a league of land, and Fordtran did the surveying for him, receiving one-fourth of the league in payment.

Ernst built a mill and planted orchards; his wife Louise ran a small inn. He was so taken with Texas that he wrote a long, glowing letter to a friend in Oldenburg, who passed it along to the local newspaper. The letter was picked up by various publications and disseminated widely. Soon Industry, and nearby settlements at Cat Spring, New Ulm, Blumenthal, and Round Top, were populated by families named von Donop, von Roeder, Kleberg, Varrelmann, Zimmerscheidt, Amsler, Wolters, Biegel, Pettus, Herder, Reinermann, and Stoleje.[7]

Boos-Waldeck toured the German farms in the company of Charles Fordtran and concluded that they offered "good black, fertile soil, prairie and woodland nicely distributed, enough water for cattle and people, but none for driving mills." After familiarizing themselves with the land, Boos-Waldeck and Leiningen rode to Washington. Sam Houston, Anson Jones, and several other members of the government were there, preparing for the Congress that was to begin December 5.[8]

Sam Houston was still in the mood to grant colonization contracts. It had been months since his spring flurry of grants to Kennedy, Castro, Pirson, Bourgeois, and Fisher, but he pulled out his old toolkit for dealing with these newly arrived dignitaries. Discussions proceeded as far as preparing a draft contract, with the names Boos-Waldeck and Leiningen inked in, but they stalled when it came to identifying the lands to be granted. "We withdrew from entering any such contract because we arrived at the conviction that such a speculation would require great expenses, versus uncertainty of compensation and complete improbability of profit," said Boos-Waldeck, making it clear that the uncertainty was "because the parts of the country that would be included in such a contract with the Government lie outside of the borders of the current population of Texas; that means either in the far west between the Nueces and the Rio Grande, or beyond Austin between the Brazos and the Colorado. The former region is exposed to Mexicans and Indians, the latter only to the Indians; therefore under the current conditions of the times, where the Government is in no position to provide protection, they are completely unsuitable for settlement." Boos-Waldeck's geography was a bit fuzzy, but his message was clear: he was not inclined to settle German colonists beyond the frontier.[9]

"After our negotiations in Washington were finished," said Boos-Waldeck, "and after our opinions about the most practicable, most secure, and—according to the current conditions in the country—most appropriate manner to invest capital profitably had matured and solidified, we arrived at the decision to purchase land and build a plantation with blacks, since that is the business that gives us the best promise of profits. At the same time we connected with it the idea of a settlement of a small number of German farmer and artisan families, all around the plantation, although the benefits arising from this for us are likewise still problematic."

Boos-Waldeck was taking a conservative, businesslike view of the nobles' prospects. He was not inclined to speculation, and he lacked the romantic streak that bloomed in younger Germans. He believed that a plantation might be made profitable, based on his firsthand inspection of plantations in the vicinity of Industry. He was willing to bring over a few German emigrants and give them land on the plantation, but he could not perceive how doing so was going to generate a profit for the nobles. After all, he pointed out, "we cannot sell the land to the emigrants at a higher price than the individual emigrant would get from a third party," and he did not believe that the value of Texas land was going to rise quickly. It was abundant, and it was under constant threat from natives and Mexico.

Boos-Waldeck and Leiningen were convinced "that the company's original plan to make a sizeable profit through the settlement of introduced German emigrants on a large purchased tract in Texas, a part of which we would reserve for ourselves, would not fulfill the intended purpose, at least not under the current conditions. On the other hand, we share the full conviction that a plantation with blacks, established at a location with adequate assessment of the soil and situated for future trade, would immediately yield certain and good profit."

And so they went forward with the purchase of a league of land—4,428 acres—in the German community near the Brazos River. It cost seventy-five cents per acre. "Splendid, healthy location, excellent soil, three running creeks, pretty woodlands of oaks, cedars and 'burch' as the American says. A first-rate league at a cheap price." They had General Woll to thank for the bargain. They named their purchase Nassau Farm, after the society's protector, the Duke of Nassau. It was January 1843, too early to put in crops, but the time for spring planting was drawing near.[10]

Boos-Waldeck and Leiningen conferred. The young Count Leiningen was planning to return to Germany soon to deliver a report on their activities. Boos-Waldeck would stay behind and begin work on the plantation. They decided to travel to New Orleans together, taking the opportunity to purchase goods, supplies, tools, equipment—and slaves—in the markets.

While Boos-Waldeck and Leiningen were scouting Texas, Henri Castro was loading French families onto boats in Europe, bound for Galveston, sometimes by way of New Orleans. Auguste Frétellière, who had marveled at Castro's sumptuous quarters on the Rue de Lafitte, was better educated and better situated than the typical Castro colonist, but he traveled to Texas as did many of the others—aboard a Belgian bark fitted with two square-rigged masts, a gaff-rigged mast aft, and triple jibs on the bow spar. The shipping company provided only water and fire for cooking, so he needed to stock food and utensils for the journey. An agent of the shipping line guided him to "their principal grocery store, where we were permitted to taste whatever we pleased in the excellent stock. Trusting in the honor of the merchant, we asked him to send some of everything aboard; but when we were on the sea we found that we had been grossly cheated. The butter was rancid, the cheese full of worms, in short, only the potatoes were good, and that merely because they were so cheap and so abundant that bad ones could not be found."[11]

Frételliѐre was young and resilient, and he did not complain of the quarters on the *Jean Key*. Passengers lived in steerage, a low space inserted between the cargo hold and the surface deck. Crude double-deck bunks, tightly packed in rows, were designed to hold at least two passengers. They often held more. Next to each bunk was a box for clothing, food, and utensils that passengers used on a daily basis. The remainder of their baggage was stacked in the center of the cabin. There was no kitchen, only a firebox and grate on deck. The ship provided kindling and firewood, but it was up to the passengers to tend their fires. Emigrants lined up for their turn at the fire and bickered over who was next. When the weather was foul, cooking was impossible and the passengers were confined below decks.[12]

Frételliѐre's ship sailed directly to Galveston, without stopping in New Orleans. The journey took seventy-four days.

> Desiring to satisfy the greatest number of emigrants, the captain ordered the pinnace [a longboat] lowered. About thirty men and several ladies embarked. We had cleared scarcely one hundred yards when she began to leak. We tried to bail out the water with our shoes, our hats. We could not get the situation in hand; the water rose to our waists, and since the boat touched bottom we resolved to take to the water immediately. We gathered on the beach without further accident, amidst the acclamation of the inhabitants. Other little boats brought to shore the remaining emigrants, and our trunk arrived in good condition—which enabled us to change our clothes.[13]

Those colonists who landed in New Orleans before transferring for Galveston heard tales of what lay ahead. They learned how primitive conditions were in Texas, and how far from civilization Castro's grant was situated. And they undoubtedly heard the local opinions of the character of Henri Castro. Many abandoned the venture there.

When the remainder arrived in Galveston, they heard the same stories and were informed that they needed to book passage to Lavaca, on Matagorda Bay, another 150 miles down the coast. From there they would travel another 150 miles by Mexican oxcart, or on foot, to San Antonio—the nearest settlement to Castro's land grant.

The colonists had no idea that an additional difficult journey would meet them in Galveston—and no idea that additional expense would be involved. They expected to reach Texas, ride into the countryside, and begin farming. Many—typically as many as half—decided not to make the journey, deterred by the cost or by tales of what lay ahead. Some went to Houston to seek their fortune. Others remained on the coast. Many suffered cholera and fevers; many died. Others, lacking any means to support themselves, became paupers.[14]

Word of the arrival of the colonists spread quickly, soon reaching Sam Houston's ears. Instinctively, he knew the difficult situation that they faced. Learning that Maj. George T. Howard, a veteran of both the ill-fated Santa Fe expedition and the equally ignoble Somervell expedition, was interested in assisting the new arrivals, he penned a note asking Howard to go to Galveston and "impress upon them the lively disposition of the Government to facilitate their location and give them every possible accommodation, until they shall be better able to make a permanent settlement in the colony." Knowing something of the conditions they would find in ravaged San Antonio, Houston authorized Howard "to inform them that they can proceed at once to San Antonio and select and occupy the vacant houses in that place, and cultivate such farms as may be unoccupied, taking due care not to interfere with the rights of any citizen who may wish to do the same."[15]

Those who decided to travel onward from Galveston transferred to shallow-draft boats and sailed for Lavaca. Depending on their ship, the tides, and the weather, some anchored offshore and were transported to Lavaca by skiffs. From the moment that their ship left the Gulf and began navigation of treacherous Pass Cavallo into Matagorda Bay, the chances of running aground, snagging, or capsizing were great.[16]

Here is how Frétellière described Lavaca:

> The first view was not very attractive. It encompassed a wharf on piles, one hundred yards long, leading to a not very large frame warehouse. We went along the coast about fifty feet and came to the town. It was composed of a frame residence with a kitchen and poultry shed. This was the boarding-house and the principal mansion of the place. At some yards was a wooden cabin which had probably been constructed for the Negroes. But as it was empty for the moment, our agent rented it, and we made our headquarters there. A wooden shanty fifty paces away was occupied by Captain Smith, a Texian veteran who sold lequin [wine], tobacco, sugar and coffee.

> Two or three empty cases formed a counter. A demi-john of whiskey and another of gin made up the stock, and half a dozen glasses completed the installation. As you can see, it was very primitive.[17]

There were 114 colonists on the first ship, the *Ebro,* which landed at Galveston on January 9, 1843. Another 142 followed close behind. Even though only a fraction of the French families persevered to Lavaca, the meager accommodations there were quickly overwhelmed. People camped in tents or slept outdoors. As was the case in every Texas seacoast settlement, provisions were expensive, conditions unhealthy, and disease rampant.[18]

They were still more than 150 miles from San Antonio, the nearest settlement to Castro's land. They would have to make the journey in two-wheeled Mexican oxcarts, and the inventory of carts and teamsters was inadequate to take the group. They had to proceed in relays. Gradually the colonists straggled into San Antonio. It had never been much of a town, but after the violence of the revolution and the raids by generals Vásquez and Woll it was a pitiful wreck. The German- and French-speaking immigrants found themselves lost among English and Mexican tongues. There were no suitable accommodations, no possibility of traveling on to the land grant, no employment, no business opportunities, and no alternatives other than to stay and suffer or make the arduous trip back—if they could afford to do so. Most of the colonists—those few who survived out of those few who journeyed beyond Galveston—hunkered down, cursing their luck and Henri Castro.

CHAPTER 6

# *France Sours, Germany Ponders*

Jules Edouard Fontaine, Viscount de Cramayel, was forty-four years old when he arrived in Texas to temporarily replace the indisposed Dubois de Saligny as chargé d'affaires. Born to wealth, he had enlisted in the diplomatic corps at age twenty-two and served for eleven years in minor positions before returning to private life. Eleven years later he petitioned the foreign minister to resume his diplomatic career.

It was a rude surprise when he was awarded the post in Texas. Cramayel was a cultured European and had never before visited North America, much less the West, and apparently he had no desire to do so. He accepted the commission with the understanding that it would be a brief interim position.[1]

Cramayel arrived at Galveston on December 22, 1842, about two weeks before the first of Castro's colonists would disembark from the *Ebro.* Houston's revocation of the wine tariff exemption had occurred the day before, but Cramayel did not know it. And, of course, Houston had not known that Cramayel was about to step ashore, but the timing was brutally bad. Considering the difficulty of loan negotiations in Paris, the revocation was a terrible idea. If Houston somehow thought that he could revoke the favor so that it could be granted again as a loan incentive, then he had clearly lost his tactical touch. More likely, his motive was simpler and more venal: Houston was against anything Lamar favored or had done. Wiping out the tariff reduction meant wiping out a vestige of Lamar's administration. Texas did not import much French wine, thus the money at stake was small, but there is nothing more precious, more symbolic to the French than their wine. Revoking a favorable French wine tariff was an insult, nothing less.[2]

Cramayel did not learn of the revocation until after leaving Galveston for Washington. The trip was not of the sort to put him in a good mood. "I shall not try to describe for Your Excellency [Foreign Minister Guizot] the difficulties of travel at this time of year through the midst of primitive forests, on land partly flooded by rivers, or across the flat and endless plains that are here known as Prairies. As a result of torrential rains that have ravaged the countryside this year, these prairies, blanketed with a tall dry grass, have turned into one continuous swamp completely covered with a sheet of water, devoid of marked roads, and pitted with quagmires so deep that the horses can scarcely pull themselves out."

When he reached Washington, there was little to lift his spirits. "At the moment when the government and Congress were unexpectedly transferred to this town, the some thirty or forty log cabins of which it consists had been virtually abandoned for several years and were in a state of almost complete dilapidation. In the short time since this honor was conferred upon them, these houses could scarcely be put into condition to offer even a rude shelter against the elements, and now they are choked with crowds of men brought here by the Congress."[3]

If Cramayel was expecting a grand reception, he was disappointed. Secretary of State Jones was not in Washington. President Houston was ill. The moment Cramayel dismounted, he was greeted without ceremony by William Daingerfield, the secretary of the treasury and intermittent diplomat for Texas. Houston received Cramayel the next day and apologized for not being able to provide decent lodging or a proper reception. Houston's own residence, Cramayel reported, "is no more than a little wood cabin on one floor divided by a partition into two rooms, one of which serves him as an office and dining room and the other as bedroom for himself and his wife, who is ill at the present time. The furniture is in keeping with the dwelling. He himself seemed very tired and attributed his illness to his long vigils at the bedside of his sick wife."[4]

Cramayel did not linger long in Washington. "In a place where I could not even find a room to myself and where the members of the government and the Congress crowd into barracks and sleep two or three in a bed, I could stay no longer than the conventions of courtesy required. Therefore, I was obliged to follow the example of my colleagues, the chargés d'affaires of England and the United States, and return to Galveston." There, he soon turned his attention to Henri Castro.[5] He wrote Foreign Minister Guizot:

> Your Excellency will recall that Mr. de Saligny in his correspondence several times alluded to a certain Mr. Castro who first came to Texas as the agent of Messrs. Basterreche and de Lassaulx and then subsequently profited by this circumstance to work for his own interests and engaged in all kinds of intrigues here. He ended up by obtaining a considerable concession of land from the Texian government and even the position of consul general in Paris. However, on the request

of the Legation of the King, which had obtained detailed information on the antecedents and conduct of this individual, this post was taken away from him. . . .

Mr. Castro returned to France where he tried in vain to recover his post of consul general of Texas. After exhausting every possible expedient, including an attempt to obtain a loan for Texas after he had ingratiated himself with the House of Laffitte, and numerous other underhanded intrigues, he now comes forth again to use Texas as the blind for a racket whose center is in France and whose victims are French nationals.

"The game of Mr. Castro and his agents, whom he dispatches to the departments with misleading handbills, is to recruit families of farmers and other rural people and send them to Texas, where they will in all probability meet only with destitution instead of with the riches promised them. Only recently 120 of these luckless individuals, almost all of them natives of Lorraine, arrived here as the vanguard of the three hundred families who are to follow in stages to settle the lands granted to him by the state. Mr. Castro promises them land for cultivation; and indeed he does have land to give them. But he is careful not to tell them that this land lies between San Antonio de Bexar and the Rio Grande in an area where the authority of Texas has never been firmly established and which since the beginning of the war has been continuously exposed to the incursions of the Mexicans and, worse still, to the depredations of the bands of Texian volunteers.

Not satisfied with this misrepresentation of the lands to be settled, Mr. Castro arranges matters so that his victims, all of whom have at least some financial resources, pay him in advance before their departure, and with this money, in addition to what he makes on their passage in bargaining with the ship owner, he ends up with a tidy profit. In return for their advance he supplies them with drafts drawn on people who are not to be found in this country or who have no business connections with him, so that this paper has absolutely no value for the bearer.

I am told that three ships are expected here any day. They are the continuation of the emigration begun by the arrival of the American vessel *Ebro* out of Havre. Apparently Mr. Castro has scheduled the departures so that the first arrivals here will not have time to warn the others still in France of the fate that awaits them.

It is greatly to be desired that such immoral speculations be fore-

> stalled so that a hardy and vigorous people can be spared a miserable fate and saved for a more useful service for us either in France or in Africa.
>
> Your Excellency will decide whether official warnings should be published or special measures be taken; but in the interests of my fellow citizens I believed it my duty to report these facts.[6]

Meanwhile, as Castro's reputation suffered under Cramayel's attacks, Secretary of State Jones elected to send a diplomatic representative to the Netherlands, Belgium, and the Hanseatic League. To undertake this effort to advance Texas' search for financing and friends, he chose lawyer, farmer, and secretary of the treasury William Daingerfield. Educated at the University of Virginia, Daingerfield moved to San Antonio in 1837 and became prominent in local political affairs. He served as a senator from Bexar and in early 1842 was named secretary of the treasury. In periods when Anson Jones was ill or absent, Daingerfield served as interim secretary of state.[7]

Jones directed Daingerfield to travel to Washington, D.C., and confer there with Isaac Van Zandt, who was the Texas chargé d'affaires to the United States. Daingerfield was authorized to linger in Washington and Virginia for two weeks to visit with family; after that he was to sail for London and Paris (where he could spend a month consulting with Ashbel Smith and acquainting himself with the prospects for financing). After a month in London he was to travel to the Hague and seek recognition of Texas. Just as important, he was to search for loans in the Netherlands, Belgium, and among the Hanseatic League.[8]

Before departing Texas in February 1843, Daingerfield stopped briefly in Galveston. He had dinner with friends; it was an odd, small moment when all the moving pieces of Texas international relations came together. It must have been at the Tremont House, virtually the only oasis of dignity and grace in the uncultivated town. In the early dark of a brisk winter evening, as cold Gulf waters lapped at the wharves, the Tremont's staff served dinner by the light of oil lamps and candles, in a dining room heated by a great fireplace. The small room was crowded. The air was thick with tobacco smoke, speculation, and rumor.

At the table were Charles Elliot of Great Britain, the Viscount de Cramayel of France, Count Victor of Leiningen, and George Hockley, the Texas secretary of war who was enmeshed in the Cozumel intrigue. When wine was served, it was enough to set Cramayel railing against Houston's revocation of the tariff exemption. Daingerfield tired quickly of the Frenchman's monomania. To the Texian, acutely aware of France's failure to do more than talk about helping Texas, Houston's declaration had been more a reproach of the condescending French than a diplomatic blunder.[9]

Cramayel had a different impression of the evening. He thought Daingerfield had "a very obvious air of depression and anxiety, noticeable to everyone," that made Cramayel "suspect some secret motive for his journey." So Cramayel listened closely as "Daingerfield made no attempt to disguise the deplorable state of affairs and readily recognized the disasters that [Texas had suffered]. As for a solution, he confessed that he knew of none and said that if some great power like France or England did not come to the aid of Texas and compel Mexico to recognize it, he saw no hope for his adopted country."

Cramayel quizzed Daingerfield about the affairs of Texas and about annexation to the United States. "From the open manner in which he replied and discussed this question with me, I could no longer doubt that he was actually going to the United States to seek once more the active protection of the North Americans and, as a last resort, to join the Union by means of annexation if they would consent." After that, if circumstances permitted, Cramayel believed it was possible that Daingerfield would go to Belgium to open diplomatic relations, to the Hanseatic League to open commercial relations, and to northern Germany to seek financing.[10]

Cramayel was wrong. It was Belgium and the Hanseatic League that were first on Daingerfield's agenda, along with financing from whatever source it might be found. There was no secret mission. Daingerfield would travel by way of Washington, D.C., and would consult with Van Zandt there, but his greater interest was in visiting his family in Virginia. There was no need for a covert effort to beseech the United States for support and protection. Van Zandt was already doing that openly and regularly. It was his purpose. And Van Zandt fully understood that at some point the discussion might turn to annexation. In all likelihood, French foreign minister Francois Guizot knew that, even if Cramayel did not.

The most acute listener at the table may have been the young Count Leiningen. He was on his way back to Germany to report to the nobles' association. If Texas was destined to join the United States, that made his project much less interesting, for the United States would bring government, discipline, laws, tariffs, and soldiers that would choke off the torrent of opportunities in an untamed Texas. What was Cramayel reporting to Paris? What was Elliot telling London? What were the odds of peace with Mexico? How could the German nobles support a stumbling Texas and gain an advantage in the process? There was much at stake and many parties who could move to block—England, France, the United States, Mexico, even the nobles themselves.

Boos-Waldeck was traveling with Leiningen but does not appear to have attended the dinner, for reasons unknown. The next morning, when Daingerfield and Leiningen boarded the *Neptune* for New Orleans, Boos-Waldeck was along. Discussing what to report to the nobles, he and Leiningen concurred that developing a plantation was the proper beginning for the nobles' association. The plantation—Nassau Farm—could serve as a staging area for future German emigrants and for the nobles' business enterprises. It would be a place for testing and refining ideas and for learning lessons in a controlled environment.[11]

The two nobles traveled to New Orleans together, where Boos-Waldeck bid Leiningen good-bye, then set about purchasing tools, equipment, and other necessities for carving out a plantation. He returned to Galveston with eleven slaves, three wagons, and some twenty thousand pounds of gear. From there he transshipped the cargo and people up Buffalo Bayou to Houston, where he planned to buy oxen for the wagons. But Boos-Waldeck was new to the business and hadn't realized that the price of oxen would soar when a German nobleman was in need of more than a dozen at once. He got his beasts, but at an inflated price.

Charles Fordtran, whom Boos-Waldeck had hired in Industry as an advisor, met the count in Houston. It was February, and as they traveled north the weather turned nasty. A slashing wind added to the sting of rain that quickly turned to ice. They were met at Nassau by Wilhelm Etzel, the newly hired plantation overseer. The group (minus Fordtran, who returned to Industry) made miserable camp in tents while they constructed permanent shelter. When the work began, it turned out that Boos-Waldeck didn't know much about buying slaves. He had acquired a blacksmith, a bricklayer, and a cook, but no one who knew anything about felling trees, erecting buildings, splitting rails, or farming. Everything took longer than it should have. It was two weeks before a crude smithy was constructed; Boos-Waldeck and Wilhelm moved their belongings there, leaving the tent to the slaves.

Nassau Farm was within the Blackland Prairie, a rolling tallgrass expanse laced with post oak mottes. Broad swaths of little bluestem, big bluestem, grama grass, and switchgrass melded into groves of sugarberry, elm, sycamore, cottonwood, and pecan that grew in the stream bottoms. The winters could be cold and wet; the summers, hot and humid. The soils were fertile, but they were also dense and high in clay.

Boos-Waldeck had neither enough oxen nor enough talent to plow the heavy soil. After futile attempts, he took Fordtran's advice and leased eighty cultivated acres for planting the first year's crop of corn. But that land was eight miles from Nassau. Boos-Waldeck ordered the slaves to stay in the leased fields, return to Nassau on Saturday, and then journey back to the plowed lands on Sunday afternoon.

And so, mistake by mistake, lesson by lesson, Boos-Waldeck set about building a plantation for the nobles' association. His story reads like that of most frontier farmers. Crop failures, market failures, extreme weather, and fevers. Cabins and storehouses and livestock and crops. But through it all, Boos-Waldeck watched a horizon more distant than that of most pioneers. He was looking for large-scale investments suitable for the association. He reported back on the prospects for corn, cotton, sheep, horses, and cattle. He noted Texas' negative balance of trade and consequent shortage of cash, and he predicted that the condition would continue until peace with Mexico was cemented. Only then would Americans and Europeans begin to return to Texas. In time, though, a new era would dawn.

The opportunity that most seemed to interest Boos-Waldeck was—of all things—soap making. Castor beans grew wild at Nassau, and a mill could be built to extract their oil. Fordtran, who claimed to have owned a soap factory in Europe, thought that castor oil might be used to make soap. But he wasn't certain, so he needed to research the process and the market. Boos-Waldeck envisioned a wind-powered oil mill producing soap that could be exported down the Colorado River to within a few miles of Matagorda Bay, then overland to the bay and by water to Europe. It seems a long way to ship soap.

Boos-Waldeck was constantly considering the prospects for colonization. When he left Germany, he—and the rest of the nobles—believed that they could gain enormously by purchasing land. As land values soared, so would profits. But Boos-Waldeck discovered that Texas had abundant fertile and well-watered land and few settlers; true, the best land was already claimed, but many owners were eager to sell. It would be a long time before land prices began to increase.

After talking with Sam Houston and Anson Jones, Boos-Waldeck concluded that the Texas colonization program was not promising. Potential grant lands were those that, "to be sure, are drawn on the map as property of the Republic, but that are owned in reality by wild Indian tribes, or belong to their hunting grounds. The idea of transplanting German colonists into such areas, where they and their children would always be exposed to the scalping knife, would hardly be considered a charity by them."

And reality on the ground had convinced Boos-Waldeck that the costs of subsidizing mass colonization—even if land were free—would be immense. "It is true," he concluded, "that different grants in the west were recently given to the English and the French, which, however, is no proof at all that those contractors are going to fulfill the obligations they have assumed, since that is something that, to my knowledge, no empresario in Texas has managed to this day, except General Austin, the first of them, who had a choice between all the estates of the country twenty years ago."

Boos-Waldeck urged the nobles to continue with Nassau as a plantation, "a home base for Germans who emigrate to Texas on their own initiative, a base from which these shall be supported with counsel and, as much as possible, with deed." By doing so, by keeping its efforts on a manageable scale, the association could avoid "being drawn into risky experiments, which, if they failed, would result in the loss of the capital, the misery of the immigrants, and would attract, as a natural consequence, mockery, scorn, and ridicule, and rightfully so."

While Boos-Waldeck was analyzing the ways to support German emigration, while he was learning how to grow corn in Texas, matters in Europe were evolving. The developments in France were not reassuring. Alexander Bourgeois d'Orvanne was complaining to Ashbel Smith that revocation of the wine duty exemption had killed the chances of the $1 million loan. Smith received private letters from Guizot and Cramayel confirming their discomfiture, with Cramayel expressing "an opinion decidedly hostile to the negotiation of any Loan for Texas, in France." Smith thought he could convince the French that Texas held no ill will toward France, but he was certain that a French loan was now entirely out of the question.[12]

The situation was perhaps better in Germany. At Mainz, Count Carl of Castell—the vice-president of the nobles' association and its driving force—was doing his own thinking about how to profit from Texas while doing good. "In general it is acknowledged here more and more as a necessity that Germany should not allow its emigrants to disperse so widely," he wrote Boos-Waldeck in May, "but should make a large acquisition of land in one place in America and colonize it, so as to create direct trade ties between this colony and Germany." He recognized, however, that buying enough land would be prohibitively expensive, and he was leaning toward seeking a land grant from Texas. The association would ask Texas to lower tariffs on German imports and exports in return for Germany settling six thousand colonists. If terms of that sort seemed likely, Castell would approach the German Confederation and seek official government support, further reducing the association's capital commitment. Castell envisioned the association acting as an intermediary or a broker, profiting from a position in the middle.[13]

Castell wrote his letter over several days, as was common then. He commenced on May 24 and was still penning thoughts on June 1, when Count Leiningen returned from Texas, full of news and stories and bearing a report from Boos-Waldeck. Even though Boos-Waldeck was inclined toward a compact plantation that supported immigrants without full-scale colonization, Castell—after talking to Leiningen—leaned the other direction. He stayed with the idea of colonization of a large land grant. Leiningen had told him of Henry Fisher's grant and indicated that Fisher was amenable to selling out for the right price. Castell thought that was worth pursuing. He thought of another selling point to press upon Texas: if Germans colonized, an entirely new trade route would open between Germany and Texas, "which would not be the case with a trade agreement with England or France, for which reason it would be good for the time being to keep that matter secret from the ambassadors of those nations."[14]

In April 1843, Ashbel Smith decided to travel from Paris to London. The chances of obtaining financing in France had been ruined by the wine tariff imbroglio. The opportunities in London seemed better. Bourgeois was to meet Smith in London and was confident that something could be worked out there.[15]

But two weeks later Smith was still in Paris, writing Guizot to complain about a circular published by the Prefect of Doubs, where Castro had recruited many of his colonists. The prefect asserted that the first colonists had exchanged their money for drafts payable in Texas, but when they arrived in Galveston they found no one who would honor the drafts, leaving them without resources. Smith protested the allegation, informing Guizot that he had checked with Bourgeois and Castro and "received assurances that they have drawn no drafts on Texas, much less in the manner stated above."[16]

It was the first trickle of a torrent of complaints about Henri Castro. Ashbel Smith never saw evidence in Europe that Castro was operating other than honorably, but the feedback from Texas was damning. Guizot made it clear that it was Castro about whom the Prefect of Doubs was complaining. He asserted that Castro "has not made adequate provision for the reception and comfort of the emigrants on their arrival in Texas." At about the same time, Anson Jones wrote Smith from Texas to mention a "general complaint in relation to Mr. Castro, that his immigrants are brought to the country destitute in some measure of the necessary means for enabling them to settle either upon their own lands or others and much consequent dissatisfaction is said to exist on the part of those immigrants with the country and with Mr. Castro."[17]

And, of course, the Viscount de Cramayel was chiming in from Galveston: "The French merchant ship, the *Louis Philippe,* out of Dunkirk, has recently arrived in Galveston with some forty French immigrants sent by the same Mr. Castro. They have left in the direction of San Antonio de Bexar to join those that had preceded them, about whom I spoke earlier.

Faced with the impossibility of settling on the lands promised to them by Mr. Castro, they are forced to rely either on their own resources or what they can obtain from the local residents." Observing that "the lands granted to Mr. Castro for colonization are located in regions still unoccupied by Texas and in the hands either of Indians or bands of Mexican freebooters," Cramayel asserted that "some other families also started out for Texas but came by way of New Orleans. There they learned something of the fate that awaited them, and they decided not to continue."[18]

Castro's neglect of his colonists further damaged the reputation of Texas in Europe. "When Mr. Bourgeois was in London a few days ago since," reported Ashbel Smith from London on June 16, "he endeavored to make some arrangements for carrying into effect his Contract for colonization. I have some reason to apprehend that so long as the present unfavorable accounts continue to be received from Texas, emigrants of a desirable character will with difficulty be persuaded to remove to our country." And it was not just colonization that was suffering: "The present mail will bring you letters from Monsieur Bourgeois concerning the Loan. Under ordinary circumstances, it could be negotiated without any difficulty. I am not now sanguine of success. I have impressed upon Mr. Bourgeois the propriety of avoiding to give this subject any publicity."[19]

What Ashbel Smith did not know was that Sam Houston had declared an armistice with Mexico only the day before. That news would have brightened his outlook, but when he did learn of the armistice he reminded Anson Jones that "since my arrival in Europe I have not been sanguine of the practicability of a Loan on favorable terms, and I suspect that the negotiations now in progress for taking that of Mons. Bourgeois will be found to be contingent on a definitive peace." A mere armistice would not attract financing. But it might help another Texian goal: "Since the armistice Texas has attracted much larger and more favorable notice especially as connected with emigration."[20]

Bourgeois got wind that the armistice was having a particularly beneficial effect in Germany, which remained entranced with a romantic vision of Texas. His efforts to find financing, and to secure colonists, had been largely confined to England and France. Bourgeois traveled to Germany in the late summer of 1843 to acquaint himself with the potential there. It did not take long for him to learn of the nobles' association in Mainz. By September he was in discussions with Count Carl of Castell, and a most intriguing possibility emerged. The count was interested in both Bourgeois's colonization contract and the loan that he was working to place. By coincidence, William Daingerfield, the new Texian emissary to the Netherlands, Belgium, and the Hanseatic League, was also in Mainz, trying to learn more about the nobles' association. He already knew Bourgeois, having met him—and Castro and Saligny—during a layover in Paris. He met with Bourgeois again in Mainz, and with the leading members of the association: the Duke of Nassau, Prince Carl of Solms-Braunfels, Prince Carl of Leiningen, Count Carl of Castell, and Count Victor of Leiningen. Count Leiningen had returned from Texas three months earlier and was likely the source of the association's increased interest in colonization.[21]

Daingerfield learned that Bourgeois was already in negotiations with the association, but neither the nobles nor Bourgeois would tell him the details of their discussions. He chafed at the exclusion. Because he doubted that Bourgeois could perform his colonization contract on his own, he urged the nobles to purchase Bourgeois's contract, and he pressed for more information. Who, exactly, were the members of the association? What were their plans?

In mid-September, Solms, Leiningen, and Castell delivered a list of the members of the association and a proposal for a relationship with Texas. The society would send between twelve hundred and ten thousand colonists to Texas, according to the wishes of the republic; it would obtain a loan of $1 million to Texas; and it would procure trade concessions from the Zollverein, a German trade cartel. In return, Texas would make a grant of fertile land in proportion to the number of colonists introduced, under the Bourgeois contract or otherwise, and it would allow the association to import into Texas goods valued at $200,000 per year duty-free for a period to be negotiated.[22]

Daingerfield was optimistic: "Of their ability to carry out any contract which they may undertake the undersigned has not the slightest doubt or question. Of their strong desire to enter into some arrangement with his Government he is equally convinced. In submitting these views of this association to your Excellency the undersigned, *at the earnest desire of the association,* would respectfully suggest the propriety of his being vested with powers touching this matter, to such an extent and in such form as to your Excellency may seem best." Daingerfield had managed to insert himself into the negotiations between Bourgeois and the association, and he asked for authority to take over the matter entirely.[23]

But after making the proposal to Daingerfield, Castell made a slightly different proposition to Bourgeois: the nobles' association would loan the $1 million to Texas in exchange for the right to bring six thousand Germans to a colony in Texas that was favorable for commerce, health, and agriculture, and in exchange for an exemption upon import duties for goods valued at $200,000 per year, for ten years. There was no mention of reciprocal trade advantages for Texas, which, of course, would have been of less interest to Bourgeois than to Daingerfield.[24]

No doubt thrilled, Bourgeois relayed the proposal to Ashbel Smith in Paris, who forwarded the offer to Anson Jones in Texas. Smith did not recommend accepting either deal in its present form, but Bourgeois assured him that necessary modifications could be negotiated. Jones pointed out to Bourgeois that, because of the way the statute authorizing the $1 million loan was written, final negotiations had to occur in Texas, not Europe, and he "impressed on him the uselessness of an Agent proceeding to Texas unless he should be authorised to draw for the Loan or a portion thereof immediately upon conclusion of the negotiation."

The Texas secretary of state was pleased that Bourgeois had made progress in Germany, but he remained fundamentally cautious: "If the armistice results in the establishment of a solid peace, Texas will be able to obtain a Loan on favorable terms. Until that takes place I shall not be sanguine of the success of any negotiation."[25]

Despite Daingerfield's ambition to negotiate with the nobles, it was Bourgeois who managed to close the deal. In November he informed Daingerfield that his arrangement with the association was final, but—frustrating Daingerfield again—he would not reveal the terms of the transaction. In fact, the arrangements were not final, but Bourgeois and the nobles had decided to work together, without involving Daingerfield in their plans.[26]

During the negotiations with Bourgeois, Castell wrote Boos-Waldeck in Texas to let him know how matters were progressing. Castell assured Boos-Waldeck that he agreed about limiting the use of the association's capital to improving and enlarging the plantation rather than funding large-scale colonization. But—enclosing a copy of his proposal to Daingerfield—he made it clear that a grand project was still possible, so long as it was subsidized by Germany and Texas. "Our intention is to colonize a grant, but only with money from the governments, so that the profit will belong to *us;* if they do not contribute anything, then we will not colonize." And, "in order to be able to commence preliminary negotiations with our government, we have conditionally taken over the grant on the Medina, which has been given to Mr. Bourgeois d'Orvanne; that is, we have stipulated that he must obtain an extension and that we reserve four months' time before we take over the grant definitively."[27]

The mention of an extension was a gloss on a very serious matter. Bourgeois's contract was dated June 3, 1842, and required him to settle at least four hundred colonists within eighteen months—by December 3, 1843, less than three months from the date of Castell's letter. It was obviously impossible to meet the deadline. But Henry Fisher had already obtained a renewal of his contract, and Bourgeois was confident that he would be able to do the same, especially since his arrangement with the nobles was the first solid evidence that a $1 million loan might be gotten in Europe. Bourgeois was working hard to produce two of the things Texas needed most—financing and settlers—and the republic would be grateful for his accomplishments.[28]

Castell's letter to Boos-Waldeck was written in mid-September. Because of the slowness of mails, it was November before Boos-Waldeck replied. He was in New Orleans, on his way back to Germany. He had left Nassau in the hands of Fordtran until a replacement agent of the association could arrive. Boos-Waldeck penned a vigorous message to Castell:

> My main purpose in writing you today is to give you a well-meant warning not to let yourself be misled by either Col. Daingerfield or Mr. Bourgeois d'Orvanne. These gentlemen will deceive you with the most beautiful words and laugh up their sleeves if they are able to mislead yet another German. . . . You, my friend—I must express this to you plainly because your fervor and haste cause me dread and anxiety—are on the direct path to becoming the dupe of such people. You appear to be so caught up in your project that you are moving with dangerous haste out of the fear of being late. Believe me, none of the grants allotted by the government will get away from you, because none of the contractors will fulfill their obligations. Henry Fischer, who apparently still has the best-situated grant, will get in touch with you because he would like to dispose of his grant for very limited compensation. Just take care not to enter into any binding arrangement with one of these gentlemen, which could cause you great embarrassment.

Boos-Waldeck made it plain that, having given fair warning, he was washing his hands of responsibility for the consequences of dealing with Bourgeois and Daingerfield. "Had I not already been resolved to return to Europe, [then upon receiving your letter] I would immediately have made the decision that we could not hold out in Nassau any longer, as I have the fear in my heart that in spite of my warning we are on a course that will result in unforeseen embarrassment and loss."

Boos-Waldeck's agitation may have been a symptom of burnout. He had traveled far, endured a laborious challenge, and suffered repeated fevers. For treatment, doctors had given him doses of calomel, a dense yellowish-white chloride of mercury. It is a diuretic and a purgative, and it is toxic.

"Well, all the best to you, most respected friend," he closed his letter to Castell, "do not be offended by my candor, but it is my duty to tell you the truth, or at least that which I perceive as such. I will have to remain in Havana at least six to eight weeks, since my entire nervous system has been affected by the ridiculous mercury, all sleep long since departed, and my digestion ruined. My best to you."[29]

CHAPTER 7

# *Setbacks and Preparations*

Paris prepares for winter in October, when the warm autumn days become gray and rainy. Trees shed their leaves, days grow short, and pedestrians wrap their cloaks tightly about them as they bustle along the Rue de Rivoli. Carriages clatter on wet streets and the odor of coal smoke permeates the air. Ashbel Smith, from the Texas embassy in an opulent mansion at Place Vendôme, wrote his superior Anson Jones, whose offices were in a crude, drafty cabin in Washington, Texas. Francois Guizot, reigning over the formidable foreign ministry at Quai d'Orsay, issued instructions to the Viscount de Cramayel in his rented house on the sandy island fronting muddy Galveston Bay. Alexander Bourgeois d'Orvanne ventured forth from the Rue Faubourg to meet with the Duke of Nassau at his palace on the Rhine, where they discussed loans and colonies. Henri Castro recruited colonists from his apartments on the Rue de Lafitte and dispatched a second wave of French citizens to Texas.

Much of the winter correspondence between France and Texas concerned Castro, whose first group of colonists had suffered badly. Ashbel Smith, as usual, was the most forgiving. He reported to Anson Jones from Paris that "I continue to impress on [Castro] the liability of entire failure in his enterprise unless he shall make adequate preparation for the comfortable reception etc. of his colonists on their arrival. In other respects his activity and energy appear deserving of commendation, and I am informed his colonists are persons of good character."

But overall Smith was not optimistic about the results of colonization. He predicted that the Peters Colony on the Red River, authorized by Lamar, would be a failure because the English principals were entangled in some sort of disagreement. On the other hand, he thought that Kennedy's contract might be salvaged: "Mr. William Pringle and others have taken to execute the terms of Mr. Kennedy's 'concession'; and should the concession in question be prolonged or renewed I feel great confidence they will do so faithfully and efficiently." Of course, his mild optimism about Pringle's chances was pinned on a renewal or extension, putting Pringle in the same tenuous position as Bourgeois.[1]

Several days later William Daingerfield wrote Smith from the Hague to report on an exchange of correspondence with Castro. Daingerfield had reproached the Frenchman, reminding him "that it would be injurious to the Country, to cast upon its shores a band of paupers, consumers, incapable of adding to the productions of its soil or the development of its resources, whose inevitable sufferings would cause them to render disastrous accounts to their friends in Europe, and thereby check further emigration, that as these emigrants landed under circumstances could never reach their destination, they would not aid him in the performance of his contract of Colonisation, that humanity and justice towards the emigrants themselves forbade a course fraught with so much evil to them."

There is some reason to suspect that Daingerfield suffered diplomatic insensitivity: "I am sorry to say that Mr. Castro in his reply manifested a good deal of anger, and instead of taking my letter in the friendly way in which it was intended, he volunteered the absurd intimation that I was inimical to him and his enterprise; How this absurd notion could have entered his brains since I have at all times treated him with Courtesy I am at a loss to imagine unless, as I am inclined to suspect from the tone of his letter of to day it has its origin in a feeling of jealousy towards Mr. Bourgeois d'Orvanne."[2]

Of course, in Texas the Viscount de Cramayel was doing his best to undermine Castro. In Paris, Ashbel Smith picked up the scuttlebutt: "I have understood from sources which appear to be deserving of credit that Mr. de Cramayel has represented the 'grant' of Mr. Castro as a sterile plain, not even in the possession of Texas; that the colonists are exposed to the attacks of Mexicans and Indians and to be pillaged by Texian Volunteers." And Foreign Minister Guizot heard from Cramayel that the Castro colonists' "condition is pitiable, that a large number have died from the influence of the climate, that the survivors apply daily at the French Legation for the means to return to Europe; etc."[3]

The biggest problem with assertions of that type was that, although Cramayel may have exaggerated some, they were in the main true. On December 1, 1843, he reported that "every day a few more stragglers from that group of unfortunate Frenchmen sent out and abandoned by Mr. Castro arrive in Galveston. Those who have been able to escape illness and destitution come to implore the Legation of the King to help them to get back to New Orleans. Already more than one fourth of them have died. Others have left Texas, and very likely all those able to depart will do so successively in the future."[4]

Smith understated to Anson Jones that "the colonization enterprise of Mr. Henry Castro is as you are aware, not favorably regarded by the French Government. The objections to it are chiefly connected, I believe with Mr. Castro; tho' I do not think this Government are disposed to favor any foreign emigration except to their own colonies." Smith also brought Jones up to date on other matters, mentioning that Bourgeois was in Germany working on the $1 million loan and his colonization contract.

By January 1844, Jones wrote Smith that the people backing the Peters Colony were mending their disagreements, but "it has appeared to me for some time to be doubtful whether under present circumstances the contracts for colonizing from the continent of Europe would result in introducing a large and valuable emigration into our country." And, he continued, "I am not sanguine of the success of the Loan until peace shall be definitively established." It is not difficult to imagine Jones letting out a sigh as he penned the words.[5]

During the last half of 1843, a small circle of people in Texas—Houston, Jones, Cramayel, Elliot, and a few others—were keeping their eyes on the effort to find financing and colonists in Europe, but most Texians were talking of annexation to the United States. The impetus was a surge of apprehension about British interference in the republic. The concern originated in the United States and was amplified by William Sumpter Murphy, the American chargé d'affaires to Texas.

Cramayel—who said that Murphy had "distinguished himself only by his freakish dress and boorish manners," and who considered him "truly mentally deranged"—complained that Murphy "did his best to spread the absurd stories about English influence and her ambitions in Texas, and then went so far as to echo the barroom talk in Texas and to say everywhere that General Houston was negotiating with England to sell out the country for money." The rumors were so virulent that Houston was obliged to stand before the congregation of a Presbyterian church and publicly deny that he was delivering the republic to the British for a bribe of £5,000.[6]

It was in this atmosphere that the Eighth Congress of the Republic of Texas met in December 1843 and January 1844. They were wary of foreign intervention, wary of the British, wary of the French, wary of a mysterious group of German nobles. Sentiment was swinging toward another attempt at annexation; many Texians wanted immigrants from the United States, not elsewhere. The Congress saw the so-called colonial empresarios as rank speculators. They resented the giveaway of Texas land. They wanted no more debt—except, perhaps, for attacking Mexico. And, for many of the members of the Congress, if Houston was for it, they were against it. Two legislative acts strongly demonstrate that sentiment: a bill revoking authority for the $1 million loan, and another bill prohibiting any new colonization contracts or extensions of existing ones.

President Houston may not have been surprised by the revocation of authority to borrow; after all, the Congress had ruled out the $5 million loan a year earlier, and it had been up to Houston to dig up old statutory authority for the $1 million. But he was wounded by the idea of terminating his colonization program. He wrote the Congress that "to curtail [the empresarios'] rights as provided for in the bill, would, the Executive conceives, be not only a violation of the constitution, but work great loss and inconvenience to those who have invested capital and expended labor in endeavoring to carry out their respective undertakings in good faith." In his view, "nothing, certainly, exerts a more detrimental influence upon the prosperity and happiness of a nation than instability in legislation."

Houston saved his strongest argument for the last. "A very powerful and wealthy association at [Mainz] in Germany, is on the eve of commencing the introduction of a large number of German families into western Texas. By affording a few facilities and observing a strict regard for the laws, much may be done toward the settlement and protection of that portion of our vacant territory by a population distinguished for its industry and thrift."[7]

Houston's four priorities for an independent republic were to achieve peace with Mexico, settle hostilities with the natives, secure financing, and attract colonists. Now two of those priorities were under attack from within. Without European financing, without European colonists, and unless the Mexican armistice could be transformed into a permanent peace, a weak and desperate Texas would have no alternative but annexation. Exasperated, Houston knew that the future of the republic hung in the balance.

The Congress turned decidedly away from Europe and decidedly toward the United States. The law revoking authority for the $1 million loan and the law prohibiting colonization contracts passed in January 1844. The loan revocation may not have overly bothered Houston; according to Anson Jones, "Our finances are now in a very flourishing condition, the exports exceeding the imports, and the ordinary income being sufficient to defray the expenses of the civil list." But the attack on colonization struck at the core of Houston's effort to populate the state. He protested loudly and pointed to the German nobles' deal with Bourgeois as an example of a potentially beneficial development. Houston believed that his policies of seeking peace with Mexico, financing for the republic, and settlers for the frontier were beginning to take effect.[8]

But the legislators talked openly of annexation and railed against British interference—in no small part because Britain was linking its support to abolition of slavery. Getting the forceful message that the Congress had soured on Europe, feeling the consequences of his tiff with the Senate, and perhaps sensing that the future of an independent republic was dimming, Houston began to maneuver. On January 20, he stood before the Congress to deliver a secret message. Though he professed to offer no opinion on annexation, he openly invited the Congress to approve moving forward on the matter. But Houston cautioned that, if talks with the United States were commenced and ended in failure, England and France would find out, would be suspicious, and might withdraw their support.

And so Houston and Smith swung their gaze to the United States. "The laws authorizing a public loan having been repealed," wrote Anson Jones to Ashbel Smith, "you will inform Mr. Bourgeois of the same, and that his contract for a Loan has expired by limitation and been annulled." He continued, saying that "the system of colonizing this country by emigrants under contracts of the character of Mr. Castro's has not been so successful as could have been desired, and the Laws authorizing the granting of such contracts has been repealed. It is believed that nearly all the contracts with Europeans made by the President have already or will soon be forfeited by a non-compliance on the part of the contractors with the conditions contained in said contracts, within the specified time."[9]

But Henri Castro's second crop of colonists was already coming ashore at Galveston. With them was Louis Huth, a competent manager. Thirty-one years of age, Huth was the son of Ludwig Huth, a French insurance company owner and wine merchant. The Huths had reached an arrangement with Castro that allowed them to ship merchandise on Castro's ships; in Texas, Louis Huth would sell the merchandise and use the proceeds to purchase hides and cotton for the European market. Castro also engaged Huth as a colonial manager, charged with shepherding the colonists to San Antonio.[10]

Huth sailed on the *Jean Key* from Antwerp in October 1843. With him were fifty families and single men (totaling 128 people) bent on colonization. As with the previous year's group, most of the colonists were from Alsace and Lorraine; some were Swiss, and some were Germans from Baden and Nassau. On January 1, 1844, they entered Galveston harbor. Castro had assured Huth that agents would meet him in Galveston and arrange for onward travel. But there were no agents to be found, for Castro had neglected to pay them. Huth felt burdened with responsibility, because the colonists—contrary to what Castro had assured all concerned—were "in a pitiable state." Using his merchandise and his own possessions as collateral, Huth borrowed money from merchant H. A. Cobb and booked passage for the colonists to Lavaca on Matagorda Bay.[11]

At Lavaca, Huth found that no arrangements had been made to feed or shelter the colonists or to move them to San Antonio. In the midst of sorting out the mess, word came from Cobb that a critical crate of merchandise was nowhere to be found; Cobb thought it must have been carried off by the colonists. But it was not in Lavaca, so Huth caught a boat back to Galveston, where he settled the matter of the missing crate and procured provisions for the colonists. When he returned from Galveston, he was in for a surprise: "During my absence, the colonists took forcible possession of all my property, stole a good portion of it from me, were at the point of dividing it among themselves when I returned! Who would not have been frightened by such behavior in that lawless place? But by my determination and cool-headedness, supported by the presence of [Charles DeMontel], I forced them to return to me anything still intact!"[12]

DeMontel, a Texas surveyor of Prussian extraction who had changed his name from Carl Scheidemontel, lived in San Antonio and had been engaged by Castro to assist with establishing the colony. With his help, Huth assembled the colonists and transported them to San Antonio on two-wheeled oxcarts.[13]

Another group of 136 colonists arrived in February aboard the *Heinrich;* Huth guided them to San Antonio. In April, he traveled with Texas Ranger captain Jack Hays to inspect Castro's land grant. He reported back to the colonists that the lands were suitable, and they decided to set up camp there as soon as enough colonists had arrived. But while in San Antonio they were in no better circumstances than the colonists of the year earlier. There were no jobs, no support, little housing, and scant provisions. Huth, who found the first shipload of Frenchmen to be "pitiable," was disappointed at the arrival of the second group, "a good many of them without any money." He loaned the pilgrims what he could, but conditions worsened.[14]

Castro was still in Europe, gathering and sending colonists. In April, the *Ocean* sailed for Galveston with ninety colonists, followed by thirty-nine colonists sailing on the *Jeanette Marie* in May. In all, 393 colonists landed in Texas in 1844, following the 256 scattered, miserable, and deceased colonists of 1843. They lacked the money, supplies, equipment, and tools needed to commence colonization, thus had no choice but to wait in war-ravaged San Antonio, hoping that Castro would appear. Disease and hunger took their toll. Disappointed colonists began to drift away.[15]

Castro nemesis Alphonse Dubois de Saligny returned to New Orleans from France in mid-January 1844, replacing the Viscount de Cramayel. Though Saligny was reoccupying his post of chargé d'affaires to Texas, he would execute his mission from the more civilized realm of New Orleans. Other than brief visits, Saligny would never again reside in Texas. Even from New Orleans, though, he quickly detected the Texas drumbeat for annexation. His impression of Sam Houston was that the Texian president was intent on peace with Mexico and an independent republic. The information coming out of the Texian peace commissioners to Mexico was encouraging. "Certainly he would not choose this moment to enter into negotiations for the entrance of Texas in the American confederation. He has expressed himself too often and too explicitly for doubt to exist on that score." He was correct: Houston would not *choose* that moment for annexation negotiations, but his hand had been forced, and negotiations were under way. By the end of March, they were public knowledge.[16]

Hope for peace with Mexico was dashed in February. The peace commissioners returned with a proposed treaty that ended hostilities but declared Texas to still be "a department of Mexico." Houston and Jones rejected it.[17]

On April 22 annexation seemed more certain than ever; a treaty was concluded and sent to the U.S. Senate for confirmation.[18]

Nonetheless, in the spring of 1844, the future of Texas was taking shape not only at the two Washingtons but also in Mainz, on the Rhine River. Alexander Bourgeois d'Orvanne was there, his hopes of a loan dashed but his colonial aspirations still alive—despite the congressional extinguishment of colonization contracts. He believed that the nobles' association, financially strong, connected to the German Confederation, with access to an abundant supply of colonists, was his ticket to contract renewal.

The nobles' association was itself changing. When Leiningen returned in June 1843, the association turned toward large-scale colonization, despite the warnings of Boos-Waldeck. When Boos-Waldeck returned to Germany in the spring of 1844, he issued a lengthy report that argued against anything other than establishing a small plantation at Nassau to assist individual emigrants. But the other members of the association disagreed. Turmoil ensued. Boos-Waldeck and his brother ended their membership. The association raised new capital for its venture by bringing in new members. It reformed on March 25, 1844, and renamed itself the Gesellschaft zum Schutz deutscher Einwanderer in Texas (Association for the Protection of German Immigrants in Texas). It assumed a high profile, publishing broadsides and calls for colonists. It was seldom called by its formal name; it was known for what it had always been: the Adelsverein—the nobles' association.[19]

The new Adelsverein embraced Bourgeois, but its members had their eyes open. They fully understood that his contract had expired and that renewal might be problematic. They were relying on his representations that renewal would not be difficult, but they were also keeping their eyes on other potential partners. They had already heard of Henry Fisher through Count Victor of Leiningen; Bourgeois would need to perform or get out of the way.

The association made plans. Its members listened to Bourgeois's descriptions of Texas and his ideas of how colonization might proceed. They calculated how much money it would require. They made inquiries of the German government about subsidization. But it quickly became apparent that the first priority was to get a team on the ground in Texas. Unlike Castro, they would not load colonists onto ships and send them to Texas to fend for themselves. That would hardly fit their three declared purposes: improvement of the conditions of the working classes and a decrease of pauperism; opening new markets for the products of German industries; and development of maritime commerce.[20]

And, unlike Castro, they would not expect the colonists to be self-sufficient. The very point of the Adelsverein was to protect and assist German peasants and proles in establishing a new German colony in Texas. The Adelsverein announced that it would provide generously:

> The verein will provide large and commodious ships as well as enough wholesome and inexpensive food for the trip across the ocean. It will have agents in Texas to assist the emigrants when they land and it will furnish enough wagons to transport them and their belongings to the settlement. Care will be taken of their needs on the way. As soon as they arrive at the settlement, each family will get its own house built after the fashion of the country, of logs laid and fitted upon one another. Warehouses filled with provisions, gardening and farming implements, and seeds and plants of all sorts, will provide the emigrants with all they need for working and living. They will find also all the necessary oxen, horses, cows, hogs and sheep. All of these will be sold cheaper at the warehouses of the verein than they can be bought at the nearest market.

And that was not all: "The Society regards it a sacred duty to provide for the moral and religious education of the emigrant children and will cause schools and churches to be erected in the colony according to the needs of the settlers. The verein will care for the employment of doctors and druggists and will look after the erection of a hospital."[21]

All of this would be provided free for a small number of truly impoverished families. The others were expected to have at least $120 for a single man or $240 for a family to meet their expenses. It was a bargain, an act of charity.

There was a lot of advance work to be done in Texas: cabins and wharves to build, warehouses to erect and stock, wagons and horses and oxen to buy, and a thousand small details to make everything ready for the colonists, who were to arrive in the autumn. The Adelsverein directed Bourgeois to return to Texas to make arrangements. He would serve as its colonial commissioner. They appointed Prince Carl of Solms-Braunfels as commissioner general; he would accompany Bourgeois.[22]

CHAPTER 8

# *Solms*

It was almost midnight, and Solms was weary. He stepped from the two-horse coach into a wispy fog that hovered just above the cobbled street. Flersheim and van der Bergh alighted behind him. Bourgeois, the unctuous Frenchman, stood at the curb, awaiting his arrival. A soft glow came from inside the grand townhouse. With van der Bergh at his elbow, Bourgeois and Flersheim following behind, Solms left his servants to look after the luggage while he attended to brief formalities with Minart.[1]

The small hotel was perfectly suitable for nobility. It was one of the elite London establishments that catered to the highest strata of society. Solms preferred Minart's to the similar property operated by Claridge on Brook Street. Still, he chafed at the idea of paying for lodging in London. It reminded him of why he was not in the family's apartments at St. James Palace.

He was Carl Friedrich Wilhelm Ludwig George Alfred Alexander, Prince of Solms, Lord of Braunfels, Grafenstein, Muenzenberg, Wildenfels, and Sonnenwalde, His Imperial Royal Apostolic Majesty's Captain in King Friedrich August of Saxony III's Cuirassier Regiment, Knight Grand Cross of the Royal Hanoverian Guelph Order and of the Ducal Brunswick Order of Henry the Lion, and Knight of the Order of St. George of Lucca.

More to the point, the handsome, impeccably dressed thirty-two-year-old with the handlebar moustache was the son of Queen Frederica of Hanover. The Hanovers had ruled Great Britain for 143 years. Solms's mother, born Princess Frederica Louisa Carolina Sophia Alexandra of Mecklenberg-Strelitz, was the aunt of reigning Queen Victoria of the United Kingdom and was the niece of the late King George III and Queen Charlotte, who had held court in Buckingham Palace for fifty-seven years.

Frederica had married well, thrice. At age fifteen she wed His Royal Highness Prince Ludwig of Prussia in an elaborate state ceremony at the royal palace in Berlin. She bore the prince three children (two princes and a princess) but divorced him just three years later, shortly before his death at age twenty-three. After four years she remarried, a bit lower. Her new spouse was His Serene Highness Prince Friedrich William of Solms-Braunfels. Prince Carl was the sixth and last of her children with Prince Friedrich and the youngest of her four Solms princes.

The Solms family dated back to the twelfth century, taking their name from the ancient castle of Solmissa in today's Oberndorff. Historically, they married well and moved easily within the complex royal society of the Holy Roman Empire. Their principality, Solms-Braunfels, was small but respected.

In 1803, Napoleon's army, using its might to unify Europe under liberal social and political ideals, had pushed east to the Rhine, absorbing many of the jumbled statelets that constituted the empire's Upper Rhenish Circle. Solms-Braunfels was safely on the east bank of the Rhine, but its existence was nonetheless in peril.

In 1806, Napoleon gathered Germanic states on both sides of the Rhine into a confederation. In the face of a French ultimatum, Holy Roman Emperor Francis II declared the empire at an end. As a part of the restructuring, dozens of small principalities, duchies, and city-states were mediatised—divided and merged—into larger states. Solms-Braunfels disappeared into the two large Germanic states (Austria and Prussia) and two of the middle-sized states (Hesse-Darmstadt and Wurttemberg). The Solmses became a family of princes without a principality.

Prince Solms was born in 1812, six years after the extinction of his family's domain. His father—the last prince of Solms to rule a realm—died just two years later, leaving his mother Frederica with four surviving children.

Fourteen months after Prince Friedrich's death, Frederica married for a third time. Her new husband was His Royal Highness Field Marshal Prince Ernst Augustus of Hanover, who also held the British title of Duke of Cumberland. He was the eighth child and fifth son of King George III and Queen Charlotte, Frederica's uncle and aunt. The two cousins married first at Frederica's parish church at Neu-Strelitz and again at Carlton House, London.

The Hanovers had assumed the British crown in 1701 in a parliamentary maneuver meant to keep Catholics off the throne. When Solms's mother married his new stepfather in 1815, Hanoverian patriarch and monarch George III still ruled. But King George was seventy-seven and quite mad.

George III had an abundance of legitimate children, thus there was little risk that the crown might leave the family. But there was a problem with the children—particularly the sons—of George III. They were irresponsible, philandering, dissolute drunks. And of all George's sons, Solms's new stepfather was the worst. One historian described him as "ugly, vindictive, vicious and surrounded by dark, evil rumors of murder and horrifying debaucheries." A London newspaper quipped that he had committed every conceivable crime except suicide. He was particularly well known for sexual assaults upon the wives of other nobles. He was said to have murdered four men; it is certain that he killed his valet, but he managed to escape conviction. His sinister demeanor was complemented by his one-eyed glare; he had lost the other in battle.[2]

Frederica's principal duty in her marriage to the Duke of Cumberland was to deliver an heir. Because she had already borne nine children, she was considered up to the task. In 1817 a daughter was stillborn, and again in 1818. In 1819, Frederica gave birth to Prince George of Cumberland, who would assume his father's mantle. Ironically, Prince George lost the sight of one eye during a childhood illness, and an accident blinded his other eye when he was fourteen.

King George III died in 1820. First son George IV assumed the thrones of Great Britain and Hanover and lived for ten more years without fathering an heir. He outlived childless second son Frederick, thus the crown passed to third son William IV in 1830. William IV lived another seven years, outlasting fourth child Princess Charlotte and fifth child Prince Edward.

The gap between the throne of England and the reviled Ernst Augustus, Duke of Cumberland, was growing smaller by the year. As matters turned out, he would have become king of Great Britain in 1840 but for the birth of a daughter to Prince Edward in 1819 at Kensington Palace. Though Edward died before getting a chance at the throne, the rules of cognatic primogeniture passed the crown to his sole surviving child, Victoria.

Victoria became queen of the United Kingdom in 1837 and would have become queen of Hanover as well, but for one difference between England and Hanover: royal succession in Hanover was still governed by the Salic Law, an ancient code dating to the fifth century. The Salic Law forbade women to succeed to family titles or offices. The kingship of Hanover skipped Victoria and her two aunts—Augusta and Elizabeth—and vested in Ernst Augustus, Duke of Cumberland and now king of Hanover.

Frederica became queen of Hanover. Blind Prince George became heir apparent to the throne. And Prince Carl of Solms became the youngest of three stepson princes living in the Hanoverian palace in the shadow of a despised one-eyed tyrant and his blind son.

Perhaps because of the pressures surrounding him, Solms displayed a rebellious streak as a young man. At age twenty-two he secretly married. It was a morganatic marriage, meaning that he married beneath himself and that his wife and children had no right to his titles or estate. Which means that he married for love. He fathered three children, but the marriage suffered under pressures from both families. In 1841 he divorced his wife, generously pensioning her as the Baroness Luise von Schonau, an invented title.

It was during his marriage that he joined the Austrian military. In 1839, two years before the marriage fractured, he was sentenced to four months in prison for having abandoned his command without leave. Perhaps the two events were connected. Nonetheless, the year of his divorce also saw his promotion to captain of cavalry in the imperial army of Austria. Perhaps those two were connected, as well.[3]

Solms was too young to have participated in the Napoleonic Wars, but he served well in prestigious assignments in the Rhineland, the Balkans, and Bohemia. By the time he emerged from his rebellious years, he was a sound officer. In fact, for all of his titles, for all of his family's history and connections, all that Prince Carl could truly claim for himself was that he was a lightly smudged captain in the Austrian army.

It sounds harsh, but Solms had no purpose unless he could invent one. In the early hours of May 17, 1844, after relaxing over tea, he slipped beneath the crisp sheets of his bed in Minart's Hotel, believing that he had done just that.

In a nearby room slept L. H. Flersheim, a Frankfurt banker who had joined Solms for the channel crossing from Ostend to Dover. Flersheim was overseeing the financial end of Solms's venture but did not plan to accompany him farther than Liverpool. They had changed to the ship *Hotel* for the voyage from Dover to London, traveling north along the English coast, entering the mouth of the Thames, and pushing upstream to come ashore at Bricklayers' Arms. The dockside had been in disarray; engineer William Cubitt was guiding construction of a nearby railway station. Cubitt was better known for building canals, but his project for the South Eastern Railway would soon link Dover to Bricklayers' Arms by rail. From the docks, the travelers took an omnibus (a two-horse streetcar) into the West End, then a coach to Minart's.

In another room at Minart's was Albert van der Burgh, a Dutch noble and business associate of Solms who had also joined the group in Ostend. And finally there was Alexander Bourgeois d'Orvanne, the unlikely Texas colonial empresario who met Solms on the steps of Minart's Hotel.[4]

The next day, Friday, Solms took Flersheim and van der Bergh to settle a few business matters in London. The flowers in London's royal parks were in full bloom; the three visitors took time to stroll the paths across the greensward, admiring the beauty of London in the spring. Westminster bustled with commerce and government, the streets crowded with merchants, clerks, nobles, and clergy.

The West End was a place of style and grace, but this was the London of Dickens, and the working-class East End was someplace else entirely. In the 1840s, London's population doubled, surging by more than a million new residents. The Industrial Revolution had knocked the pins from under the working class; emerging factories, railroads, and vast docks drew laborers to cities and intensified their toils without enriching their lives. London had no city government, thus it had no municipal system of sewers or water. Open ditches emptied effluent into the Thames. Squalid tenements lined both sides of the Thames below the Tower of London.

Solms's world was far removed from the miseries of the working classes, but he was neither ignorant of the enormity nor unsympathetic to the victims. To the contrary, the acute and unique distress of Germany's working classes and peasantry had long since registered on Solms and his associates, who had resolved to relieve the pressure in a way suited to their abilities and interests. It did not diminish their resolve when they realized that their good intentions created commercial and political opportunities as well.

Spurred by idealistic notions of his mission's dignity, cosseted in his world of privilege, Solms spent Saturday in relaxation and correspondence. Most important to Solms was the letter he wrote to his betrothed, Princess Sophie of Lowenstein-Wertheim-Rosenberg. Sophie was the widow of Prince Franz of Salm-Salm, who had died seventeen months earlier, making her Sophie of Salm-Salm, engaged to become Sophie of Solms. She was, if nothing else, sibilant.

In an age of romance, the undeniably romantic Prince Solms was helplessly infatuated with his Sophie. She was his Roxanne, his Dulcinea del Toboso. Just six days into a long journey, he already missed her desperately.

Sunday evening Solms, Bourgeois, Flersheim, and four servants boarded the London and Birmingham Railway at Euston Station and traveled northwest. Not quite six years old, the railroad was the first to connect London and Birmingham, where passengers could change to the equally new Liverpool and Manchester Railway and travel on to the port of Liverpool. With railroads still in their infancy, early locomotives were so underpowered that a stationary steam engine at Camden was used to haul trains uphill from Euston by cable, from whence they proceeded under their own power.

The chuffing, clanking, screeching locomotives that gathered in Birmingham were an impressive and frightening sight, but no more so than the hellish glow and belching smoke of the industrial city's around-the-clock iron smelters. It would be another eleven years before Henry Bessemer developed a process for mass-producing steel; the coke-fired blast furnaces at Birmingham were turning out cast iron, and their sister puddling furnaces were converting it into wrought iron. Solms marveled at Birmingham's lurid, orange, flickering sky as he waited for his luggage to be transferred. It was already a journey of new experiences.

After changing trains in Birmingham, Solms and his retainers reached Liverpool at 5:15 in the morning and checked into the Adelphi Hotel for a few hours' rest. Solms, Bourgeois, and their servants were booked on the *Caledonia,* which was leaving that night when the tides turned.

Liverpool was a hard-working port on the banks of a Mersey estuary that opened into the Irish Sea. Far northwest of London, it flourished on textiles and—in its early years—the slave trade. Massive imports of cotton from the United States and Texas brought rapid expansion of its docks in the early decades of the nineteenth century. Warehouses, chandlers, and multistory merchant houses lined the Mersey for seven miles. Wide wharves and plazas that separated the docks from the streets teemed with horses, wagons, stevedores, and cargo. The waterfront was a tangle of masts and rigging.

Even in May, the wind off the sea had a cold edge that sliced through layers of clothing. A miasma of coal smoke darkened the sky and tarnished the building stones. For every bank there was an almshouse, for every prosperous trader five burdened stevedores. Because almost two-thirds of children died before age five, the average lifespan for a Liverpool laborer and his family members was fifteen years, and for tradesfolk twenty-two.[5]

Solms saw no more of Liverpool's inner workings than he had of London's. The Adelphi Hotel, built in 1826 by James Radley, was the finest in the city. On Ranelagh Place at the center of town, it was comfortably east of the clamor and odor of the docks. Solms finished up some correspondence, then entrusted Flersheim with his letter to Sophie and another to his business partner Count Carl of Castell. The banker accompanied Solms and Bourgeois to the docks, then watched as they boarded and cast off for North America.

The *Caledonia* was a steam packet ship, as novel a contraption as the steam locomotive. Around 1830 a Quaker by the name of Samuel Cunard had conceived of transatlantic commerce by steam, only to be laughed at. After becoming a partner in a Boston shipping company, he began lining up supporters and investors. In 1840 his company launched the first of four steam packet ships. They missed by a year or so being the first scheduled transatlantic steamers, but they benefited by a bit of genius: Cunard's *Britannia, Acadia, Caledonia,* and *Columbia* were identical. For the first time, passengers knew in advance the accommodations that they could expect.[6]

The Cunard Line's *Caledonia* was less than four years old when Solms stepped aboard. Her gigantic lever-driven sidewheels, powered by enormous steam engines that rose through three decks amidships, were the latest technology in ocean travel. Because her furnaces consumed thirty-eight tons of coal each day, because weather in the North Atlantic could greatly complicate travel, and to accelerate her pace whenever possible, she was fitted out with three masts and spars for square or gaff-rigged sails.

Steamships were the newest, fastest, and most expensive way to cross the Atlantic, accessible only to the wealthy. The *Caledonia* accommodated only cabin passengers; there were no steerage quarters for immigrants. She was 207 feet long, more than seventy feet of which was consumed by her engines and boilers, and she measured just thirty-four feet wide inside the paddlers. She carried 115 passengers and 225 tons of cargo, making her way through the ocean swells at just over eight knots per hour.

The deck of the *Caledonia* was stacked with cages of poultry—fresh food for the journey. A special padded stall held the ship's cow—fresh milk, cream, and butter. On her aft deck was a saloon where passengers and crew dined separately. Forward was the small officers' mess. Passengers' staterooms—including a separate section of cabins for single ladies—were below.

Her massive steam engines hammered the paddle wheels into motion and the *Caledonia* churned slowly from Liverpool's harbor. Solms, exhilarated by good weather and the excitement of the journey, stayed on deck until three in the morning. He watched the ship's sharp prow cut through the waves and marveled at the phosphorescence of the sea in the moonlight. He thought of Sophie.

Later, lying in his bunk, his thoughts turned to Bourgeois, and to the Frenchman's troubles. He wondered what was left of the colonization contract. His thoughts kept coming back to another Frenchman on board whom he and Bourgeois had not expected to encounter: Henri Castro, the schemer with his own colonial vision. Castro's mismanagement of his colonists had already cast a shadow over Solms's project, and his days as a nemesis were far from over.[7]

Prince Solms mingled as an equal with the denizens of European diplomatic salons. He understood the forces that were oppressing the German peasantry and proletariat, pushing them to emigrate. He saw the rifts that still trailed the Napoleonic Wars. He understood why the continent's attention was increasingly directed outward, to the United States of America. He knew of Madison's doctrines, Tyler's hesitance, Clay's caution, and the jousting among Jackson, Van Buren, and Polk. He had met the emissaries of the fragile Republic of Texas, and he recognized the equally challenging circumstances of their sworn enemy, Mexico. He appreciated the changes brought by Sam Houston's return to the presidency. Perhaps most important, he realized that Texas was not a prize yet grasped the contradictory truth that to lose Texas risked creation of a vast United States that could render Europe a collection of second-rate powers forever.

Solms and more than twenty of his fellow nobles had joined together in the powerful Adelsverein, and he sailed from Liverpool as their representative. The association's public image was entirely benevolent. Privately, there were competing agendas that exploited the grand jumble of interests that was Germany, Texas, the United States, Britain, France, and Mexico.

Solms couldn't yet be certain whether he could compound the right potion, but the elements were surely there. He needed to see Texas in person, needed to meet its leaders and assess its circumstance. He needed a vast expanse of land, whether through Bourgeois or otherwise. If conditions seemed right, he would need to convince the British of his logic. Solms knew he had the access necessary to make his case.

American elections loomed just six months away. An election gone wrong might not doom his plan, but it would make matters more difficult. He could do little but wait.

The Mexicans' tenuous cease-fire with Texas seemed to be holding. That was good, for it denied the United States an excuse for aggression, but it was bad, for it signaled Mexican weakness. The British and French were pressuring Mexico to compromise with Texas, hoping that removal of the Mexican threat would bolster Texas independence and stave off annexation. But peace with Mexico would never be enough to preserve the Republic of Texas. And it would never, by itself, thwart the Americans.

Solms saw the same possibilities that other students of the moment did, but two years of working with the association—two years of agents on the ground in Texas, two years spent watching the Americans, British, French, and Mexicans warily circle Texas—had given him a perspective that few others shared. Solms knew that pressure applied at just the right point could change the equation entirely.

Yet, for all his thinking, for all his planning, Solms had only a glimpse of what lay ahead. Believing wrongly that Texas had been well reconnoitered by representatives of the association who had gone before him, he was in fact proceeding into a deep unknown. Little would be as he expected. The youngest prince in a family without a principality, a stepson in a cruel corner of a primogenital royal society, a vestige of a collapsed empire, a man with something to prove, a man with a grand scheme—and, for better or worse, a man of traditions, standards, and principles—he would be tested.

CHAPTER 9

# *The Journey*

A week out of Liverpool, Solms spotted the first iceberg, drifting down into the North Atlantic. Soon there were more, plowing through choppy seas, driven by frigid, biting winds. A fog descended. The seas rose.[1]

The *Caledonia* pushed ahead, gigantic paddle wheels frothing the cobalt waters. Almost ten knots per hour, more than two hundred nautical miles per day, through ice fields populated by fifty-foot bergs that concealed another five hundred feet of ice below. As night fell, everyone aboard feared for their safety. The ship rolled and lunged so angrily that Solms could not sleep. Resigned to his fate, he lay awake in the dark, thinking.

On his last day in London, the prince had learned that the United States and Texas had signed an annexation treaty. Annexation would be disastrous for the Adelsverein's plans. Analyzing the situation, he concluded that ratification by the U.S. Senate was unlikely. "The United States Congress is going to reject the annexation, because it would result in a declaration of war by Mexico, or worse, by England, France and Russia. The American, whose finances are ruinous and who could not endure a war, is not that unwise."[2]

The pitching ship left Solms queasy. For most of the trip he was either bedridden or unable to walk on the gyrating decks. When he could, he dined in the ship's salon and conferred with Bourgeois over steaming cups of tea. The Frenchman seemed unfazed by the expiration of his colonization contract. His relationship with Ashbel Smith left him supremely confident that it would be renewed. Even if renewal proved elusive, Bourgeois felt that they could step into Kennedy's contract or acquire an existing Mexican land grant. According to Bourgeois, Kennedy's partner Pringle recommended that the association proceed with settlement of the Bourgeois grant, even though it had expired, thereby pressuring Texas to renew the contract. But Solms was wary of that approach; he didn't want to begin by flouting Texas law. Curled up in his narrow bunk, blanketed against the frigid air, rocking with every wave that crashed across the bow, he calculated the risks. There were many.[3]

The next morning he saw Henri Castro at breakfast. To Solms, he appeared a typical middle-class Parisian, the sort one might find sitting on a bench in the Jardin des Tuileries, fussing with an umbrella. As was their custom, Solms and Bourgeois studiously ignored their competitor, keeping their distance to avoid any possibility of guilt by association. It seemed to Solms that no one ever spoke to the balding opportunist with the drooping eyes and sad, wide mouth.

The weather brightened in the morning, and the waters calmed as the *Caledonia* crossed the outer banks of Newfoundland. The ship's engineer took time to shoot a few ducks over a flat sea. In two more days, they entered the narrows at Halifax. Citadel Hill loomed two hundred feet above the channel; the fortifications at York Redoubt bristled from its crest, commanding the harbor within.

Halifax was a miserable sight, a cluster of wooden buildings clinging to a low shore rimming its busy harbor. It was a working town, nothing more. Humble dwellings for its almost twenty thousand residents spread inland. Smoke curled from their stone chimneys, then hovered low in the cold air. Two or three church steeples rose above the clutter. The *Caledonia* lingered only three hours, but Solms took the opportunity to walk over to the eight-pointed star-shaped fortress that the English had been building for sixteen years. Unfinished, it was still more than a dozen years from its completion and christening as Fort George.

The *Caledonia* departed at nine o'clock sharp in the morning. A bright sun warmed the day, and Solms felt reinvigorated to the point of engaging in calisthenics on deck. From the rail, he watched whales breaching and spouting in the ocean. That night, "spectacular moonlight! Oh, the memories! Where was I at the last full moon? At Sophie's heart! And today on the cold ocean."[4]

The morning of May 31 dawned foggy, and the fog refused to clear. The ship reached the entrance to Boston harbor by evening light, but the captain would not risk navigating the rocky passage in the fog. The *Caledonia* anchored, then entered Boston's harbor in the morning.

Boston was a proper city, with a population of more than one hundred thousand. Tall, white, wooden church spires jutted from the green hills above the harbor. Stout red-brick buildings lined the wharves and streets beyond. Long Wharf, more than a third of a mile in length, extended the line of King Street deep into the harbor. But Boston, squeezed between the Charles River and the harbor, and topographically hemmed in at its rear, was already making room by tearing the tops off the hills and using the soil to fill the harbor front. Long Wharf was shrinking as Quincy Market and other waterfront commercial centers grew.

Eager to stretch, Solms hiked up Beacon Hill to the "new" State House, built fifty years earlier. As sometimes happens with every tourist, he was a bit disoriented, believing himself to be standing atop Bunker Hill. And, as with many visitors to Boston, he complained, "Climbed the hill, my poor legs!" He took time to post a letter to Count Castell in Germany, enclosing a report from Bourgeois. After an afternoon dinner and good-byes to some of his fellow passengers from the *Caledonia,* Solms joined Bourgeois and their two servants—Torczinsky and Brockhald—and caught the Norwich & Worcester Railroad's four o'clock train from Boston to Norwich, Connecticut.

Though the line was only four years old, the train was crude by European standards. The smoky, wood-burning engine was little more than a cylindrical boiler mounted on iron wheels, its stovepipe chimney emitting sparks that threatened to ignite the countryside. There were no conductors or staff; Solms boarded and fended for himself. The passenger car was small and cramped, holding just twenty travelers, and it lurched side to side along the uneven tracks.

Solms watched the springtime countryside pass by. He marveled at the abundance of creeks, ponds, and lakes along the way and noticed oak, sycamore, maple, and conifers. The villages were tidy: "Everything is painted, mostly in white. In each community there are two or three, sometimes even more, churches." In Boston, the houses were brick or stone, but the country houses were clapboard.[5]

It was dark by the time he reached Norwich. There he immediately transferred to the sidewheel steamship *Worcester;* his $5 fare included combined rail and ship transport from Boston to New York. With five hundred beds, the *Worcester* struck Solms as possessing "unbelievable size." The moonlit night was beautiful, but he was homesick and missing his Sophie.

At half past six in the morning the *Worcester* docked in New York. Solms found the city and its harbor striking. It was a metropolis of over a half-million citizens, possessing a certain cosmopolitan air—not entirely American, not entirely European. It was the New York of John Jacob Astor, whose American Fur Company had earned millions. Exercising his refined taste, Solms chose to stay in the hotel Astor had built six years earlier. Solms described the ornate Astor House as "colossal, but very eerie." It was Sunday, and quiet. Solms crossed the Hudson to Hoboken, then returned and walked along the New York harbor front.

New York existed for commerce, for the accumulation of wealth. The New York Stock & Exchange Board—brought indoors from the streets in 1836—was abuzz with the invention of the telegraph; Samuel Morse's new device would allow rapid communication with distant investors and brokers.

The city was beginning to turn its attention to less material matters. Grace Church, designed by twenty-four-year-old James Renwick Jr., was rising above Broadway, but a lack of funds meant that the spire was wooden, not stone, and plaster and lath served instead of carved stone inside; John Cox Stevens, George Schuyler, and Hamilton Wilkes were raising money for the clubhouse of their New York Yacht Club; the Board of Education had just opened its first school; the polka made its U.S. debut at the Chatham Theatre; and the New York Gallery of Fine Arts was created to house the art collection of the late Luman Reed. But New York was also a city of oppressive poverty and crushed dreams; two-thirds of the city's population earned only about a dollar a week.

Monday morning, New York sprang alive—carriages, carts, and pedestrians bustling on Broadway. Solms and Bourgeois took care of formalities, calling upon the Prussian consul and John Brower, the New York merchant who was serving as Texas consul. With both, the topic was annexation of Texas. Schmidt, the Prussian consul, felt that annexation would not get through the U.S. Senate on the first try but that it might succeed at a later time. Brower analyzed it in commercial terms: the United States would assume $7 million in Texas debt, receiving in return all the public lands of Texas, another star on its flag, and a monopoly on trade with Texas. It was the trade advantages, reasoned Brower, that had to make the deal for the United States, because the new star was going to provoke war with Mexico, and possibly with England or France.[6]

Even though annexation would increase the value of any lands that the Adelsverein might acquire in Texas, Solms saw the benefits of an independent Texas as greater. Texas trade would swing to Europe; the nobles' association would be in a position to capitalize on exports of raw materials to the homeland and imports of manufactured goods into Texas. Solms knew that the terrible state of Texas credit meant that its $7 million debt could be settled for much less, perhaps a quarter of its face value. After rejection of annexation, he said, "we will take ever stronger hold in the country, in this rich country that is just sitting there to be cultivated in order to bear immense profit and to provide rich resources. German trade and German merchant shipping can reblossom. If we leverage the envy of England and France for commerce, their involvement in Texas will afford as much protection as a German fleet."[7]

Bourgeois was beginning to get on Solms's nerves. The little functionary, with manners that were, well, bourgeois, came across as annoyingly unctuous. The way he tagged along, fretting about his colonization contract while earnestly supplicating the Adelsverein to fulfill his dreams of land

and wealth, reminded Solms of some parasitic insect. Bourgeois hadn't the slightest concept of the potential of the enterprise. He was focused only on himself. The prince began referring privately to colonial commissioner Bourgeois d'Orvanne as *Wanzen:* Bugs.[8]

On Tuesday, Solms, Bugs, and their servants caught a train to Philadelphia, then left in the morning by steamboat to Wilmington, Delaware. Next, by train to Baltimore, arriving in the afternoon. After a poor dinner at the Exchange Hotel, Solms strolled the city and the shore of Chesapeake Bay, killing time. It appeared to him that at least 40 percent of the residents were German.

Solms had a most interesting revelation in Baltimore. From a local physician, he learned of a nearby insane asylum populated almost entirely with German Protestants. A Catholic himself, Solms lamented to Count Castell that in America

> all Protestants, especially the lower classes, are so badly seized with the reverie spread among the populace by the innumerable sects, that eventually their senses become completely confused and exhausted. A lonely life in the wilderness contributes to promote this exhaustion. You hear this said, and it is unfortunately corroborated by many examples. That is why I not only advise, but urgently ask that you not send me any sectarians or people like that initially. Have the first arrivals be Catholics. There has to be a capable Catholic priest on the first ship.[9]

On Thursday—three weeks after sailing from Liverpool, three steamships, three trains, and six American cities into his journey—Solms took yet another train: the Baltimore & Ohio Railroad along the Potomac River valley to Cumberland, Maryland, stopping at Harper's Ferry for a mediocre dinner. Though the B&O had been in service for sixteen years, it had only penetrated to Cumberland two years earlier.

Halifax, Boston, Norwich, New York, Philadelphia, Baltimore, Cumberland. Except for New York, the longest layover had been a night's rest. The prince was obviously intent on making mileage, but it seems a most peculiar way to get to Texas from Liverpool. Solms, however, knew what he was doing. He was heading for the Ohio River.

Arriving in Cumberland at four-thirty in the afternoon, an hour later he was on a stagecoach for Uniontown, Pennsylvania, sixty-five miles distant—a rough, rattling, fifteen-hour trip. "Sky was threatening when we departed. Soon there was a thunderstorm. It poured. There were precipices, primeval forest, sky-high trees, all this during lightning and thunder, the air filled with electricity, the road as awful as the coach. It was not an enviable night, the worst that I have yet encountered; the danger was rather great."[10]

The next day, eleven more miles by stagecoach to Brownsville, on the Monongahela River. Almost twelve hours on a riverboat through coal-mining country dotted with simple farms, to Pittsburgh. Solms, Bourgeois, and their servants had finally reached the Ohio River. From there the journey would be simple, or at least simple to describe. Down the Ohio to the Mississippi, then to New Orleans, which was practically Texas. Finally, a steamship to Galveston and the Lone Star Republic.

A simple trip, perhaps, but twelve long, monotonous days of pounding engines, bad food, and worse accommodations. In shallow stretches, the flat-bottomed riverboats constantly scraped sandbars, jerking the boat and tossing passengers and furniture to the deck. To pen letters on the vibrating, lurching vessel, Solms was reduced to sitting on the deck outside his tiny stateroom and writing on his knees. The days of icebergs were over; mid-June temperatures on the river soared to one hundred degrees. Progress was impeded by innumerable stops at small towns to load and offload cargo and passengers.

Solms reached into his vest pocket, pulled out a clipping from the *Cincinnati Daily Inquiries & Messages,* and read it with bemusement: "A live Prince. There is at the Broadway Hotel—so Johnson says—a bona fide live Prince, who lords it over a principality in Germany called Salms or Solms. He is making the tour of the United States and is now on his way to New Orleans. He is tall and rather good looking, dresses fashionably, wears red hair and mustachios of much the same color—and it is said that he has the strange peculiarity of eating when he is hungry. Queer, isn't it, ladies?" He tucked the article into a letter to his beloved Sophie.[11]

In his travels after Cumberland, it seemed like conditions worsened every day. Disembarking at Louisville to portage around the Falls of the Ohio, he described the Hotel Galthouse as "dirty and terrible." The steamboat from the docks below Louisville departed late; "food is horrible. The captain is a drunkard. What prospects! . . . The days that followed were just like before and the nights were the same. Heat and mosquitoes, fleas and roaches; lice."[12]

Solms was moving beyond the limits of comfortable civilization. He was going to a place that was, in his words, "a few degrees away from the equator, amidst Indian tribes and in the lonely jungle and the hot prairie—and with people on whom one needs to keep an eye." He was a downstream Marlow, steaming the perilous river, watching the wilderness pass:[13]

> Going up that river was like traveling back to the earliest beginnings of the world, when vegetation rioted on the earth and the big trees were kings. An empty stream, a great silence, an impenetrable forest. The air was warm, thick, heavy, sluggish.[14]

But instead of Kurtz and his ivory camp, this river led to a most remarkable mélange of the civilized and the brutal, the urbane and the savage, the cultured and the crude, the sacred and the profane: New Orleans, the farthest city, the jumping-off point into Texas.

The original French city of New Orleans remained the gracious home of conservative Creole families, steeped in tradition, mixing French, Spanish, and Caribbean cultures. Above Canal Street was the American enclave—rough, boisterous, and chaotic. Below the French Quarter was the Faubourg Marigny, a family plantation that had been divided to pay gambling debts incurred by Bernard Marigny, who is generally credited with bringing the game of craps to America. Here all elements of New Orleans society mingled: Spanish, French, free Africans, Creoles, Italians, Germans, and Irish.

When Solms and Bourgeois arrived in New Orleans, its population was over one hundred thousand—about the size of Boston. It had more than five hundred licensed saloons, taverns, and cabarets and uncounted unlicensed establishments. One historian reports "five hundred gambling houses, between five and six hundred places selling liquor, perhaps almost as many brothels. . . . Pickpockets, footpads, burglars, greater and smaller thieves of all sorts, confidence men, every sort of grifter down to the thugs who rolled helpless drunks were commonplace."[15]

Malaria, yellow fever, smallpox, and cholera raged too frequently in the humid, semitropical environment. There was no effective refuse removal, no common sewers. Everywhere was garbage and excrement. Stagnant gutters, canals, and ponds bred clouds of mosquitoes. The fashion of long pants was pioneered in New Orleans, where men tried to protect their calves and ankles from bites.

One historian describes it as

> a strange city of strange contrasts, and beside the vast sea of degradation and vice and human greed there were oases of dignity and grace and beauty. If the streets were quagmires underfoot they were also channels of moving, living color that could be matched nowhere else in America. The multicolored stucco and brick walls of the French Quarter were weathered into the loveliest of pastel tints; the door-

> ways and fanlights were models of wooden grace; the handwrought ironwork of grilles and balconies and street lamps has hardly been matched elsewhere in the United States. If the land on which the city stood was marshy it was also fertile almost beyond belief and everywhere, practically the year round, there was a riot of foliage and flowers.[16]

The Saint Charles Hotel opened in 1837, just as a great financial panic rocked the economy. It was architecturally eccentric but the most substantial and impressive structure for many hundreds of miles. Solms, true to his discerning taste, checked into the Saint Charles after arriving at seven-thirty in the morning and headed directly to the bath for a thorough scrubbing. Eager to break the boredom of the river voyage, he wasted no time contacting key figures in the business and diplomatic community. First was a conference with Wilhelm Vogel, a prominent merchant and consul for Prussia and Hamburg, from whom Solms learned that the U.S. Senate had rejected the Texas annexation treaty ten days earlier. Elated, he next called on Ambrose Lanfear, a member of a distinguished New Orleans family and the Adelsverein's U.S. banker.[17]

Armand Ducos, Bourgeois's partner, was already in New Orleans and met Solms at the Saint Charles. With him was Dr. Labatut, one of the seven children of Jean Baptiste Labatut, who arrived in New Orleans in 1781, served with distinction in the Battle of New Orleans, and sat on the board of the Bank of Louisiana. The Labatut family had a sprawling plantation in Grand Coupee Parish, upriver beyond Baton Rouge, and had connections throughout Louisiana.

Also at the Saint Charles was Henri Castro, who had arrived five days earlier by taking a combination of trains and coastal packet ships, avoiding the river journey. In his words, he had traveled "as fast as the postal service." The remark was apt because everywhere he was surrounded by bags of mail: "We are packed in with enormous sacks of letters whose continuous movements caused by the horrible routes which one must travel make the journey unbearable. Add to this picture the brutality of the conductors, who do not worry any more about the passengers than they do about the letters, and you will have an idea of what one must endure."[18]

Castro's welcome to New Orleans had not been entirely cordial. The colonists who had lost faith and refused to continue to Galveston, and some who had gone to Texas and returned, met him at dockside and demanded a refund of their money. There was a commotion, but Castro somehow made amends and emerged unscathed. Recording the moment for posterity,

Castro wrote: "I made them understand that I was not a man, as they could well see, who would allow himself to be taken advantage of by anyone, and that I was determined to punish those among them who might lack the respect which was due the act of devotion which I had just performed by sacrificing my life and my fortune in order to protect them. I received assurances from all of them that as soon as the Colony was founded, they would come to settle there." Subsequent events suggest that Castro may have been putting an overly optimistic spin on the encounter.[19]

Castro had already paid his respects to Ambrose Lanfear and the appropriate local merchants. Although Castro was in a way a competitor of Solms, that was the case only because Solms had aligned himself with Bourgeois. It was Bourgeois and Castro—the two empresarios—who were competing for the attention of the Adelsverein or anyone else who could deliver colonists to Texas. Castro viewed Solms as an ostentatious dandy, but he reserved his greatest disdain for Bourgeois.

Lanfear invited Castro, Solms, and Bourgeois to dinner at his home. There, Castro made a point of letting the prince know that he had the warmest affection for him and the greatest distrust of the "schemer" Bourgeois. Castro mentioned that he had some letters of introduction for Solms, and they agreed to meet the next day. While delivering the letters, Castro pitched Solms, pointing out all the advantages that could accrue from a joint effort. Castro thought Solms seemed interested, "but Bourgeois, by his crafty slander, prevented any further communications and things stayed right where they were, because I did not think that it was worth taking another initiative."[20]

Solms, Bourgeois, and Ducos spent several days making contacts and arrangements, preparing for the final leg to Texas, and waiting for the steamer *Neptune,* which would carry them to Galveston. They met with Alphonse Dubois de Saligny, the French chargé d'affaires, who had returned from his sick leave in France.

On Sunday, Solms's fourth day in Louisiana, Robert Urquhart—a young Creole of Scottish descent who owned a sugar plantation—took Solms and Bourgeois alligator hunting in the bayous. The Urquhart family was well established in Louisiana: Robert was a member of the third generation. His father, Thomas Urquhart, had been president of the Bank of Louisiana while Jean Baptiste Labatut served on the board.

Solms, armed with a large-caliber Altenburger rifle that he called his "Elk Catcher," shot three alligators, one measuring nine feet long—"a grandfather of all crocodiles." Dr. Labatut was along, and he shot a five-foot specimen. After it had lain in the boat for more than an hour, the creature suddenly leapt to its feet and started thrashing around. In the mad scramble to get out of the beast's way, Solms somehow had the presence of mind to bash the reptile's head with the butt of his Elk Catcher, ending the episode.

Writing Count Castell that evening, Solms derided Bourgeois: "Our Colonial Director in a gray-blue old summer tail coat, with the waist up above his bosom, looks delightful. He was with us on the flat boat to 'process' some caiman. Fired two shots, too, but into the air." Calling Bourgeois irresponsible, reckless, and insecure, he sarcastically labeled him "as pleasant a traveling companion as he otherwise is in every respect." Bourgeois, according to Solms, possessed a true French character: all the foam of Champagne, without the strength of wine.[21]

After talking to a Houstonian named Wilson and conferring with Levi Jones, a Galveston physician and a representative in the Texas Congress, Solms came away convinced that Texians had turned against annexation and that the Bourgeois-Ducos colonization contract would certainly be renewed. "What matters now is to forge the iron while it is hot. That is why there is a fire burning under my shoes to . . . call on the president of Texas without delay, and to put the thread through our needle an inch at a time."

Solms was circumspect in his letters and reports. It is difficult to tell the degree to which the needle-and-thread metaphor is meaningful, but it suggests that the association's plans were going to unfold incrementally—that there was more than met the eye. From his conversation with Wilson he took the idea that population was wealth to Texas; since Germany had a surplus of population, there was a mutual benefit to be had. There is nothing particularly obscure about that relationship, but Solms was thinking of something more when he broke his usual circumspection and told Castell, "Just between the two of us, I am convinced that if one could tell President Sam Houston, for example, 'the German Federation will take over the debt or guarantee its payment and leave you with a salary of fifty thousand florins,' then Texas would submit to the sovereignty of the German Federation tomorrow." Solms was not thinking small.[22]

On the other hand, Solms *was* thinking small. In a June 19 personal letter and again in an official letter on June 20, he reminded Castell to make sure that the Duke of Nassau sent a set of china and silverware for twenty-four: "It would be a scandal if he did not keep his word."

The prince spent his last few days in New Orleans gathering tools and equipment that he would need in Texas. He was already thinking ahead to when the colonists would arrive, making plans for their accommodation. He meant to assemble a force of forty or fifty workers and begin construction of houses as soon as possible. They would be built of logs, with a window, a door, and an outside hearth for cooking; he felt the climate would be too hot for cooking indoors. As usual, he had a litany of complaints about Bourgeois, whom he had given a second nickname: "The Colonial Pretender, who had his hair cut off completely bald so that he looks classier than ever, still doesn't want to take any of the tools with us, and believes that he will be able to build everything with ten workers, or twenty at the most; in short, he is handling matters quite irresponsibly."[23]

The morning before Solms departed for Galveston, letters arrived for him from Germany. One from Castell mentioned that the Adelsverein was meeting with Henry Fisher, who was looking for someone to back his colonization contract. Fisher, unlike Bourgeois, had secured an extension of his contract. Solms dashed off a reply: "It is beyond doubt that we are going to receive land, so I ask you not to make any deals with Fisher."[24]

The more important letter, though, was from Sophie: "At last! . . . Enclosed was a strand of her hair. The smell of the pomade delights me. What an angel, my Sophie!"[25]

The night of Saturday, June 29, Solms and his retinue sailed for Galveston on the steamship *Neptune,* which made regular runs between the two cities. Inevitably, Castro was on board too. "Unbelievable heat, poor food, very crowded," complained Solms. "Poor company, as always. Spent the night in the open, slept on top of beer and whiskey kegs."[26] Watching the coasts of Louisiana and Texas pass, he now surely felt like Conrad's Marlow:

> I watched the coast. Watching a coast as it slips by the ship is like thinking about an enigma. There it is before you—smiling, frowning, inviting, grand, mean, insipid, or savage, and always mute with an air of whispering, Come and find out.[27]

CHAPTER 10

# *Welcome to Texas*

Galveston Bay is an overgrown puddle, measuring seventeen by thirty miles across but less than ten feet deep. It was named for Bernardo de Gálvez, who governed Spanish Louisiana beginning in 1777 and battled British troops in support of the American Revolution. The Trinity and San Jacinto rivers empty into the bay, as does languid Buffalo Bayou, which descends from Houston. The bottom of the bay is mud. Brown, torpid waters lap at low shorelines overgrown with cactus and scrub. The bay and its estuaries and marshes are a rich biological breeding ground for oysters, shrimp, redfish, speckled trout, flounder, turtles, snakes, and alligators. Those same estuaries and marshes breed prodigious quantities of dragonflies, mosquitoes, and other insects that hover and dart in the coast's heavy, humid, heat. Undisturbed, the bay is an abundant, voracious food chain.

The entrance to Galveston Bay is framed by Bolivar Peninsula to the north and a long, low barrier island to the south. One of the first Europeans to set foot on that sandbar—Galveston Island—was Álvar Núñez Cabeza de Vaca, the pitifully lost Spanish explorer who drifted ashore as his improvised horsehide boat began to disintegrate. He dubbed the island Malhado—the Isle of Misfortune. It is not an entirely inappropriate name.[1]

Galveston Island is just three or four feet above sea level, extending twenty-seven miles along the coast but never as much as three miles wide. It faces the Gulf of Mexico and backs up to long, skinny estuaries on the south side of the entrance to Galveston Bay. It is naturally barren; until settlers began planting, there were less than a dozen trees on the island's expanse of sand, shell, sea grass, and scrub.

Jean Laffite took control of Galveston in 1817 and used it as his headquarters for smuggling and piracy, but his reign lasted only three years. A handful of habitations stood on the island when Mexico declared it a port of entry in 1830. The Galveston City Company was incorporated in 1836, but by 1837 there were still just seven houses on the island. Then change came on the heels of Texas independence. By 1839, sailing ships crowded the port; steamships shuttled to New Orleans and traveled Buffalo Bayou to Houston.

In 1841, three hundred houses spread across the island, sheltering probably two thousand inhabitants. The modest public buildings included a customs house, a courthouse, a jail, an armory, and a hospital. William Kennedy reported

> three large warehouses and fifteen retail stores, six licensed taverns and coffeehouses, two printing offices, reading rooms, consul's, lawyer's, doctors,' notaries public and magistrates' offices; druggists,' confectioners,' and fruit stores, bakeries, slaughter and oyster houses, and shops occupied by carpenters, masons, painters and glaziers, cement and wooden cistern makers, turners, cabinet makers, ship joiners and plumbers, sail makers and riggers, tin and sheet iron manufacturers, black-smiths, gun-smiths and armourers, watch and trinket menders, saddle and harness makers, cord-wainers, tailors, milliners and dressmakers, barbers; also boarding houses and private houses, and several lumber yards, replete with materials to build more.[2]

By 1842 a cash trade emerged in Galveston, replacing the former credit-and-barter system. At the two-story brick Tremont House, travelers could use their cash to purchase a mint julep, chilled with ice brought from Boston. One traveler admitted that "this is naturally almost a barren island, there is abundant pasture, but only three clumps of young trees," and allowed that "the temperature is rather too elevated," but otherwise he painted a flattering picture of the creature comforts available in Galveston. After walking or bathing on the seashore in the early morning, he would take "a most excellent dejeuner a la fourchette" at the Tremont House, then "retire, light the gentle Havana, discuss the politics of the day—a small amount of whittling going on." Midday, billiards or nine-pins before dinner prepared under the supervision of the Tremont's Captain James Seymour. "Moreover one may enjoy a bottle of wine, as the duties are low." Then an afternoon of fishing or riding, followed by a "tea supper à la fourchette—a quiet smoke in the Verandah—long chats—and then each one off to some evening party or other—where if there be no dancing there is music and singing—pretty good hours are kept—but it does not require much persuasion to sit for an hour or two and in the cool of the evening, sip a mint julip or two—touch the guitar and sing the song most loved."[3]

Solms, Bourgeois, and Ducos stepped ashore at Galveston on July 1, 1844. They were welcomed by members of the French delegation—vice-consul Henry Cobb and secretary Flavio Arcieri. Also there was Samuel

Maas, a wealthy German immigrant, merchant, and ship chandler who had married Isabella Offenbach, an opera singer and the sister of composer Jacques Offenbach. One historian observed that Isabella had "left the salons of Europe for the saloons of early Texas."[4]

Solms's group had an afternoon dinner at the Tremont House, then went horseback riding to the point of Galveston Island that overlooked the channel into the bay, where the Texians had emplaced a dozen cannon. That night, a visit by Arcieri. Retiring to his room, Solms got a taste of Texas: "Chased roaches and in the morning ants."[5]

The next day Solms received several visitors. William Kennedy, now British consul at Galveston, paid his respects. George Washington Hockley, the Galveston resident who served as Sam Houston's secretary of war and backed the Cozumel adventure, visited the prince.

Notably absent were French chargé d'affaires Alphonse Dubois de Saligny and British chargé Charles Elliot. Solms had met with Saligny in New Orleans, so his absence in Galveston was not problematic. The gossip in Galveston was that Saligny was recovering from a wound received in a duel.[6]

Elliot had fallen ill and gone to New Orleans for treatment. He no sooner returned than his child took sick, requiring another absence from Texas. Except for a few days in April, Elliot was in the United States during 1844.

The first six months of 1844 had been a particularly bad time for Saligny and Elliot to absent themselves. If France and England were interested in forestalling annexation, or achieving abolition, or doing anything else that might annoy the United States, it was a grave liability to be underrepresented in Texas during annexation negotiations. Even though annexation was defeated, forces were set in motion—and attitudes and fears were generated—that gave momentum to the pro-annexation faction.[7]

Bourgeois knew this, as one of his first diary entries after landing in Galveston shows: "The absence of England's and France's diplomatic representatives at the time when the annexation was proposed had much to do with the unwise decision by the head of state. It would be prudent, if both governments could be influenced, so that they force their representatives to stay at their posts. This is of the greatest political as well as general importance."[8]

Another diplomat who failed to connect with Solms was outspoken U.S. chargé d'affaires William Sumter Murphy. But Murphy had two excellent reasons for not linking up with the prince. One was that the United States had revoked his credentials when annexation failed. The other was that he was suffering an attack of yellow fever. The disease would take his life in a few days and would rage through Galveston and Houston.

Despite the absence of the principal diplomatic representatives, Solms accumulated a good amount of intelligence in Galveston. His most interesting visitor must have been James Grieve, an Englishman who had replaced Kennedy in the colonization contract co-owned with William Pringle. Grieve was accompanied by William Bollaert, an adventurer who had been drawn to Texas by Kennedy's book. The two had just returned from an expedition to inspect the land grant, which lay immediately south of the Bourgeois block that the Adelsverein meant to invest in.[9]

It took Grieve and Bollaert a month to travel from Houston to San Antonio and prepare to venture farther southwest. Legendary Texas Rangers Jack Hays and Ben McCulloch counseled them, and they proceeded in a group of nine that included a friend of Grieve named Stephenson, Bexar surveyor John James, guide and hunter Tom Hancock, muleteer Felipe Jaime, and newly arrived San Antonio surgeon George Cupples, plus guests and servants. Three days out of San Antonio they were within the boundaries of their grant.[10]

Grieve and Bollaert found the tract varied. Here a blanket of wildflowers, there an impenetrable thicket. Abundant trout, catfish, and perch in cool rivers, dry expanses of prickly pear cactus. Always on the watch for Comanches and Mexican *cortadores*—troops that prowled to cut off smugglers and nab stray Texians—they proceeded carefully. Much of the land would require irrigation for successful farming. Antelope, deer, wolves, hares, wildcats, turkey, quail.

They proceeded deep into the grant, encountering one section where "the many varieties of *chaparral* (acacia or mimosa) thrive to the great horror of the woodsmen and it requires considerable of *woodcraft* to pursue one's course. We are perhaps the first to traverse this section of the country. Even the Indian would not venture to travel thro' it." They reached the Nueces River—the far boundary of their grant—and camped.

> After sunset the gnats and small flies nearly blinded us. The effluvia from the slough nearly choked us. Frogs (bull), crickets, and such like small fry commenced their inharmonious notes. No breeze and very sultry. No sooner had we had supper and bethought to seek repose upon our pallets, with the idea that a few snakes, scorpions, centipedes, and lizards—independent of wolves, panthers, and such like—when myriads upon myriads of "galley-nipper" mosquitoes commenced their discordant buzzing and stinging—which was kept up until morning. No one slept altho' much fatigued.[11]

As rough as the country was, there were portions that Grieve and Bollaert felt would make fine sheep ranches, cattle pastures, and farms. But the land needed taming. Dams, wells, and irrigation ditches would have to be built. Mexicans and Comanches would have to be dealt with. No one had ever said that it would be easy. On June 18 they ended their inspection and headed for the struggling settlement on Corpus Christi Bay, where they caught a ship for Galveston, which they reached one day after Solms.

Henri Castro had arrived in Galveston on the same ship as Solms and Bourgeois and was making much the same diplomatic and commercial rounds, though his initial welcome had been no more hospitable than he experienced in New Orleans. In his own words, "When I disembarked, I was surrounded by my colonist-deserters who, according to the rumors, were supposed to make an attempt on my life. I had made up my mind, and I was ready for any emergency, equipped with good weapons concealed on my body." Castro managed to soothe the angry mob, promising to refund their money if they were unhappy, trying to explain why the colony was not yet ready for settlement, transferring as much blame as he could to the agents who had abandoned his project, and inviting the strong to follow him to the colony. When he received a briefing from Louis Huth, Castro was annoyed to learn that sizeable sums had been expended just keeping the colonists alive in San Antonio, and that Huth considered occupation of the concession impossible. Castro complained that his colonists were "at San Antonio, without protection."[12]

Castro seems to have been entirely contradictory—annoyed by expense but expecting that the colony should already be occupied, or at the least that the colonists should have been better cared for. Huth, who was convalescing from an illness, was frustrated by Castro's ingratitude. To his way of thinking, he had shepherded the colonists to Lavaca only to find that the promised agents were nowhere to be found, obliging him to spend colony funds and his own to get the group to San Antonio, a town in a shambles with only the poorest accommodations available. Without adequate funds, equipment, tools, or weapons, there was no possibility of beginning colonization. Castro had left him in the lurch.[13]

Castro, Bourgeois, Grieve: it was a veritable colonization convention. Solms must have felt some anxiety at traveling so far only to find himself surrounded by competitors. Grieve was not so much a bother, because he was not yet actively recruiting colonists, and his emigrants would come from England. Castro was a different matter: he was recruiting colonists from the same regions as the Adelsverein. It would not be wise to alienate him until Bourgeois's contract extension was secure. If no extension was granted, an alliance with Castro might be necessary—but Castro's negligent management was giving colonization a bad name in France and Germany. Everything Castro did contaminated the Adelsverein's efforts.

As much as anything, Solms disliked that Castro and, to a lesser extent, Grieve were stealing the limelight. Their presence in Texas made it more difficult for the nobles' association to be heard and to gain respect. Now, when Solms needed the undivided attention of the Texas president, his cabinet, and the Congress, when he needed to work out arrangements with any number of provisioners and service providers, when he needed to make every sort of arrangement for his colonists, there was Castro, nipping at his heels, competing for attention, creating controversy.

Solms, Bourgeois, Ducos, and their entourage left Galveston for Houston on July 3, taking a nine-hour steamboat ride across Galveston Bay, around Morgan's Point, and up Buffalo Bayou. Forty-five miles inland from Galveston, Houston had most of the disadvantages of the coastal city, except perhaps that it had trees and was removed from the direct impact of hurricanes. Houston was flat, laced with bayous, marshes, creeks, and woods. The humidity hung visibly, unstirred by any coastal breeze. For the six cool months of the year it was a tolerable place to live, often pleasant. But for the hot six months, it might as well have been the Amazon River basin. Day after monotonous day the steamy heat weighed down the oaks, pines, and magnolias, forcing mortals to constrain their active hours to morning and evening. Solms and Bourgeois had the misfortune to visit in July.

There were only two brick houses in Houston. All else was of wood. The town's only hotel was the former capitol building, a two-story frame structure not in the best of condition. Solms found his room bad, his supper worse, and his bed linens dirty. A devout Catholic, Solms called first on Bishop Jean Marie Odin, the prelate of Texas; he was introduced by Abbé Jean Pierre Ogé of Galveston, who had arrived on the same steamship as Solms.

And of course Castro was in Houston, along with Louis Huth. Castro, too, had an audience with Bishop Odin; he reimbursed the bishop for expenses he had advanced to help stranded and destitute Castro colonists.

There was not much business to be done in Houston, the peripatetic Texas government having relocated sixty-five rough miles northwest to Washington. Solms spent the next day exploring and was pleased by a twenty-one-gun salute. Although the prince and Bourgeois both reported the salute as being in Solms's honor, it must be noted that the date was July 4.

On the fifth, Solms purchased a $100 dapple-gray horse for himself and $25 mustangs for Bourgeois, Ducos, and the servant Torczinsky. Solms, a cavalry captain, was a magnificent horseman and relished the saddle. The party split up: Ducos, with two aides and a cook, rode toward Nassau Farm; Solms, Bourgeois, Torczinsky, and surveyor William Hunt (who had only recently been set free from a Mexican prison after serving with the Santa Fe expedition) set forth for Washington. It was a critical moment: Solms meant to figure out whether Bourgeois was going to be able to get an extension of his colonization contract.

Solms: "What a procession of riders. In the lead, Hunt, land surveyor on the Red River, on a small mule which kept an unbelievable pace! Bugs on the Indian pony, Tory on the roan and I. What a sight. Through woods and prairie."[14]

Solms made no mention of his party's attire, likely because he found it unexceptional. But people whom he encountered found it absurd and made a point of recording their thoughts. A military man, the prince required his entire retinue to dress alike. The uniform was high leather boots, spurs, a brass-buttoned doublet with upturned collar, a wide belt holding a long military sword, gauntlets, and a flat-topped, wide-brimmed hat of gray felt, turned up on one side with a feather inserted. Castro derided it as a costume from the Middle Ages. But Solms was royalty, he was an Austrian army officer, he was a romantic, and he had come unstuck in time.[15]

Fortunately for Solms, this was frontier Texas, not yet cowpoke Texas, and variety in dress was common. Sam Houston had delivered his first presidential farewell speech dressed as George Washington, wearing a frock coat, knee breeches, and a powdered wig.

Departing in the evening, Solms's nattily attired team made less than ten miles (inside the city limits of today's Houston) before accepting the hospitality of the Tuckham family. As Bourgeois put it, "Here began the harsh lessons in Texas with the terrible suppers and terrible beds." It wasn't the beds that bothered Solms: "A night without comparison, mosquitoes, fleas, lice."[16]

The group had crossed Buffalo Bayou and reached the Brazos River, which they would follow to Washington. On the morning of the third day, two miles outside Washington, they crossed paths with Henri Castro. Planning ahead, he had brought a horse and cabriolet with him from New Orleans. While in Houston, he had met Texas secretary of the treasury James Miller and offered him a ride to Washington in the light, two-wheeled carriage with a canvas top. Miller accepted, and they left a day before Solms, but the cabriolet proved ill suited to the muddy Brazos River bottoms, and they traveled slowly. Solms's group passed Castro's slower one-horse carriage.

It was Sunday, and the sleepy village of Washington was somnolent in the ninety-five-degree heat of summer. Log cabins and rickety frame buildings scattered across a rise above the river. The dirt paths through the town were empty; the residents had taken refuge from the sun. Grasshoppers leapt above bluestem. Spiny lizards lolled under rocks. Scattered cicadas droned, previewing the chorus that would come with darkness. Solms removed his feathered hat and wiped his brow.

Washington is higher than Houston, and farther north. The rolling hills offer fields suitable for cultivation or pasture, interspersed with stands of oak and pine. Its climate is better than Houston's, but not by much. Solms pronounced it "the most miserable and unhealthy place in Texas."

Germany was only six weeks behind Solms. From a world of castles, chivalry, elites, and elegance, across a treacherous ocean, through the heart of a verdant wilderness, down rivers and up, to reach this, this barbarous backwater.

No one in Washington was debating great ideas. In fact, at the moment no one was doing anything except napping or swatting flies in the shade. The Congress was in recess, and most of the government had fled the summer heat.

Solms reflected on the intellectual deprivation surrounding him. The democrats of Texas insisted on *libertie* but seemed markedly nonchalant about *egalitie* and *fraternitie.* While Darmstadt's university students debated Fourier's phalansteries, Texians slapped together a shantytown on the Brazos and declared it the capital city of a new nation. Many of the Texians were clever, some were men of letters, but the philosophical underpinnings of Texas were as simple as the words of Julius Caesar: *veni, vidi, vici.*

President Sam Houston was not in Washington; he was at his home on the Trinity River, suffering an illness. Secretary of state Anson Jones was the highest-ranking official in the vicinity. Jones was a forty-six-year-old medical doctor whose original Philadelphia practice had not prospered. He spent years in New Orleans as a merchant, again without success. At loose ends, he went to Texas, where he built a decent medical practice in Brazoria. After fighting in the war for independence, he entered politics. He would be the republic's next—and last—president.

Bourgeois and Jones were already well acquainted, having traveled together to New Orleans seeking the $1 million loan for Texas. Bourgeois penned a "Cher Monsieur" note to Jones in French, asking whether it would be convenient to meet at his farm. Bourgeois and Solms called on him that afternoon and were well received. Jones assured them that Bourgeois and the Adelsverein were in favor in Texas but reminded them that since January only the Congress—not the president—could extend Bourgeois's contract. Jones made suitably soothing noises about that, however, and the two came away reassured.[17]

Of course, Castro was right behind Solms, calling on Jones that same afternoon. His visit was even more reassuring: Jones advised him that his contract wouldn't require extension, because he had already begun bringing colonists to Texas. Fisher's contract had been extended in writing, as had the Kennedy contract now held by Grieve, and the remaining two—Bourgeois and Pirson—were at the mercy of a Congress that was no longer enamored of colonization. As Castro observed, "The current-day politics and the interests of the country made any donation from the public domain unpopular."[18]

Solms and Bourgeois met with Jones again the next morning and had supper with him in the afternoon. In the course of their discussions they asked about the Castro contract. Jones candidly made it clear that Castro was in a different circumstance than Bourgeois: Castro had colonists, bedraggled as they might be, and his contract was secure; Bourgeois had nothing but plans, and his fate was up to the Congress. Bourgeois bristled: "This part of the discussion became rather lively; fortunately, it did not stay on the subject for long."[19]

With Houston absent and the Congress in recess, there was no reason for any of the colonizers to linger in Washington. Solms and Bourgeois left as the heat dissipated in the evening, their destination Nassau Farm. Castro lingered a day, then turned west toward San Antonio, where a destitute clutch of colonists awaited his arrival.

CHAPTER 11

# *West to San Antonio*

Bourgeois's problem was this: his colonization contract had expired in December 1843; the Texas Congress had banned all new colonization contracts and extensions in January 1844; the Congress had adjourned in February and would not reconvene until December; it was now July; Adelsverein colonists were scheduled to start arriving in September; the president and the secretary of state both lacked the power to extend his contract; and the Adelsverein was under no obligation to colonize his lands without an extension.

Before departing Washington, Bourgeois had penned a long report to President Houston. He claimed that "it would have been easy for me to send to Texas several thousand individuals. The material was not wanting in Europe." But the Mexican raids on San Antonio in 1842—which had marched through the Bourgeois, Kennedy, and Castro grant lands—had made that the wrong thing to do. "Was it prudent, was it for the interests of the Republic or the emigrants, and worthy of my character as an honest man, to have dispatched European emigrants to take possession of land which I could not, and which the government itself could not, put them in possession of? No, this would have been the act of a fool, or a man devoid of principles or morals." Of course, that was exactly what Bourgeois's competitor Castro had done, sending colonists even though the colony could not be occupied, and it was that arguably foolish, unprincipled, and immoral act that had secured Castro's contract while Bourgeois's expired.

Bourgeois expounded upon the plans of the Adelsverein and his association with them: "Preeminently moral and philanthropic, our association has not taken its course without a calculation of all the risks. It has resolved that it will commence its first expedition in the month of September next, so that the emigrants may avoid the danger of acclimation during the warm seasons."

He asked Houston for an extension or renewal of his contract, knowing full well that the president lacked that authority. If that could not be done, he said, then "we pray your excellency to authorize us, provisionally, to place our emigrants upon the lands of my concession on the Medina, with the assurance always that the lands on which they may be settled cannot be taken from them." After all, "our emigrants [are] arriving in a short time, it being indispensable to us to construct for them houses into which they can go upon their arrival, to prepare for them the means of subsistence and labor, to provide them with the means of transportation to the interior, and in time to realize our plans of colonization." Surely Houston understood "that all these preparations require considerable expense and that they cannot be made unless the association has assurance that they can be made with the power to enjoy them."[1]

By the time he reached Nassau Farm, Bourgeois had reflected on his interlude in Washington. Stress had taken its toll. His last meeting with Secretary of State Jones had not been entirely pleasant. Bourgeois had let his temper show, had been too blunt with Jones about Castro's performance. But why should Castro's contract be considered still in effect, when all he had done was send over a few hundred colonists and leave them stranded and desperate in San Antonio? Castro's colony was as unpopulated as Bourgeois's, but Castro was receiving preferential treatment.

But, thinking it over, Bourgeois realized that demanding that Castro's contract be cancelled would do nothing to secure the extension of his own contract. Castro's status was irrelevant. It was important to curry favor with the government of Texas and to get them to understand the importance of granting an extension.

But the Congress would not meet until December, and the colonists would arrive before then. Meanwhile, Solms seemed intent on inspecting the grant, assembling a colonial management team, and preparing for the colonists' arrival. The sine qua non of the entire enterprise was a habitable tract of land. It looked like the Adelsverein would have to choose between settling colonists on Bourgeois's dubious grant or finding someone with a more reliable title to their lands. Bourgeois feared what Solms's decision might be. He had to shore up his contract somehow.

First, Bourgeois needed to mend his fences with Anson Jones; he penned a personal apology in French: "In my English jargon, I may have been a little sharp. . . . Only my native tongue will allow me to use expressions naturally more soft and less rude than those which my knowledge of English furnishes me." He continued, "I ought to address the Secretary of State a note of explanation, and my good friend Doctor Jones some apology, if, in my bad English, I said anything too hasty to him. I hope he will permit me to retain the same place in his friendship which I have hitherto occupied."[2]

His apology made, Bourgeois wrote a longer, official letter to Jones, again in French, again suggesting that "my ignorance of the English language has perhaps not enabled me to explain myself sufficiently with regard to the concessions made to me by the government." Bourgeois pleaded for renewal of his concession and asked that he be treated no differently than other empresarios whose contracts had been renewed, mentioning Fisher and Kennedy but not Castro.

Bourgeois fretted to Jones about holders of land scrip or headrights locating claims within his grant before the Congress had a chance to grant him an extension. He argued that they should not be able to do so and that, if they could, then the president must use his inherent powers to protect Bourgeois's rights by extending the contract. Since holders of scrip and headrights had always been able to locate within the Bourgeois grant—there had never been any prohibition—it is difficult to see how this argument would have much leverage. Nonetheless, he ended by pleading for "that which the law, justice and equity, without respect of persons or the relations of friendship, require upon the part of the executive power."[3]

While Bourgeois was scribbling his letters, Solms was inspecting Nassau Farm. He was unimpressed. Bryan, the overseer whom Boos-Waldeck had left in charge, proved to be a drunk. Charles Fordtran, functioning as supervisor in the absence of an association member, had replaced Bryan with a man named Denman, who was capable but was already lobbying for more pay. The first cotton crop, planted by Bryan, had failed; a second crop was struggling. The slaves had run away under Bryan's mismanagement; two of them had been shot and killed while attempting a robbery. ("Therewith an investment was lost," said Solms.) The manor house was still a work in progress; its log exterior was unchinked, allowing wind and rain to penetrate. Overall, there seemed to have been a great waste of money.[4]

Nassau Farm held little interest for Solms; he felt it should be divided into eight parcels and sold. He meant to settle hundreds of colonists by spring, and thousands of colonists after that; the league of land at Nassau was entirely inadequate. And Nassau Farm was much too close to non-German settlements, too close to the influence of Houston and Austin. Foremost in Solms's mind was rigorous preservation of the colony's German culture, language, and religion. He would linger at Nassau only long enough to compose a report to the Adelsverein's directors and recruit a few members of the staff he would need before the colonists' arrival. Then west, toward San Antonio and Bourgeois's land beyond.

Even though Armand Ducos and his companions had split off from Solms's group outside Houston, bypassing Washington and heading separately for

Nassau Farm, they had gotten bogged down in the Brazos bottoms and arrived there a day after Solms, spending the night with Charles Fordtran before rejoining the prince at Nassau.

Solms's arrival stirred the German community that surrounded Industry, New Ulm, Round Top, and Cat Spring. People wanted to know what the prince planned. Some hoped for adventure, or another chance to begin anew. Solms painted grand pictures of the future of his colony; he invited his fellow Germans to join the cause.

A Swiss physician named Emil Meyer had arrived at Nassau with Ducos. Noting Meyer's experience with tropical diseases, Solms added him to his team. That night, twenty-six-year-old Ludwig Willke arrived to meet the prince. Willke had been in Texas less than a year; he had come with his brother Herman, who, like Ludwig, had been a lieutenant in the Prussian army. He struck Solms as "a respectable and brave person." The two brothers enlisted in the cause; in the end, Solms decided that Herman "is a bit frivolous and requires supervision."[5]

The next day Abbé Ogé arrived, following Solms from Washington. On Friday, July 12, Solms visited Charles Fordtran's farm. In a bit of wit playing off the village of Industry, Fordtran's farm had been given the nickname Indolence. Abbé Ogé and Dr. Meyer came along. It was a social occasion, at least until it came up that Fordtran's five children had not been baptized. Apparently, Fordtran made it known that if baptism was in the future it would be in a Protestant faith. As a result, in Solms's words, "things got heated up."

Departing Indolence in the afternoon, Solms et al. visited Friedrich and Louise Ernst in Industry. There they met the Reverend Louis Cachand Ervendberg and Ferdinand Lindheimer, two of the more interesting people in the early German Texian community. Solms thought that both of them would be valuable to the colonization project—though not of much immediate use—and he invited them to join him when the colonists began to arrive later in the year.

Solms described Ervendberg as "a Protestant minister who in payment of one cow and a calf will baptize [Fordtran's] children. He is the teacher to the Ernst children, candidate and demagogue of the Frankfurt Putsch [a landmark German liberal protest against Metternichian absolutism]." What Solms did not know was that Ervendberg was an assumed name; the pastor's real name is lost to history. He adopted his pseudonym before leaving Germany, likely to avoid the consequences of participation in the liberal movement. There is also some question about whether he was a minister—several contemporaries commented on the low quality of his work—but one historian concluded that "he almost certainly received some theological training—probably at an Evangelical seminary, of which Germany has a number."[6]

In 1837, the mild, gentle Ervendberg had been an Evangelical pastor in the small town of Chicago, Illinois. He ministered to congregations in Chicago, Teuto, East Prairie, and Schwemm's Grove. In total, his flock numbered more than 275, but it was the time of the 1837 economic crash, and his recompense was miniscule. In the Hanoverian enclave at Teuto, he met Maria Sophie Dorothea Muench, whom he married in 1838. When their first child died in the fall of 1839, he was crushed. Adding to the misery, church tithes dwindled with the economy, as prices rose. The Ervendbergs decided to seek better times in Texas.[7]

Traveling down the Illinois and Mississippi rivers to New Orleans, then to Galveston and Houston, they arrived in the fledgling shantytown around December 1839. Ervendberg bought a small plot of land, meaning to plant a market garden in the spring. He quickly assembled a congregation of Germans in Houston, preaching his first sermon within a month of arrival. He was the first German preacher in Texas.

A year after arriving in Houston, Ervendberg migrated north to Blumenthal, fifteen miles west of Industry. As the only German preacher in the area, he soon established a circuit of congregations in Industry, Cat Spring, Biegel, La Grange, and Columbus.

The Ervendbergs were blessed with the birth of a daughter, Anna. Infant mortality rates on the frontier were depressingly high; Anna soon died. This loss of a second child seems not to have slowed Ervendberg's drive to evangelize Texas: by the time Solms met him, he had persuaded the Texas Congress to charter the German Texian Hermann's University, to be located near Blumenthal or Industry, with Ervendberg as its president. But by that time it was already becoming clear that raising the necessary capital in cash-starved Texas was a dubious proposition. Doubtful of the success of his university, Ervendberg lived with his wife on a simple homestead outside Blumenthal. The quiet, bespectacled, trim-bearded minister with a sharp jaw and a receding hairline seemed the image of piety; it was impossible to foresee that he would fall in love with an orphan girl in his care, that he would abandon his wife, that he would flee to Mexico with his seventeen-year-old lover, or that he would be murdered in a tiny Mexican village.

It seems odd that Solms latched onto the good Reverend Ervendberg. After all, Solms had made it clear to Count Castell that he wanted no Protestants among his colonists. Why was he not pushing the abbé or the bishop for a priest? The likely explanation was that the prince, as romantic and idealistic as he may have been, was at some level a realist. He knew that Protestants would be among his colonists, and he knew that spiritual support would be critical to their success in difficult circumstances. And he probably *was* asking Odin and Ogé for a priest, but without success, thus that effort went unmentioned in his diaries and reports.

Like Ervendberg, Ferdinand Lindheimer was a liberal who left Germany out of a sense of self-preservation. He had attended the University of Wiesbaden, the University of Jena, and the University of Bonn, where he won a scholarship in classical philology, and he had taught at Frankfurt's Bunsen Institute. An agitator for reform, he watched in dismay as the government closed the institute following the Frankfurt Putsch, and he recoiled at the sentencing of six of his fellow teachers for sedition. By 1834 it was clear that Germany was the wrong place for him to be. He sailed for the United States and, like Ervendberg, ended up in the German communities of Illinois.[8]

Among intellectuals reacting to industrialization and pursuing the romantic, naturalism became a significant movement in the mid-nineteenth century. Being a naturalist—being close to nature—was a popular and noble pursuit, rather like being a philosopher. Lindheimer followed the trend. His interest in nature dated back to a university friendship with botanist Georg Engelmann, who also fled to Illinois, then migrated to Missouri.

After a few months in Illinois, Lindheimer made a pilgrimage to El Mirador, the legendary Vera Cruz hacienda of Carl Sartorius, which had become the preeminent destination for botanical explorers of Mesoamerica. Lindheimer spent sixteen months there, collecting plants, managing a distillery, and overseeing a banana and pineapple plantation. But Lindheimer had not rid himself of the urge to resist tyranny and fight for freedom. The reactionary chaos in Mexico and the cries for independence north of the Rio Grande stirred him to action. He joined a company of Alabama volunteers and marched for Texas.

Lindheimer arrived too late to experience battle in the revolution. He blended into Texas, then left for St. Louis, where he spent two years working with his botanist friend Engelmann. With Engelmann's help, he entered into an arrangement with Harvard professor Asa Gray in which Lindheimer would return to Texas to gather, mount, and label botanical specimens and ship them to Harvard in exchange for $8 per hundred plants. And that became Lindheimer's occupation. When he met Solms, he was in the midst of a season-long collection expedition between the Brazos and Colorado rivers. He spent at least three months working out of Industry and Cat Spring. A local resident described him: "He lived in a miserable little hut, which was crammed full of specimens of animals and plants. On his little

Mexican cart he would sally forth on excursions into the wilds of the Brazos bottom, returning with a wealth of new and strange forms of plants and animals. He was a fine gentleman and a splendid scholar."[9]

Lindheimer is credited with discovering several hundred plant species; forty-eight species and subspecies bear his name. Among his discoveries are a prickly pear cactus, a rock daisy, a milkweed, and a locoweed—all characteristic of Texas. His plant collections can still be found in such diverse places as the Komarov Botanic Institute in St. Petersburg and the British Museum in London.[10]

In his later years, Lindheimer became publisher and editor of the *Neu-Braunfelser Zeitung,* a German-language paper published in New Braunfels, Texas. True to his liberal past, he was a fire-breathing social critic, but when the issues of secession and abolition came to the fore Lindheimer took an uncharacteristically moderate stance, arguing that Germans were obliged to fit into the community they had adopted and should not try to force their anti-slavery views on Texas. Perhaps Lindheimer had tired of fleeing controversy. All this—and much more—was still before him when Solms entered the picture.

The prince, on the other hand, was not at all concerned about fitting into Texas. He meant to transport a piece of Germany to the Lone Star Republic, intact. His clothing and his retainers advertised his disposition. The Ernsts' daughter, Caroline Ernst von Roeder, reported that "the prince had a considerable retinue of horsemen, dressed mostly like himself, after the fashion of German officers. Among the company was an architect, a cook, and a professional hunter." Her brother Fritz signed up with Solms, joining his entourage.[11]

Her sister-in-law Rosalie von Roeder Kleberg was another who met the prince in Industry. Rosa was thirty-three years old; in Germany, she had married Robert Justus Kleberg on the condition that he move with her to Texas. No stranger to German nobility, and no stranger to Texas, she did not take well to Solms's peculiarities: "Prince Solms-Braunfels came to our house one day and wanted me to make coffee for him. He was attended by a number of persons on horseback and was dressed like a German officer. He impressed me as a conceited fool. He was unwilling to eat at the same table with other people—a manner of conduct which, I fancy, did not serve to raise him in the estimation of the American farmers."[12]

Rosa Kleberg may have been unimpressed, but Solms had no difficulty engaging a handful of new employees from among her fellow Germans. Most remained behind until Solms needed their services; a guide named Jordt joined his riding party. Tuesday, July 16, the riders and a mule-drawn wagon set forth for San Antonio. The group was Solms, Bourgeois, Ducos, Meyer, Ogé, Fordtran, Jordt, a cook, and servants Torczinsky and Brockhald.[13]

Solms felt anticipation and trepidation about the journey, but he covered his emotions with bravado:

> Bugs rides reasonably well, but he is more easily fatigued than I because he is not as used to it. If I were to believe half of what he blathered on about yesterday about Indians and marauders, I need more than a lion's courage to continue the journey. I guess I will see and take my precautions. It seems to be dangerous indeed, but then again the idea is for me to win or die. Bugs is full of courage, and I am sure we will have the matter on proper footing by March or April. The most difficult thing will be to see eye-to-eye with the Indians, but I am going to accomplish that—otherwise I never want anything else to do in this world.[14]

The trip was largely uneventful. The wagon repeatedly bogged down crossing rivers; twice they had to borrow oxen to pull it loose. Fordtran left the group at his father-in-law's property on the far bank of the Colorado River. Solms spotted a few Indians.

West from Industry, the land seems to rise before you, giving a sense of increasing altitude while permitting few glimpses of the change. High hills tumble into deep, wide river valleys. Oak, hackberry, and pine cluster into groves. Gradually, somewhere beyond the Colorado River, the land descends and the topography becomes more gentle. Mesquite replaces pine; pecan trees offer their bounty; mulberry bushes grow into trees. The forests thin, oaks gather into mottes, the horizons spread apart, the gullies lose the musty smell of woodlands. Though both ends of the journey can be verdant, and both can be parched, mentally the distance paints itself in a shifting palette of colors and shapes. East of the Colorado River all is olive, moss, and viridian; the mind remembers leaves and trunks and vines. By San Antonio, the mental hues are ochre, bright green, and buff; grasses and brush linger in the memory. Industry could be mistaken for Arkansas or Missouri, but San Antonio is distinctly the West, at the edge of the Southwest.

Solms was traveling on the old Spanish Camino Real, not through untracked wilderness, and there were farms, ranches, and villages scattered along the route. But there were no inns or hotels; nights were spent under the stars and among the mosquitoes. Solms was wary of Indians and other dangers. "The guard was set up at two hour shifts. I patrolled every fifteen or twenty minutes; everyone was up at three o'clock. You call out 'Halt!' If there is no answer, shoot. Throughout it all I didn't sleep an hour but I did not forget to kiss Sophie's picture and her locks or to say my prayer. The saddle and pistol case served as a pillow. Didn't take off my jacket."[15]

At Brown's Settlement on the Lavaca River, Solms met missionary priest Edward Clarke, who was hosting Bishop Odin from Houston. Brown's Settlement was one of several tiny farming hamlets strung along the riverbanks. Bourgeois observed that "almost all [of the settlements] are inhabited by American Catholics from Missouri. The Catholic priest appears to have a strong as well as beneficial influence upon them. It seems that Catholics are easy to lead. It would be nice, if in the beginning the Society could send only Catholics to settle this land."[16]

There, far into the frontier, among a few struggling pioneer farms, the bishop—in vestments—celebrated Sunday mass for the travelers and locals, assisted by the abbé and the missionary priest, in "a pitiful church which serves also as school, living quarters and whatever." As unlikely as that may sound—a Catholic bishop and two priests assembling in the remote western reaches of pioneer Texas—Catholic priests had been in Texas since 1682 and passed through the area of Brown's Settlement before 1718—the year in which the first mission was established in San Antonio.[17]

Henry Castro and Louis Huth preceded Solms to San Antonio. Castro had already faced groups of angry colonists—"colonist-deserters," he called them—in New Orleans and Galveston, so he must have been braced for confrontation. If Castro's version of events can be believed, however, he had an amazing knack for talking his way out of trouble. None of the colonists in New Orleans or Galveston had followed him to San Antonio, but many of them—according to Castro—said that they would join him as soon as the colony was established. The destitute bunch in San Antonio—the ones who were sticking with the colony, waiting for Castro—might be the least hostile. Or the most.

In contrast to Solms and his grand procession, Castro and Huth traveled to San Antonio alone, stopping at La Grange, Gonzales, and the home of Michael Erskine on the Guadalupe River near the Capote Hills, twelve miles outside the five-house settlement at Seguin. Unencumbered by a wagon, their journey took just six days.[18]

"My arrival in the capital of Bexar County caused a great sensation. People had spread so much slander about me. The colonists had been assured so many times that I would never come back to Texas that everyone wanted to see this ogre who devoured children raw with one bite." Exhausted from travel and heat, Castro found meager lodging and prepared a proclamation that he would read to the colonists in the morning.

The proclamation was meant to be inspirational: "In order to enjoy the resources which have been offered to us, what are we supposed to do? Work with fortitude and perseverance, and in unity. Therefore, let us get down to the task at hand without hesitation and especially without losing any time."

Not everyone was convinced, least of all those first-year arrivals who had been waiting for twenty months for him to appear. Castro's journal for July 20–24 reads, "Numerous visitors. Refunding of deposits. Explanation of my plans. Preparation to go visit the lands of the Grant."

But for their deposits, most of the colonists surely would have scattered before Castro appeared. Those who had intercepted him in New Orleans and Galveston wanted their money back. Despite Castro's claim that many of them said they would join him when the colony was established, it is telling that none of them decided to ride with him to San Antonio. Many of those who were in San Antonio to greet him were out of funds and without any other option; they were enduring hardship in the hope that Castro would appear and return their money.

Castro's decision to make refunds without quarrel had its advantages. It was a show of good faith that might convince some colonists that there was still hope for the venture. Still, the best that can be said is that not every colonist took his money and left San Antonio. Some lingered to see what might evolve.

Castro had in his pocket a letter from Secretary of State Jones to Captain Jack Hays of the Texas Rangers, ordering Hays to support Castro's colonization effort. Hays, seemingly like much of the population of Texas, was recovering from an illness, but he was able to arrange an escort for July 25. He wrote Jones that "I will do every thing in my power to effect his object (the establishment of his colony) as soon as possible," but he cautioned Jones that "the small force that I have under my command will not be sufficient to afford the colonists much protection in their new settlement."

Jack Hays provides a reliable glimpse of the conditions in Texas' western frontier in 1844. He had been based in San Antonio, fighting Mexicans and Comanches, for more than five years. Just weeks before Castro's arrival, Hays had received intelligence indicating that a Mexican force of six hundred soldiers was preparing to march on San Antonio. When he took fifteen rangers south along the Nueces River to investigate, he found no Mexican army but did learn of a band of Comanches raiding near Corpus Christi. Hays pursued and attacked and, in what was almost an unexceptional event in his career, dispatched thirty warriors, at a cost of several wounded rangers. He returned from that excursion to find Henri Castro requesting his services.[19]

It is tempting to imagine Hays and his men as the sort of cowboy Texas Rangers who became iconic in the late nineteenth century, but that would be an error. Hays and his rangers were an entirely different breed. To begin with, firearms in 1844 were nothing like those of the later cowboys-and-Indians days. There was no such thing as a repeating rifle; that innovation would not emerge until the Civil War. Long firearms were either muzzle-loaders or single-shot breechloaders. It was challenging to get off more than three shots in a minute.

Pistols, with one exception, were also single-shot weapons. That one exception was the .36-caliber five-shot Patterson revolver patented by twenty-two-year-old Samuel Colt in 1836. Despite its technological superiority, it did not sell well, and its manufacturer went out of business in 1842; the weapon was rare until production resumed after the commencement of the Mexican-American War. Jack Hays and his rangers had gotten their hands on a few. Their revolvers did not hold cartridges; the rangers loaded gunpowder, wadding, bullets, and wax into each chamber of the cylinder and placed a percussion cap on each of the five nipples that protruded from the back. The advantage was not that reloading was fast—if anything, it was detailed and tedious—but reloading was only required after five shots. When pursuing someone on horseback, with reloading almost impossible, that was a tremendous advantage. Armed with this innovative firearm, "Captain Yack," as the Comanches called him, became the bane of marauders of every stripe.

It was not just the primitive weaponry that sets Jack Hays's rangers apart from the iconic Texas Ranger image. They were a most irregular and unpredictable bunch. "Discipline is almost wholly lacking," said one observer, "but its lack is made up for by the unconditional devotion to the leader, who by example leads all in the privations and hardships they usually endure."[20]

Hays's rangers supplied their own clothes, weapons, horse, saddle, and a rawhide riata for roping. Weapons of choice were a long gun, two pistols, and a Bowie knife. They wore sombreros to deflect the sun, buckskin leggings and high boots to protect them from cactus and chaparral. Their sturdy trousers were always tucked into the tops of their boots. A short jacket was typical, perhaps accented by a colorful scarf. In cold weather, they tossed a serape or blanket over their shoulders. The appearance was that of a vaquero, not a soldier.[21]

In addition to leading his company of rangers, Jack Hays served as the Bexar County surveyor. The two roles fit well: both required time in the field and an intimate knowledge of the countryside. Serving in both capacities made Hays the definitive source of information in Bexar. No newcomer wanted to venture out of San Antonio without the company of Jack Hays, and even long-time residents were prudent enough to get his advice before riding forth. They checked with him for danger as we might check the weather before traveling.

Hays dispatched five of his rangers to accompany Castro and six associates on a six-day visit to the Frenchman's grant. Also along was John James, Hays's deputy surveyor. The summer sun took its toll on the travelers: two of the group suffered heatstroke. But, overall, Castro was pleased: "I covered a distance of 160 miles over terrain which can only be compared to an English park deserted of inhabitants. One does not encounter there any dangerous animals at all, only some deer and some wild horses traveling in herds. Supplied with coffee, sugar, whisky and flour, we lived in luxury from the products of our hunting and fishing. There was excellent honey in which we were never lacking."[22]

Solms arrived in San Antonio on July 25, while Castro was still in the field. He was shocked by what he found: "Bexar looks like one great ruin from Spanish times—the Álamo, all the splendid Spanish-style monuments, the missions of San José, La Concepción, San Juan and La Espada lie in ruins. I truly am here like Scipio at the ruins of Carthage. And amid all this rubble there is nothing but misery—all these poor Alsatians and Rhinelanders, sent by Castro, hurt me in my soul. Many from the previous year are dead, including twenty-five Frenchmen, all of them for a lack of money and thus a lack of food."[23]

Rumors of a Mexican invasion plagued the town, but the invasion would have been purely symbolic, for there was no more to be gotten from the bones of San Antonio. Solms set about finding quarters. "We leased a house from Cassiano. It was full of trash. We slept in the yard close to our horses." José Cassiano, born Giuseppe Cassini in Italy, had been in San Antonio since the 1820s. A merchant, he supplied and quartered the Texian revolutionaries during the 1835 siege of Bexar. Over time he accumulated expansive landholdings and was known for extending hospitality to visitors such as Solms.[24]

Naturally, Solms's first call was on Jack Hays. With Hays was Johann Jacob Rahm, a Swiss who had joined Hays's company. Solms had already met Rahm just outside San Antonio, where the prince's group encountered some of Hays's men. In San Antonio—from Hays, Rahm, and the destitute Alsatians—Solms learned that when Castro's colonists were stranded at Lavaca, without money, food, or housing, Rahm had persuaded Hays to help him arrange and fund their transportation to San Antonio, doing what they could to ease their plight.

Solms was truly stricken by the misery of Castro's people: "The Alsatian families are left by Castro in deplorable condition. . . . So much misery and ruin everywhere spoil everything for me." He directed Dr. Meyer to do what he could to alleviate their suffering. Solms's official report to the Adelsverein lamented, "Mr. Castro pushes his inhumanity to extremes; he does not concern himself with these poor people who have been brought to this unfortunate condition through him. He does not visit them or furnish a doctor or support them." Relating all that Rahm had done to alleviate their suffering, Solms reported to the directors that "this gallant, sincere man interested his superior in these unfortunate Germans and fed them with his assistance and with what he, although poor, could secure. After some grew well, he procured employment for them so that they could provide their own scanty needs. He still is providing for the sick. I therefore propose that Colonel Hays's and Johann Rahm's services for the unfortunates be recognized by the Verein and that, as a token of appreciation, a combination rifle-shotgun be sent to the former and a shotgun to the latter." Solms asked that each weapon be inscribed with a personal dedication.[25]

Solms also met Maj. George Howard, a soldier who had been on the disastrous Texian Santa Fe expedition and who was currently serving as the sheriff of Bexar County. Earlier, Sam Houston had asked him to make vacant buildings available to Castro's colonists. Howard joined Solms, Bourgeois, and Bishop Odin on a tour of the five missions surrounding San Antonio. Mission San José seemed in relatively good shape, but the others were tumble-down shells. Bourgeois was so taken with Mission San José and its surroundings that he imagined making the first colonial settlement there, taking advantage of the walled compound, buildings, and mission church.

Solms and Bourgeois had never gotten along well, but their meeting with John William Smith on Sunday, July 28, may have been the first moment when their interests concretely diverged. Smith, nicknamed "El Colorado," was a notable figure in the governance and development of San Antonio and the Republic of Texas. At various times he was the town's mayor (thrice), alderman, tax assessor, court clerk, probate county clerk, land commission clerk, treasurer, and postmaster. At the state level he held eleven different commissions over time, including Indian commissioner and state senator, an office he occupied when he met the prince. It did not escape Solms's notice that Smith also owned more than fifty thousand acres of land, or that the bilingual Smith often served as a middleman between Tejano owners of land and headrights and English-speaking land speculators. Jack Hays knew the land; El Colorado knew the landowners and the land market.[26]

In his usual circumspect way, Solms never reported much about his meeting with Smith. But from Bourgeois we know this: "A sensible and intelligent man, he is of the opinion that we should wait until the concession is renewed before we undertake anything on that land. On the basis of this sensible advice the commissioners decided to talk to the various landowners. The Society has to be sure that it can have ready a settlement for the first group of immigrants."[27]

Solms had repeatedly expressed the opinion that Bourgeois's grant would be renewed, and perhaps Smith did nothing to undermine that opinion, but the meeting brought home the fact that Bourgeois's grant was useless unless it was renewed. Solms was going to have to purchase land for the first colonists and, once settled, they would not be inclined to pull up stakes and move elsewhere. Bourgeois came away from the meeting thinking that nothing had changed, that the grant would be renewed and that the Adelsverein would make some interim arrangements for the colonists. Solms must have come away wondering about the prospects of the alliance with Bourgeois.

CHAPTER 12

# Competition

During both of his administrations, President Sam Houston emphasized peaceful relations with natives as part of his four-element plan to stabilize the republic. He reached a treaty with the Tonkawas at San Antonio in 1837; peace with the Lipan Apaches, Comanches, Kichais, Tawakonis, Wacos, and Taovayas came in 1838. The progress made during his first administration was significantly undone by Lamar—most notably by a dishonorable incident in San Antonio known as the Council House Fight—but Houston resumed his effort when he returned to office. In 1843 he signed a permanent treaty with the Anadarkos, Biloxis, Cherokees, Chickasaws, Delawares, Hainais, Kichais, Tawakonis, and Wacos, but the Comanches (victims of the Council House Fight) and Wichitas refused to attend the peace council.

Peace with the Lipan Apaches fractured in 1842. Of the roughly four hundred tribe members, two hundred fifty moved to Mexico, where they aligned with Mescalero Apaches and began cross-border raiding. The remaining members of the tribe remained in central and south Texas, many of them near San Antonio, and continued an uneasy peace.

When Solms and Bourgeois visited San Antonio in 1844, the Lipans were present and peaceful, but they were treated with a measure of disdain by the Texians. When a group of Lipans came to town on Monday, July 29, Solms watched with interest and concluded that they were being cheated by merchants and roughly treated by the Texians. In his usual paternalistic and naïve way, Solms took them under his wing, offering lodging to three chiefs he identified as Oketown, Roon, and Ltzeti. They joined him for breakfast. Solms met another chief on Wednesday and four more on Thursday. The plethora of chiefs reflected the Lipan Apache social structure, in which the largest integrated unit was the band, not the tribe.

Perceiving an opportunity to formalize his own mini-peace with the Lipans, Solms arranged a breakfast reception for them at the San Antonio armory on Friday. The bishop was there, dressed in his purple vestments. Weapons, saddles, and tack were laid out to impress the natives. Solms's entire retinue attended, in their official uniforms, wearing wide belts but omitting their usual sidearms. Solms not only donned his uniform and his feathered hat, he decked himself out in all of his medals, which he had brought from Germany for just such an occasion. Bishop Odin, serving as translator, introduced the prince as a great chief from across the ocean where a large tribe followed his commands. The bishop made a speech with the customary noises about peace and friendship, then Solms passed out trinkets. The Lipans played their parts correctly, responding in kind about peace and friendship, inviting the visitors to come to their village, and promising to let the Comanches know that the great prince was coming.

For all of his initial feelings of brotherhood for the Lipans, Solms was not looking forward to more grand receptions for them: "I had to kiss them. They bored me throughout the day with their constant begging." It may have eventually dawned on Solms that what the Lipans wanted even more than peace and friendship was breakfast.[1]

His purpose in San Antonio was not to make friends with natives. It was to inspect Bourgeois's land grant. But a detachment of Hays's rangers was still in the field with Henri Castro, and Hays could not spare another. So Solms was obliged to wait until Castro returned, but—at least from Bourgeois's point of view—there was much to be done. Bourgeois wanted to buy lands for the initial colonists—who would arrive before his colonization contract could be extended—and he meant to do so before Castro returned to San Antonio, lest Castro prove a complication.

Through the good offices of Bishop Odin and Senator John Smith, Bourgeois and Solms had learned of two tracts of particular interest. One was owned by José Cassiano, their landlord. The other was the property of John McMullen. McMullen had unsuccessfully tried to establish an Irish colony on the Nueces River in 1829 under Mexican colonization laws. He actually managed to bring some Irish families to Texas, but he did not fulfill the terms of his colonization contract. The Irish immigrants formed a small settlement called San Patrício, on the lower Nueces River, where the road to Laredo crossed. Because of the fighting during the revolution and afterward, the Irish fled to safer locales, leaving San Patrício a ghost town by 1844. But McMullen, with his partner James McGloin, had settled in San Antonio and accumulated substantial speculative land holdings. One was an eleven-league Spanish land grant, containing almost fifty thousand acres.

Cassiano had a tract at the confluence of Cibolo Creek and the San Antonio River, about fifty miles southeast of San Antonio, on a trail from Aransas Bay through Goliad to San Antonio. The land had potential as a stopping point or staging area for colonists on the journey to San Antonio from

Aransas Bay, where Solms planned to land his Germans. It was a bit small, but it might be useful until the contract renewal could be secured.

McMullen's Spanish land grant was adjacent to, and partly within, Bourgeois's grant. It was on the Medina River, on the side toward San Antonio, and had originally been granted to the Indians of the Mission San José for pasturing and watering their livestock. It was large and, more than Cassiano's, had potential for initial colonization pending contract extension. But it was far from the coast and had little value as a staging area.[2]

The meeting with Senator John Smith—El Colorado—had been the moment when the rift between Solms and Bourgeois split open, as Solms began to mull the consequences of the delay in extending Bourgeois's contract. The negotiations with Cassiano and McMullen pushed them farther apart. Bourgeois, with strong support from the bishop, led the talks; Solms stayed removed. By July 30, Bourgeois was determined to ink contracts for both tracts, and he wanted to do so immediately, before Castro reappeared.

But Solms was not convinced. Bourgeois had been talking to both sellers about a plan in which the Adelsverein would buy alternate sections (square miles) of land in a checkerboard pattern. The idea was to leave some of the economic upside of colonization with the seller, who would then be amenable to a lower price. This was the approach of some of the colonization contracts, but Solms realized that it pushed his colonists farther apart, reduced his colonial lands by half, and gave the seller the upper hand when it came time to negotiate the purchase of infill tracts. Besides, Solms wanted to see the lands before he agreed to purchase them, and he wanted to see Bourgeois's lands, too. If Bourgeois's grant turned out to be uninhabitable, the whole exercise might be moot.

Bourgeois pushed Solms to make a decision and agonized over what might happen if Castro returned to town while negotiations were incomplete. At Bourgeois's invitation, Solms met with McMullen and Cassiano, but he remained unwilling to commit; when Castro reappeared on July 30, no arrangements had been made.

Henri Castro was not happy with what had happened in his absence: "The Prince of Solms, his worthy companion, and a suite of ten or twelve servants or employees had arrived in San Antonio four days ago, creating quite a stir, spending a lot of money and producing the effect of a circus troupe with their costumes from the Middle Ages. They did not have any trouble in gathering most of my colonists around them. Speaking German and showing lavish extravagance, there was no longer any question but to go onto the lands of the Prince and to follow him everywhere." Castro even claimed that Solms had hired a German volunteer from Hays's company, named Rumpf—"a professional murderer, who promised him that he would kill me."[3]

Then Castro learned that Solms had been talking to McMullen. Castro had visited the McMullen tract on his tour of the countryside. He knew something that Solms and Bourgeois might not yet fully appreciate: the McMullen property held better lands than his grant, it was on the beautiful Medina River, and it was considerably closer to San Antonio than his own lands. McMullen had carved out a choice piece of Texas for himself. If Solms acquired the McMullen property, the Alsatians would surely follow Solms. "I understood that if this business deal were brought to fruition, I would be ruined."[4]

Castro wasted no time contacting McMullen, whose price predictably began to rise. Bourgeois grew anxious. As McMullen grew more demanding in his terms, Bourgeois began to rationalize his circumstance, accepting that he lacked the authority from the Adelsverein to make the purchase, mentioning that large tracts of land could be purchased for much less, and deciding that there was nothing to do but hope that Castro's negotiations would fail. But still Bourgeois chafed as Castro progressed toward moving colonists to his grant. He felt that Solms had been wasting time that could have been spent inspecting his grant and Cassiano's land. Frustrated by his disagreements with Solms, he observed that "the willpower of one is better than that of two."

On Sunday, August 4, Odin celebrated Mass. The ceremony was modest, for San Fernando Cathedral, built in 1755, had been devastated during the revolution and subsequent raids. Half its roof had collapsed; swallows and bats swooped through its remains. The tumble-down cathedral, as much as the crumbling Alamo, symbolized the sad circumstance of San Antonio.

That afternoon, Solms and Bourgeois mounted up and headed west, escorted by Tom Lyons and Samuel Walker from Hays's company and an Indian guide named Rilcipi. Ranger Johann Rahm joined them later on the trail. Ranger Samuel Walker was a stalwart presence; he would become a legend for valor and aggressiveness. He helped Samuel Colt design an improved .44-caliber, six-shot revolver that became known as the Walker Colt. The three rangers provided plenty of protection, but (according to Solms) Bourgeois and Ducos recommended against venturing forth with anything less than a guard of twenty men. The rumors of Mexican invasion were seeping into them, and Bourgeois must have been skittish on the trail.

Solms survived a dinner of squirrel meat, a breakfast of rancid bacon, an attack of chiggers, and an unceremonious dumping when the branch supporting his hammock fractured. The tour was brief—out and back in four days. In that amount of time it was impossible to see more than a glimpse of the edges of Bourgeois's grant. Solms relied on descriptions of farther points provided by the rangers and guide. His strongest impression of the lands was that many of the supposedly bountiful water supplies were dry. Only the Medina River seemed reliable in summer; according to the guides, the upper reaches of Quihi Creek and the Sabinas River were in better condition than their lower stretches.

For much of the trip, they were on McMullen's land. In Bourgeois's opinion, it was the less desirable portion of that tract, grasslands laced with mesquite growing on chalky soil. He was frustrated by the trip—so much time spent on McMullen's tract, so little spent on his own. He saw the journey as a failure. Solms, inexplicably, seemed perfectly satisfied with the information he had garnered.

It was, of course, the third sign of the growing divide between the two men. As he gathered more information from more sources, Solms was coming to believe that Bourgeois would not get his contract renewed. Even if he did secure a renewal, it would be too late to do any good for this year's immigrants. Besides, all of the good land in Bourgeois's grant had already been taken by McMullen and other speculators: "On the Medina River, up to its source, as in the Cañon de Uvalde, locations for settlement are not possible, as claimed by [Bourgeois] because from one end to the other all of these are already taken by Americans, Irish, Mexicans, etc." There wasn't much purpose in inspecting Bourgeois's grant; the McMullen and Cassiano tracts were all that mattered for now. Bourgeois, on the other hand, recognized the importance of buying land for initial colonization, but he failed to grasp that his own tract had become inconsequential.[5]

A week earlier Henri Castro had returned from his field trip to discover that Solms and Bourgeois were agitating his colonists and negotiating with McMullen. It was now time for him to return the favor. While Solms was exploring the McMullen lands, Castro signed a contract to settle his colonists on the tract. "I had struck them in the heart," he gloated. "I had had the last laugh and my formidable opponent understood the expression that there is only one step between the sublime and the ridiculous."[6]

Yet Castro was still nervous, still concerned that the prince would steal his colonists. Things worsened as a result of his case of nerves and a bad decision by Solms. August 9 was the birthday of Sophie of Salm-Salm, and the prince meant to celebrate. He gathered the Germans (many of whom were Castro colonists), requisitioned a cannon, and fired a celebratory salute. A cannon shot is loud—ear-shatteringly louder than the unaccustomed expect—and is accompanied by a great cloud of black-powder smoke. Having rattled the few remaining windows in town, Solms passed out alms to the poor. His ceremony had at least two negative consequences. First, he scared the wits out of the San Antonians, who thought the Mexicans were attacking. Some swam across the river and fled; others brandished firearms. It took time to calm them down. Second, Castro became convinced that Solms was trying to buy (with a total of $30) the loyalty of his colonists, who were among the poorest of the poor.

Bourgeois understated his opinion: "The Prince's behavior and generosity I consider to be in error." He continued with the obvious: "The unanimity which at first existed between the Commissioner General [Solms] and the Colonial Commissioner [Bourgeois] is slowly dissolving. The Prince and I do not share similar views." And he told the prince as much.[7]

Intimidated by Solms's pyrotechnics, Castro tried to energize his colonists, notifying them on August 12 that he would grant each family 320 acres and each single man 160 acres on the banks of Quihi Lake. Their houses would be free, except that they had to contribute to the common labor. He would loan milk cows, oxen, plows, and provisions until the colonists got on their feet.[8]

Quihi Lake—a spring-fed pond on Quihi Creek that empties into the Medina River—was on McMullen's tract, not Castro's. Competition with Solms, and a dash of paranoia, had prompted Castro to change his plans in a major way. Rather than pursue his colonization contract—originally the entire purpose of his labors—he had struck a bargain with McMullen and was giving land away in the hope that building a community there would make his remaining land more valuable. The land grant could be settled later, if ever. There was some sense to the expensive choice. He had cut off the competition and obtained far better land than his grant held. And there was serious doubt about whether he could muster enough colonists to meet the terms of his grant, anyway. But between Castro abandoning his contract and Solms abandoning Bourgeois's, the entire colonization picture had changed.

The summer was wearing on Solms, who lamented that "news and mail arrived from New Orleans, no letters for me. This makes me despair." The steamships that made regular runs between New Orleans and Galveston operated only in the winter, when northern ports were stormy and clogged with ice. When the weather warmed and calmed, the boats moved to the East Coast, where they could make more money. Mail service from beyond the borders of Texas became sluggish and intermittent. Solms was frustrated; he needed instructions and news from Germany. Castell had mentioned that he was talking with Henry Fisher about Fisher's land grant. Solms had discouraged Castell at the time, but circumstances were changing. What was the status of those talks?

Rumors of a Mexican invasion were soaring, but they subsided somewhat when a group of sixteen Mexican merchants arrived to do business. Solms and Bourgeois caught wind of another sort of rumor from a man who complained, "Why are these strangers here? These princes come here only to enslave us as they do in Europe." Bourgeois realized that "this man's opinion, when shared by many other like-minded individuals, could be the beginning of an angry opposition." It was a taste of the sort of anti-European sentiment that was prevalent in the Texas Congress, and it portended trouble for Bourgeois's concession.[9]

A letter arrived for Solms from President Houston. He apologized for not being able to meet Solms in Washington and conveyed his regret that Bourgeois was having to convince the Congress to grant an extension. He enclosed a copy of a message he had sent the Congress in which he vetoed the legislation that prohibited extensions. It went without saying that the Congress had overridden the veto; that fact must have reminded Solms that an extension was a risky proposition. Notably absent from Houston's letter were any reassuring words about the likelihood of the Congress accommodating Bourgeois. The omission surely caused concern.[10]

Bourgeois dashed off a letter to Secretary of State Jones that politely mentioned the unfortunate cannon incident, warned of mounting rumors of invasion, and suggested that Texas urge France and Britain to pressure Mexico into recognizing Texas independence. But his real purpose was to ask Jones to reply to his inquiry of July 10 in which (after apologies) he had urged that the president renew his contract in the name of "law, justice and equity." He was still praying for an early solution in the absence of the Congress.

On August 14, Solms, Bourgeois, their two servants, plus José Cassiano and Dr. Emil Meyer set forth to inspect Cassiano's land, accompanied by Texas Rangers Rahm and Lyons. They spent the first night at Casa Blanca, the nine-thousand-acre ranch of Erasmo Seguin. From an important Tejano family, Seguin had been born in San Antonio in 1782 and had remained loyal to Texas through all of its turmoil.

All of the ranches in the region still bore the devastating marks of the 1842 Mexican raids. Corn crops were struggling in the wilting heat. Cotton was doing better. Tough Texas range cattle were thriving. That night an Apache chief and his family appeared with, in Solms's words, "a Lipan Indian who is very wild and has no manners whatsoever."

By mid-morning on the second day they were on the banks of Cibolo Creek, one of the most beautiful streams in Texas, particularly in its upper reaches. They were above the Cibolo's junction with the San Antonio River, not yet on Cassiano's tract.

Every trip has its high point. On this jaunt, it came that afternoon. Solms and Bourgeois argued over the best way to reach the San Antonio River and whether to go to Michael Erskine's ranch near the Capote Hills. The fractious band split into three groups of disgruntled riders and went different directions. All three groups got lost, in large part because Cassiano gave directions to Capote Hills without knowing the way. All three spent the night without food and only warm canteen water to drink. Solms built a fire and accidentally set the prairie ablaze. He had two bullets in his pistols and no powder to reload. A panther cried out.

His diary entry for the next morning begins, "I recall the times a year ago! If I could only see Sophie at the Rochus Chapel again!" Somehow, Solms had remembered that it was Saint Rochus Day. Rochus was the patron saint of dogs and dog lovers. And knee problems. It must have been Sophie more than the saint that was on Solms's mind.

The prince chanced across some Lipans who kindly guided him back to Seguin's. The other two groups had straggled in earlier. Solms was coming undone. "Since I had not eaten for the past thirty-six hours, I devoured the food. Twelve Indians around me by the campfire. I slept poorly. Bourgeois and Cassiano. What will become of me?"[11]

The next day the group returned to San Antonio, sullen, exhausted, and without having actually set foot on Cassiano's tract. That plan had been sidetracked by getting lost. "Instead of handling ourselves in a businesslike manner and acting like local people, we move around like children," complained Bourgeois. "As a conscientious person I understand the importance of our mission and therefore deplore the two unsuccessful trips, to the Medina River and to the San Antonio River. I imagine that all future trips will be similar and our trips will be a waste." But Bourgeois had no alternative but to follow Solms, who held the purse strings.[12]

Solms complained of a headache and a rash on his leg. The headache lingered for a day, and his rheumatism acted up. Perhaps he prayed to Saint Rochus. "It's been a year since I was in the company of Sophie at Rheingrafenstein where she presented me with the cigar case." Homesick, lovesick, and out of sorts, he rested up for a couple of days, mulling over how to make the most of the situation and composing a report to the Adelsverein's directors. Putting the report together helped clarify his thinking.

Solms was anxious about the consequences of casting aside Bourgeois's colonization contract in favor of purchasing land privately. Buying land—buying enough land for thousands of colonists—entirely changed the economics of the venture. At times he despaired over the practicality of putting a colony on purchased land; at other times he reassured himself that land in the upper reaches of the Cañon de Uvalde could be bought from speculators for pennies per acre.

As Solms vacillated about what to do, his thoughts gravitated toward dumping Bourgeois, purchasing the Cassiano tract, and approaching the Congress for a new grant directly to the Adelsverein. He envisioned a new colonization contract that would have a longer time for colonization, require Texas to bear the cost of surveying, and benefit from lower import duties. He wanted the grant to center on the southwest section of the Medina River—closer to San Antonio than the other grants and on the two trails from the Mexican border.[13]

But Solms was still conflicted: on one page of his report he recommended seeking the new grant; on another he proclaimed, "What really are grants? All are alike; they are nothing but a farce, a bad jest. They are useful to have if one wants to defraud others. The government grants an enormous extent of remotely situated land in which the grantee receives, under the most stringent stipulations, much unfit and a little good land." The prince was grappling with difficult choices, and they seemed to be getting the better of him.[14]

Nonetheless, for all his mental clutter, Solms somehow distilled a new, aggressive and grand vision. He had learned that much of the freight that traveled through San Antonio came from Aransas Bay or Matagorda Bay on the coast, then turned southwest to Chihuahua. Silver from the rich mines of Chihuahua ran the reverse route to the Gulf coast. The remainder of San Antonio's trade was to or from settlements to the east, following the old Spanish Camino Real that Solms had taken from Nassau Farm. Most of that trade continued on to (or from) Mexico.

San Antonio was a traders' stopping point, not an origin or destination. Trade with Chihuahua was valuable—it was much of the reason Texas (and France) coveted Santa Fe. The Adelsverein could float cargo up the San Antonio River from Aransas Bay to the Cassiano tract, then freight it by wagon to the new Medina colony and Mexico beyond, circling below San Antonio.

Solms saw trade advantages in his plan. "On account of [the Cassiano tract's] proximity to the coast and water transportation, goods could be shipped at less cost to this point than to San Antonio. Merchants from Mexico come to Bexar the year around for merchandise. They would have a shorter route to this point from Laredo. They pay for everything in silver and gold."[15]

It was an audacious vision. Solms planned to snatch San Antonio's trade with Mexico. It might be possible; San Antonio was in ruins. To begin, he had to purchase the Cassiano tract, then get the Congress to give him a new colony on the Medina. But those steps were a fundamental departure from his assigned mission; he couldn't move forward on the new concept without the approval of the Adelsverein directors.

Solms became obsessive about not having received mail. He wanted to know whether the association had decided to go forward with Fisher, as hinted in the last letter from Castell. And he regretted having reassured Castell that Bourgeois would get his renewal. That was in New Orleans; this was San Antonio, an entirely different world. He became convinced that there was mail languishing in Galveston. And he needed to get his new ideas in front of Castell. He decided to send his report to Galveston with Dr. Emil Meyer, with instructions to inquire there about mail. If it appeared necessary, Meyer was then to proceed to New Orleans on the same mission. And if there was no mail to be collected, Meyer was to wait until mail arrived—possibly several months. Bourgeois thought it a complete waste of money and protested the expenditure. Solms figured that Bourgeois feared what might be in the letters.[16]

Meyer departed on August 22 but never reached Galveston. He got no farther than the Guadalupe River, about thirty miles from San Antonio, before encountering Friedrich von Wrede, sent by the Adelsverein as a special messenger to Solms. Wrede had with him a letter from Count Castell dated June 25. Like Solms, the directors had concluded that Bourgeois's contract would not be renewed. And, fortuitously, Henry Fisher had approached them, looking to form a venture. Unlike Bourgeois, Fisher had obtained an extension of his contract; he had until next March to land two thousand colonists. The Adelsverein had decided to change horses.[17]

Castell's letter gave Solms specific instructions. He was to advise Bourgeois of the new direction and give him the option of remaining on as colonial commissioner under Solms's direction and at a much reduced compensation: he would get 5 percent of the profits instead of his original empresario's share of 47.5 percent. If that proved unacceptable, then he would be paid fairly for his efforts to date, plus the cost of returning to Europe.

Castell explained that any arrangements that Solms had made should be transferred to Fisher's new block, and that any concessions that Solms hoped to negotiate with the republic should be equally applicable to the Fisher lands. It should be an easy fit, especially since Fisher's lands were in the vicinity of Bourgeois's. Fisher would be added to the future colonial council, which was planned to have five members (the colonial commissioner, the general commissioner, the engineer, the accountant, and the doctor), but he had negotiated to have three votes, making him the most powerful member. Fisher would be in Texas in about a month; Solms should return to Nassau Farm and await him there. On Fisher's advice, Solms should assume a low profile, because in opportunistic Texas making a big splash would only raise the price of everything.[18]

Solms probably bristled at the impression that Fisher seemed to have made on Castell. Fisher had the answer to everything. On the other hand, getting rid of Bourgeois was going to be a pleasure. Solms consulted Jack Hays about Fisher's grant and reported back to Castell that "it is hilly, but still choice land with plenty of good soil, well forested and watered; and since large stretches of land are still unclaimed, it is the most superior of all the grants." But, he continued, it was farther away than Castell realized: "It would be impossible to establish the first settlement on the grant because the area is too remote for transporting the immigrants and keeping them supplied with provisions, [and] although the lives of the persons in the settlement might be secure, in no event would their herds or fields be secure."

As he had before, Solms recommended establishing the first settlement closer to San Antonio. But he had to satisfy Fisher's obligation to settle two thousand colonists (one-third of the total) within the grant before March 1, just six months away. He asked Castell for ships in November, December, January, February, and March. If enough colonists were shipped, two thousand could venture beyond the initial settlement, into the Fisher grant, by spring.

Admittedly, the Comanches had the ability to harass, but Solms was undaunted: "The Comanches [are] great in number and brave, and carry on their existence [on the grant land]. I beg, however, not to bother about these people, for I shall not wait for them to look for me in the settlement, but shall politely pay them the first visit. They will either make peace terms and keep them, or I shall immediately strike them such a blow that they will be rendered harmless for a long time to come, if not forever. However, I cannot do this before winter or spring; by that time I will have sufficient men." Sufficient men, it seems, to do what Jack Hays and his company of Texas Rangers had been unable to do. Solms pictured a disciplined force of hundreds of Germans imposing order, whereas Hays headed a few dozen ragtag Texians. Solms asked Castell for "weapons of all kinds, especially cavalry arms, carbines, or short rifles, straight but not heavy swords, pistols, etc., since the prairies can only be traversed on horseback."[19]

Solms did fret about the signal disadvantage of the Fisher tract. Unlike the Bourgeois grant, and particularly unlike the Cassiano tract and Solms's intended Medina grant, "it is far removed from Mexico and the Rio Grande River for commercial purposes. This is too important a point to overlook and I shall therefore see what steps can be taken. What the attitude of the government would be toward granting commercial advantages to the Verein, I do not know." Fisher's grant was, in fact, not on the trail from anywhere to anywhere else, and that remains the case today. The land is a remote destination, not a waypoint.

That circumstance prevented the kind of Mexican trading activity that Solms had envisioned, but if the colony ended up being isolated that might suit Solms. All the better to protect his colonists from contamination by Texians and Americans. All the better to create a pure German community. And, should chaos provide the right moment, should Britain, France, or Mexico provide the opening, all the better for forming a strong, fortified, independent German colony in a blocking position on the far frontier. But commerce? Other than raising and selling crops and cattle, it was hard to envision much commerce north of the Llano River. It would be—as most colonization efforts were—a long-range land speculation.

Relations had so deteriorated between Solms and Bourgeois that the prince did not meet with him to deliver the bad news. In the tiny, wretched hamlet of San Antonio, Solms sent Bourgeois a letter by messenger. Ironically, that evening the regular mail finally arrived from Galveston. Solms received "one from Flersheim and none from Sophie! Only my belief in God keeps me going."[20]

The next morning Bourgeois sent a letter in reply, protesting. Solms wrote back and began gathering his belongings to depart for Nassau Farm. Solms and his well-dressed retinue—with von Wrede added but without Bourgeois—left town and arrived at Nassau Farm in five days, after the usual inconveniences, discomforts, and complaints.[21]

Bourgeois remained in San Antonio long enough to write a letter to Secretary of State Jones, which included an eight-page memorandum recounting his experiences with the Adelsverein. The letter was relatively circumspect, though it did accuse the association of violating its obligations to him. Optimistically, he asked the secretary of state "not to include any longer the German Company as a party in the renewal of the grant for which I have applied; I wish to have it renewed in the name of Mr. Ducos and in mine." The memorandum was more emotional. "Were it not the duty of every gentleman to expose treachery," it began, before continuing to complain that "no doubt for the sake of greater profits, and through an aristocratic feeling, which should have been laid aside in business, the [Adelsverein] thought it proper to avail itself of the late arrival of a Mr. Fisher in Germany, and has concluded with him a treaty more advantageous to themselves." Solms had informed him that he "was no longer a partner of the Company, under the pretext that my grant had been repealed, and to add the ridicule to the treachery, they offered me the office of clerk."[22]

But in all likelihood Jones already knew that Bourgeois's association with the Adelsverein was at an end. Henry Fisher had written him on June 27, just two days after Castell wrote Solms:

> I arrived in Bremen, and visited Count Castell, Count Leiningen, and other members and heads of the society, and after a great deal of exertion, and my having pointed out to them the impracticability of obtaining a new grant for Bourgeois, and our grant being now in full force and virtue, they concluded at last to enter into a contract of association with me, which was signed and sealed yesterday. They now desire much *to get rid of Mr. Bourgeois,* and that he may not succeed in getting any privileges from the Government of Texas, in order to be able to concentrate all their means for the colonization and improvement of our grant."[23]

The hint was not exactly subtle. If Bourgeois's contract was renewed, the Adelsverein could find itself in a legal tangle with Bourgeois. If it had irrevocably expired, the Germans had no obligation to the Frenchman. If Jones and Houston wanted to pave the way for the Adelsverein, they should withdraw support for Bourgeois's renewal. Since renewal was probably a lost cause in the Congress anyway, it was easy for Jones and Houston to decide to save their political ammunition for another fight.

Solms had received Count Castell's letter giving him the opportunity to rid himself of Bourgeois on August 23. On that same date, Henri Castro had finalized his deal with McMullen and written letters to each of his colonists in San Antonio, advising them that he would depart San Antonio on the thirty-first to establish a settlement at Quihi Lake. Those who wanted to be part of the colonization, and who wanted their land grants, were to sign up with him before the twenty-eighth.

The response of the impoverished, exhausted, and by now cynical colonists was not encouraging. On the thirtieth, beyond the deadline for joining his caravan, Castro was still calling for participants to join up, promising them a town lot and a free house built with communal labor; those who tarried until September 15 would receive the town lot but would have to build their own house; after that date, all contracts with colonists would be void.

A small group of Castro's colonists were making their way from Galveston, due to arrive before month's end. Forty miles from San Antonio, a straggling wagon was attacked by natives. Nineteen-year-old Ziliax Rhin was killed. The attackers cut off his hand and nailed it to a tree. Then Indians stole eleven mules from a corral just two hundred yards from Castro's house in San Antonio. Businessmen in San Antonio, fearful that Castro's new town might compete for Mexican trade, fanned the flames of the Indian scare and urged the Alsatians to stay put.[24]

Scurrying to convince colonists to come with him, Castro let his departure date slip by a day but made the best of it by hosting a grand festival on the evening of August 31. Food was plentiful, drink flowed freely, and speeches and toasts were numerous. Then it began to rain. At four o'clock in the morning Castro lined up twenty-two mule carts and tried to assemble his followers, who were loath to come out in the miserable weather. He sent out messengers to roust the laggards. As the day dawned, he refreshed the food and drink. Still the mules stood at their carts, heads down in the rain. Castro and the rangers and drovers who were to escort him took shelter under porches or crossed the muddy streets to the nearest tavern. By four in the afternoon, Castro had gathered just twenty-seven colonists, huddled in their carts, enduring a downpour.

Henri Castro had brought seven hundred colonists to Texas to populate his vast land grant. Only Castro and twenty-seven colonists remained. And of the twenty-seven, several had not enlisted with Castro in Europe. Dr. Henry Cupples, who had toured Castro's grant with him, joined the expedition to Quihi Lake. Charles DeMontel, the San Antonio surveyor who was assisting Castro, signed up as a colonist. Theodore Gentilz, a Parisian artist, embarked on the adventure. And of course Louis Huth joined the group.[25]

The wet and bedraggled pilgrims reached Quihi Lake on September 3 and set about building a village. They carved narrow streets and lanes modeled after their native Alsace. They named their settlement Castroville.

It was ignominious, but it was not the end. Henri Castro was not yet finished. And Prince Carl of Solms-Braunfels had barely begun.

CHAPTER 13

# *Missed Connections*

Prince Solms had been elated when the U.S. Senate rejected annexation in June 1844. Anson Jones had been disappointed, because he believed that the treaty had a chance to succeed and had hoped for its success. Jones also understood that failure of the treaty could alienate France and Britain. Sam Houston must have shaken his shaggy head. He had known that failure was likely. He had known that the negotiations would alarm Europe. He had known that the fervid Texas Congress would not be denied, and so he had insisted that talks be conducted in secret. The secret had quickly escaped. Texas had, once again, put herself in the worst possible position.

Houston retreated to his farm at Grand Cane on the Trinity River. From there, he directed Anson Jones to determine the positions of England and France. Jones dutifully did so but, unknown to either of them, Lord Aberdeen had already approached Ashbel Smith with a proposal.[1]

On June 24, the earl summoned Smith for a meeting. The U.S. Senate had rejected annexation, though the news had not yet reached London. Aberdeen let Smith know that Britain and France had discussed annexation and decided to work together to prevent Texas from agreeing to it. They would, if Texas resolved to remain independent, impose a peace with Mexico and guarantee Texian independence. It would be done by a "diplomatic act," according to Aberdeen; to Smith, the choice of words suggested something other than a customary treaty. Britain and France seemed inclined to declare a peace and enforce it.[2]

News of the British overture reached Texas, and Jones met with Houston in August to discuss the proposed diplomatic act. Jones confirmed to Smith that:

> should either England or France separately or both powers conjointly be disposed to make any offers to guarantee to Texas a truce of convenient form and duration, or freedom from further molestation by Mexico, or an acknowledge[ment] of our separate indepen-

dence by that power, based upon assurances from this government of maintaining that separate independence, and upon reciprocal commercial privileges and advantages, it is the wish of this government that their representatives here should be instructed at the earliest day possible on this subject and fully empowered to conclude the necessary arrangements for carrying these purposes into immediate effect. It is the desire of the President that all future negotiations connected with the subjects above referred to should be conducted at the seat of Government of Texas.[3]

But Texian diplomacy had a way of drifting off course, and—as it turned out—Anson Jones's sentiments were far from settled. Two events gave him the room to reconsider his position. First, Houston granted Ashbel Smith leave to return to Texas, interrupting discussions in London on the diplomatic act. Second, on September 2, Jones succeeded in his quest to be elected the next president of the Republic of Texas. Though Jones would not be inaugurated until December, Houston—on his farm on the Trinity—increasingly left the business of governing to Jones at Washington. And Jones, knowing that he was soon to be vested with the powers of president, felt free to handle matters his own way. Houston sent him a letter on September 24 rescinding his requirement that negotiations on the diplomatic act take place in Texas and directing that Smith—or, if he had already departed Europe, then William Daingerfield—"be instructed to complete the *proposed* arrangement for the settlement of our Mexican difficulties as soon as possible—giving the necessary pledges, as suggested in the late despatch of Dr. Smith on this subject."

It had been less than two months since Jones had instructed Smith to ask that negotiations commence immediately, but he turned over Houston's letter and wrote on the back: "The within order cannot be obeyed for it would either defeat Annexation altogether, or lead to a War between Europe & America. Besides it would directly complicate our relations and entangle us with France & England—produce disturbances & revolution at home & probably render it very difficult if not impossible for me to administer the government of Texas successfully."[4]

Jones knew that there could be war either way. "Such too, was the opinion of the European Ministers and agents here," wrote Jones in his memoirs. "The Prince of Solms, a relative of the Queen of England, told me, in December 1844, that annexation would be a *casus belli* anyhow, and I have his letter to the same effect. I know from various sources, that if France had stood up to her engagements with England, there would have been war growing out of it, as it was. Had the Diplomatic Act been negotiated, France *would* have stood by England in a war; but it was my refusal to sanction that negotiation which caused her to withdraw; and England had no idea of going to war with the United States unless she could take France with her."[5]

Solms was quietly involved with the matter of annexation. He traveled to Washington more than once to visit Jones and caution against the consequences of joining the United States. He met repeatedly with Elliot, Kennedy, Cramayel, and Saligny. When George Whitfield Terrell replaced Ashbel Smith as chargé d'affaires to Britain and France, Terrell passed through Galveston on his way to London; Solms made a point of obtaining an introduction and scheduling a meeting for the next day. During his extended stays in Galveston, Solms met and dined frequently with all the influential members of the community and doubtless spoke his mind.[6]

After he left Bourgeois steaming in San Antonio in August, Solms suspended most of his colonization work while he waited for Henry Fisher to arrive from Germany. Even though Solms had assured Count Castell in July that he would build houses for fifty families by November 1, he did nothing to advance that project. Perhaps it was as well, for in July—while he was still in San Antonio—Solms meant to build the houses on Aransas Bay, and by October he had decided to bring the colonists ashore in Matagorda Bay, fifty miles north. Still, while waiting for Fisher, he could have been procuring wagons, supplies, and implements. He could have scouted out landing sites, chosen a location, and commenced building docks and warehouses.

But he didn't. He spent September at Nassau Farm, reading Schiller, conversing with the locals, writing Sophie, celebrating her occasional missive, and recruiting and training a paramilitary company of riflemen. In early October he traveled to Galveston, stopping briefly in Houston, and spent the remainder of the month there. It was a time of meetings, visits, and horseback rides. Henry Fisher arrived on the twentieth: "Met with him at 9:30 o'clock. Talked with him, afterward went riding, then letters! Two from my angelic Sophie. Dinner with Fischer, talked until 12 o'clock." Solms found Fisher to be "a calm, thoughtful man, one who is not a schemer." Solms and Fisher lingered in Galveston until November 4. No doubt they spent a great deal of time talking through their plans, arranging matters with local agents and merchants, buying goods and supplies to be shipped to Matagorda Bay, and gaining intelligence on how best to land the colonists and move them to Fisher's land grant. But they expected their first ship of Germans in late November and they had not yet selected their exact landing point, much less begun construction of facilities. In fact, neither man had ever been to Matagorda Bay or Fisher's land grant.[7]

Solms recognized that he would not be able to have docks, warehouses, and cabins ready when the colonists arrived. He changed his plans, deciding that the emigrants could make camp on the shores of Matagorda Bay while he scouted a route inland and inspected Fisher's land grant. From his talks with Jack Hays, he believed that the grant was too far from the coast to be reached in a single step, and Fisher confirmed that impression. Solms would need to procure land for an interim settlement. And there were matters that needed to be brought before the Congress in December. It looked to Solms like it would be January before he could begin construction work at Matagorda Bay. The colonists would need to camp until then. Solms and Fisher, unlike Castro, had bought tents and supplies in Galveston and New Orleans; the Germans would not be tossed on the shore without support.[8]

While making arrangements, Solms took time to pen a brief note to Anson Jones:

> By the last steamer from Galveston I got despatches from home, by which I see that the Association [the Adelsverein] is very anxious about the annexation question, stating, by good sources, that it would be a case of war between the European powers and the United States—as I am sure you, my dear and honored sir, are best aware of. The Association requested me to write to the Government, and especially to you, dear sir, whose favorable disposition and feelings towards the Association I duly reported, to get, as far as it is possible for you to give, a slight notice whether the probability is for the independence of our beautiful Texas; whether we may flatter ourselves with the hope of a man with enlightened views, like you, dear Dr. Jones, at the head of the Government, or whether Texas should fall into the condition of a territory of the United States.[9]

On November 4, Fisher and Solms left Galveston for Nassau. There, Solms went on a geological excursion, read *Faust,* looked for horses, wrote to contacts in San Antonio, met with Fisher, managed Nassau Farm (firing supervisor Charles Fordtran in the process), and drilled his militia company. On November 16, two weeks before the colonists were scheduled to arrive, Solms and his company of riflemen saddled up and rode toward the little town of Lavaca on Matagorda Bay. Henry Fisher remained behind to work on arrangements for the pending arrivals.

The land surrounding Matagorda Bay is low and flat, covered with cactus and scrub. Wild hogs and javelina root in the shade of scraggly oaks.

Rattlesnakes hunt for mice, frogs, and lizards. Armadillos shamble along, pausing to dig for grubs.

From the north, Matagorda Peninsula wraps a protective arm around the bay, defending it from the Gulf. Toward the south end of the bay, the peninsula stops briefly, then resumes as Matagorda Island. The gap between the two is Pass Cavallo, the only way to enter the bay. The pass is treacherous. Shallow and laden with sandbars, it has claimed many a ship.

Matagorda Bay is fed by scattered smaller bays that drain into it: Carancahua Bay, Chocolate Bay, Cox Bay, Keller Bay, Lavaca Bay, Tres Palacios Bay, and Turtle Bay. Like Galveston Bay, Matagorda and its shallower back bays are fertile breeding grounds for oysters, shrimp, turtles, redfish, and speckled trout. Long-legged water birds prowl the shallows. Brown pelicans fly in formation, then suddenly dive vertically into the water.

The prevailing wind is offshore, from the southeast. In summer, the blistering South Texas sun is moderated only by the offshore breeze; on days when it fails to rise, Matagorda is scorching and at the same time soggy. In the summer and fall, the breeze may surge, swirl, and strike as a ferocious hurricane. Too often during the winter, the breeze shifts to the north, strengthens, and becomes a fusillade of ice. Life along Matagorda Bay is harsh and unforgiving.

The bay was charted by Spaniards sometime around 1680. Its first notable visitor was René Robert Cavalier, Sieur de La Salle, who anchored his three ships there in 1685, hoping that he had found the mouth of the Mississippi River. La Salle lost two of his three ships to sandbanks and shell bars. The third sailed away, stranding his party.

When Solms and his armed company arrived on horseback in 1844, decked out in their German uniforms and feathered hats, the biggest town on the bay was Matagorda, at the north end, near the mouth of the Colorado River. Founded in 1827, Matagorda had grown to more than one thousand residents, who made their livings from the port and from growing, ginning, and shipping cotton. A speck of civilization along the bay, Matagorda had theaters and hotels and boasted three academies, including the Young Ladies' School. But those are the sort of selective facts that local boosters employ; in 1844, Matagorda was about halfway to Galveston in terms of sophistication and comfort. It was a town of mud streets, plank houses, mosquito plagues, winter influenza, and summer fevers. It was a town of hard labor, rough men, drunken sailors, and dubious transactions.

Out on the tip of the peninsula was the hamlet of Decros Point. Dating back to the 1820s, it was probably named after Daniel Decrow, one of Stephen F. Austin's colonists. The Decrows were sailors from Maine. Thomas

Decrow bought land on the peninsula and began raising cattle. He built a dock on Pass Cavallo and served as a pilot on the narrow channel. In 1844 the most prominent resident of Decros Point was Gen. Alexander Somervell, who in 1842 had led an ill-fated punitive expedition into Mexico. Sam Houston had awarded Somervell the post of revenue collector at Calhoun, a town that was meant to exist on the north end of the peninsula but never took root. Somervell's home was on the point, not at Calhoun.[10]

Matagorda Bay and its contributing estuaries contain more than 350 square miles of water and many times that number of miles of shoreline. Solms's destination was Lavaca, about sixty miles northwest along the southwest shore of the bay. Lavaca sits in the neck of Lavaca Bay, where it joins Matagorda Bay. It was where Henri Castro's colonists had come ashore, and it was still little more than a few shacks and a dock. The town had been founded in 1840 by Texians fleeing from a Comanche raid on the town of Linnville. It sat upon what passes for a bluff along Matagorda Bay, some fifteen feet above the water. Lavaca was growing; it would soon surpass Matagorda and become the busiest port on the bay.

Solms arrived there on November 23. He was met by Jack Hays, who presented a letter from Captain Simpton of the Texas revenue cutter *Alert,* which served Somervell's customs house. Solms sent Hays out to Decros Point to ask Simpton to join him at Lavaca. Simpton gave Solms a thorough orientation to the bay and suggested locations that the prince might scout, then he set sail for Galveston in the *Alert.* Solms rented a forty-foot sloop named the *Tom Jack,* under the command of a Captain Parker, and scouted the bay, looking for the place where the Adelsverein colonists would come ashore. It might seem that the logical choice was Lavaca or Matagorda or even Decros Point, but Solms had something different in mind. He envisioned a port controlled by the association, populated and managed by Germans. He was going to build his own docks, wharves, warehouses, residences, and commissaries on his own land.[11]

"I was looking for a place where the best harbor could be built, and at the same time good healthful land and fresh water could be found. I also was searching for a place from which the route would be shortest for transporting the settlers inland over the bad routes on the low prairies. It is very difficult to obtain this combination." Solms spent five days cruising the bay, going ashore to inspect potential sites for his port. On November 27 he landed at Port Austin—which consisted of a single house—where he rendezvoused with Henry Fisher. Solms informed Fisher that he had selected Indian Point as the colonial mustering point on the bay.[12]

Indian Point is more a bulge than a point. Lying roughly halfway between Lavaca and Decros Point on the southwest shore of Matagorda Bay, it is low, a strip of beach with marshes and saltwater ponds behind, near the entrance to a shallow estuary known as Powderhorn Lake. Inlets such as Powderhorn Lake exist because fresh water drains into them, then moves into the bay; there was adequate fresh water for the planned settlement. Off Indian Point the bay is shallow, but it reaches ten or fifteen feet within three hundred yards. That may seem to be not very deep at quite a distance, but in the context of shallow Texas coastal bays it is deep water close to shore—deeper and closer than at Lavaca, for example. And Indian Point is closer to Decros Point, thus closer to Pass Cavallo. Cleansing water flows in and out of the pass, preventing the port from becoming stagnant. The single greatest downside to Indian Point was the same as for Matagorda Peninsula or Matagorda Island: it is low and on the seaward side of the bay, exposed to hurricanes and other violent storms.

Fisher and Solms believed that the first shipload of colonists had probably arrived at Galveston, so they set forth in Solms's rented boat, through Pass Cavallo and up the Texas coast to Galveston. It was November, and the weather turned foul. Battling against the adverse winds of a norther, they had to anchor in the shelter of shore and wait it out. It took them four days to reach Galveston, landing on December 2. When they arrived, they learned that the first load of colonists had already transshipped for Lavaca; they must have passed Solms in the night. Solms was livid. He had specifically instructed his Galveston agent, D. H. Klaener, to hold the colonists until either Solms or a special messenger arrived. Now they were bound for Lavaca, where no one would be present to greet them.[13]

That afternoon, Solms searched out William Kennedy, the British consul at Galveston, and caught up on diplomatic developments. He had dinner with acquaintances at the Tremont House. The talk in Galveston was still of annexation; everyone believed the subject would arise again, especially since the election of James K. Polk as president of the United States in November. Polk was an unabashed expansionist and a foe of Mexico. An unpredictable U.S. consul, Duff Green, was in Galveston making a stir, advocating annexation and sailing off to Mexico to try to strike some sort of bargain—or start some sort of row—by which the United States could capture Texas, New Mexico, and California.[14]

The next day, Solms contracted with Captain Simpton for passage back to Lavaca aboard the *Alert*. Then he sat down with Duff Green for a talk. Green made noises about how supportive he was of German colonization; Solms thought his words insincere. Probing for the prince's views on annexation, Green asserted that "Mexico was pledged to invade Texas—to make it a desert, and to exterminate the inhabitants, men, women, and children; not even sparing the child in the mother's womb!" Solms smiled skeptically. Green persisted and argued that Texas should launch a preemptive strike across the border, and he hinted that the United States would assist.

Green's behavior agitated Solms. Before sailing, the prince wrote Anson Jones (who would be sworn in as president of the republic in just six days) about what was on his mind: "By my last despatches, recently arrived, I am repeatedly told that annexation will and must be a cause of war between England and the United States. Gen. Green pushes this country to war with Mexico; he promises the help of the United States. Then we shall have all the old thing over again, and a large number of adventurers from the United States, and this country falling back into the old state of uncertainty and poverty." Solms was not shy; he made a bold offer to Jones: "I think it my duty, too, to put myself wholly at your disposition. I will, if you think it necessary or profitable, proceed myself to Mexico and see Santa Anna. I cannot prove more my feelings for this country in whose welfare I am so deeply interested."[15]

After boarding the *Alert,* Solms went to his cabin, thinking over the dinner conversation of the night before, replaying his conversation with Duff Green. If the United States swept through the West, capturing Texas, New Mexico, California—perhaps even Chihuahua, Coahuila, Nuevo Leon, Tamaulipas, and Sonora—the Adelsverein's ambitions might be crushed. There were realistic chances of getting trade concessions from Texas, but no chance with the United States. Texas needed foreign partners; the United States did not. Texas was generous with its land; the United States would change that. And, from his many conversations with Elliot, Kennedy, Cramayel, and Saligny, Solms understood that blocking U.S. expansion was geopolitically crucial to every European nation.

Lying on his bunk in the rolling ship, wrapped in blankets against the cold, he penned a lengthy and most remarkable letter to Kennedy: "General Duff Green who, if I am not mistaken, is on an express Mission to this Country, pushes, and urges, the people of Texas to war, promising every aid of money, or troops, from the United States, for the sake of 'Annexation'; for if the United States' troops are once within this territory, they will certainly not leave it voluntarily."

"It appears to me that there is a very obvious step to be taken," Solms continued, "and that is to fill this Country, and especially the Western part of it, as soon as possible, with a large number of Europeans. And how can this easily be accomplished?—I am disposed to believe that the [Adelsverein] could be of great use in the matter." It was obvious to Solms that:

> it would be easy to make some arrangement with the Direction of the said Association, and send, even by the end of next Spring, some twenty, or thirty, thousand individuals, well armed and equipped, to this Country. This number of men could be got in Germany, which suffers from a redundant population. . . . English and German ships could carry them to this Country,—able and active young officers, of every arm, would accompany them. English arms . . . were effective weapons in the hands of the German soldiers of the Legion. They would do as well to stop American encroachment towards the South. In fact, this force once established, I may pledge my word for the safety of the future, on this side.

Solms pointed out to Kennedy that the Adelsverein had the right to bring in colonists, and that there was no maximum limit on the number that could be landed. "So large a number, promptly established, who will dare to drive them out? This is the moment for doing it."[16]

Solms meant to plant an armed colony of thirty thousand Germans in a position to thwart U.S. expansion. This was not a plan to save Texas from annexation; it was a plan to protect Mexico and the West from the United States, whether or not annexation occurred. He envisioned importing the Germans under the auspices of a colonization contract, but the proper blocking position would logically be somewhere other than Fisher's grant. And if annexation occurred, the blocking German phalanx would be as opposed to Texas as to the United States. Solms was proposing the establishment of a true colony, a nascent nation, a territory ruled by Germans, armed and supported by England.

This was not the Solms that meddled with the management of Nassau Farm. This was the true Solms, the Solms who had proposed cutting off San Antonio from its trade route with northern Mexico. Solms thought big. He was accustomed to giving orders, not executing operations. Why did he not spend September and October buying wagons and shovels, hiring carpenters, and building warehouses? Because that was the responsibility of the colonial commissioner, not the commissioner general. It was a job for a manager, not a prince, not a captain in the Austrian army. His evenings with diplomats in Galveston had brought him into the real game being played in Texas. It was not about making soap from castor beans. It was about the future of the continent.

As it turned out, Solms did not have to mail his provocative letter from Lavaca. The weather turned even more foul; the *Alert* was forced to return to Galveston. Waiting out the storm, he delivered the letter and conferred with Kennedy and Elliot. Elliot had just arrived from New Orleans and brought a letter from Sophie that had been waiting there. He may have been taken aback by the prince's audacious proposal for a thinly disguised German-English military invasion; it was more assertive, even, than the English-French diplomatic act. It easily went as far as Saligny's Franco-Texian Bill, though it was not so focused on the mines of Santa Fe. The Congress had rejected Saligny's scheme, but Solms was in a position to create his militarized colony without congressional approval. Elliot surely remembered the embarrassment he had suffered in China; he may have been reluctant to endorse something so overtly aggressive. And he may have doubted that thirty thousand Germans—lacking supply lines, infrastructure, and reinforcements—could block an angry United States. But the Franco-Texian Bill had proposed to do so with just eight thousand men.

On December 9—a week after arriving to find that the colonists had departed—Solms was able to set sail again on the *Alert.* General Somervell was on board. Solms found him to be "a drunken bore." The next afternoon, Captain Simpton waited outside Pass Cavallo for the tide to rise, then crossed the barrier sandbar into the pass. They docked at Decros Point for the night.[17]

There, Solms met Sam and Mary Maverick, who had arrived two days earlier. They had moved into Somervell's house with the understanding that they would look after the property while he traveled on business and provide his meals when he was at home. The Mavericks were to become legendary Texans. Sam bought a ranch on Matagorda Peninsula, already stocked with cattle, but he traveled so much (he was a lawyer, land speculator, and entrepreneur more than a rancher) that the cattle—and the fences—went unattended. Slang for a stray steer became "maverick." On this night, however, they had barely unpacked their belongings at Somervell's when they met their first German prince. Mary Maverick took it all in: "General Somerville was a noted laugher. He saw the prince's two attendants dress His Highness, that is, lift him into his pants. General Somervell was so overcome by the sight that he broke out into one of his famous fits of laughter and was heard all over the point. They wore cock feathers in their hats and did not appear quite fitted to frontier life."[18]

On December 11, the *Alert* sailed and Solms made his grand entrance by sea. As the cutter passed Indian Point, it fired two cannon shots. As it drew near Lavaca it fired another four. The people on shore responded with rifle shots and shouts. Coming ashore, Solms found that the Germans had made camp about two miles from Lavaca. Visiting the camp, he found all in order. "A small group of live oak trees provides them protection against the storm and also a source of firewood. A fresh water brook is only one hundred steps from the camp. On the morning of the 12th, I rode out and welcomed them in the name of the Verein, and I immediately transferred my headquarters to the encampment. I found all of them in good health. All were satisfied with the treatment and the food except four; these, however, were soon quieted by the others."

If, in fact, only four colonists complained about their sustenance, it is a surprise. Solms reported that "the Verein's provisions supplied from Bremen are faulty, to put it mildly. The salted meat, as a whole, has a disagreeable odor and is hardly useable; the peas cannot be cooked tender. The barrel of spirits is nothing but the worst kind of potato brandy, and the red wine is of poor quality." Solms recommended that the Adelsverein reprimand the provisioner in Bremen.[19]

Between November 29 and December 30, four German brigs—the *Johann Dethard, Ferdinand, Herschel,* and *Apollo*—brought 439 colonists to Galveston under the auspices of the Adelsverein. Those Germans, plus more colonists recruited by Solms in Texas—and the survivors of nine families sent over earlier by Fisher on the brig *Weser*—sailed from Galveston to Lavaca, where they awaited creation of the settlement promised by Solms. Among the arrivals were the three key individuals who would join Solms and Fisher as members of the Adelsverein colonial council. Nicolas Zink was a civil engineer, experienced in building roads. Dr. Theodor Koester was the colony's physician. Jean von Coll served as the colony's accountant.

A plan was forming in Solms's mind. He would establish a townsite at Indian Point. From there, the settlers would move inland. There would be two or three intermediate camps on the road north, destined for a new settlement at a staging point short of Fisher's land grant. At that settlement, the colonists would consolidate, organize, and outfit for the push farther north into the grant. On the fourteenth, Solms rode out to inspect some land near the village of Texana that might serve as an interim camp. Texana was about thirty-five miles from Lavaca, near the junction of the Lavaca and Navidad rivers. It might have been possible to ferry passengers and freight from the coast on the Lavaca River, but Solms found the place "absolutely poor and unhealthful." On the journey, Solms encountered the Reverend Louis Ervendberg, botanist Ferdinand Lindheimer, and a few other men who were coming from Industry to join him at Lavaca. With their arrival, the cast of characters who would lead the colonists into unsettled lands and establish their first community was complete: Solms, Fisher, Zink, Coll, Koester, Ervendberg, and Lindheimer.[20]

Samuel Addison White, who had brought his family to Texas from Tennessee in 1830, owned the land on Indian Point that Solms was eyeing. Solms rode out to his house with four men, but White was not there. The prince and escort made camp and spent the night. Among the group was one Ewing, who was designated as the Adelsverein's "chief forester."

White returned the next day and proved amenable—if not eager—to sell a portion of his land for cash. He further assisted by leading Solms through the marshes and twelve miles beyond, to a point on Chocolate Bayou where Sylvanus Hatch owned a league of land and operated a plantation called Agua Dulce. Solms purchased 1,100 acres there for the colonists' first way station.[21]

Solms laid out the new community at Indian Point and dubbed it Carlshaven. He, Count Castell, and Prince Leiningen were all Carls. The camp on Chocolate Bayou would be called Leiningen, and another camp—not yet chosen, but at a crossing on the Guadalupe River—would be known as Castell. Carlshaven, Leiningen, and Castell would be stops on a new trail inland, which Solms envisioned as ultimately becoming a railway. The trail would lead to a site he had seen during his journey to San Antonio with Bourgeois. "An excellent and beautiful place where a Senator Smith [El Colorado] owns a location of four leagues is at the so-called 'fountains' on the route from San Antonio to Austin, thirty miles from the former. This area offers excellent land. It is a beautiful tract with first rate cedar and oak forests and water power. Its proximity to San Antonio and Seguin assures support and help in case of need. Situated at the foot of the hill country, it will be the headquarters for the colonization project, since it is equidistant from the coast and the upper portion of the Verein's land."

To Solms, it made perfect sense to carve a new trail through the land instead of taking established roads: "The route to there by the way of Victoria, Gonzales, and Seguin is like a bow to the string which would be a route on the watershed between the Guadalupe River on the one [east] side and the San Antonio, Coleto, and Cibolo Rivers on the other. For this reason it is evident that the latter route would be the shortest and the best, especially since being on the watershed, it is on a plateau." Still, in selecting the route, Solms had more on his mind than point-to-point simplicity: "It is out of the question to route the settlers by way of Victoria, Gonzales and Seguin. Firstly, every town inhabited by wicked rabble of Texas is to be avoided for a number of reasons. Secondly, this route passes through a large number of often-flooded streams over which there are no bridges. . . . Thirdly, none of these towns are our destination."[22]

But first there was the matter of getting the colonists from their temporary camp near Lavaca to the planned port at Carlshaven. They began the move on December 24—men, women, children, tents, crates, and trunks, some going overland, some on the *Alert*. Solms was feeling the strain of the project. He was annoyed that Fisher was still in Galveston, annoyed that Fisher was shirking the hands-on role of the colonial commissioner, annoyed that Fisher had argued over who should be the Adelsverein's agent in Galveston. "I can truthfully say that up to now I have had everything on my own shoulders, a thing which is almost too much for one person. I must also mention that of all the draft oxen, livestock, etc., to be obtained, Mr. Fisher has not secured one head. Wagons are being delivered very sparingly; instead of fifty, there are only fifteen so far. Thus, everything is moving very slowly; and, as a result, it will be more costly than if Mr. Fisher had hurried here and had attended to everything with zeal and energy."

Solms had no intention of running the day-to-day affairs of the colony. That was the colonial commissioner's job. Solms was the commissioner general, an executive oversight position, not an operating one. He had his own matters to attend to in Galveston, matters of much greater importance than procuring wagons. And he was disappointed in how Fisher was operating. "Mr. Fisher should never be entrusted with guidance of the Verein's affairs, even on an interim basis, since the best interests of the Verein would suffer. Even if it is only on an interim basis, a reliable and energetic man must be sent here. The earlier such a man arrives the better it will be for the Verein."[23]

In truth, Solms already had a good support staff among the colonists. Men such as Zink and Coll were capable and hard working—though they turned out to have their share of flaws. For now, though, everyone was focused on the immediate task of establishing Carlshaven and preparing for the trek inland. It was Christmas Eve. The colonists were split between the temporary camp and Carlshaven. At the camp, Solms had a small oak cut down to serve as a Christmas tree. "Walked by moonlight to the camp. Sophie was in my thoughts!!!" On Christmas morning, Reverend Ervendberg conducted services, then Solms passed out gifts to the children. The two men conducted similar ceremonies at Carlshaven the next day. Lindheimer, a freethinker and an atheist, slept quietly behind the altar.[24]

Almost five hundred Germans had reached the distant shores of Texas, where they were greeted by a prince. Huddled on a barren coast, they were peasants and workers and young idealists and political refugees, the bitter fruit of Germany's upheaval, transplanted to a strange land. Another journey lay ahead, into country unknown. It was Christmas, a time of reverence and hope. There were laughter and tears, expectation and apprehension, songs and prayers. And there were likely a few rounds of bad potato brandy.

CHAPTER 14

# *Priorities*

Prince Solms spent the first two weeks of 1845 getting Carlshaven organized, establishing a camp at Chocolate Bayou (officially dubbed Leiningen, but that name was seldom used), and putting management in motion. In the absence of Henry Fisher, who was in Washington (where the Ninth Congress of the Republic of Texas had convened December 5), it fell to the remaining four members of the colonial council to administer the colony.

Their first task was to move the colonists inland to Chocolate Bayou, away from the more severe weather and less favorable conditions at Carlshaven. Having an insufficient supply of wagons and carts, they made the trek in relays, but by January 5 all the colonists were gathered inland.[1]

A letter arrived from Fisher, who had reached Washington after an unexpected delay. The letter illustrates the tension between Solms and Fisher over the wagons and oxen, but Fisher let Solms know that he had asked Ernst and Fordtran, of Industry, to take twenty yoked oxen to Carlshaven. Fisher rubbed salt into an ongoing disagreement with Solms over who should be the Adelsverein's agent at Galveston—Klaener or Kauffman—and reported that Jack Hays was in Washington. Hays said that he had scouted out a location on the Llano River that would suit the colonists perfectly, and that he could lead the procession directly there.

But the important matter in the letter was the Congress. Fisher had put forward a bill that would extend the deadlines under Fisher's colonization contract and tweak some of its lesser provisions. Castro was in Washington, too, and he had submitted a similar bill. And, Fisher said, Kennedy and Ducos (Bourgeois's partner) were seeking deadline relief. Fisher was confident that his business would go well before the Congress, even though the Texians were fixated on annexation and the question of what town should be the capital.

Then Fisher broached a most sensitive subject: "Around here, word goes around that Your Serene Highness has raised a yellow, black and red flag (without the Texas star) in the camp. If this is really so, I ask to please incorporate the star and to avoid anything that creates the impression that we want to erect a government within the government. Your Serene Highness knows the jealousy of the Americans. There are some here who really believe we intend to conquer the country, and our opponents try everything to reinforce that prejudice." Yellow, black, and red were the colors of the flag of the German Confederation.[2]

On Sunday, January 6, Solms penned a blistering reply to Fisher: "Concerning the flag that stands before my tent, it is black and yellow and I have no desire to place a star on it, even less so because the Texans, for whose nationhood I fought battles in Europe, are about to give it away out of fear and dread. Tell whomever you want that I wrote this to you." And there was this passage: "Now, with regard to Hays's company, as well as all the other Americans or other foreign elements, I entreat you, once and for all, to keep them out of the verein settlements because this is absolutely necessary for many reasons, and because the opposite is impermissible." Solms was not only building a little Germany, he wanted to exclude non-Germans.

Solms blamed Fisher for failing to foster a pro-colonial spirit in Washington. By arriving there late, he had let the negative influence of Duff Green, Henri Castro, and Armand Ducos poison the atmosphere. The prince demanded a full accounting of the $11,000 in Adelsverein funds that Fisher had been given. He accused him of providing insufficient wagons and oxen. And, firing a shot that landed amidships, he informed Fisher that "with regard to the settlements on the Llano, I am of the opinion that they are too high up in the country to have a connection to the sea, and are out of contact with other settlements as well, and I will announce my decision about this to you when we speak." Fisher's grant was entirely above the Llano. If Solms did not settle there, Fisher's contract would not be fulfilled.

Turning to the matter of annexation, Solms advised Fisher that he was coming to Washington to deal with the Congress personally, but in the meantime, "this is what you tell the members of Congress in my name: that I have already spent a lot of money for Texas, and that I am prepared to even undertake the enormous expense of a wooden train [wooden rails] from the sea to the upper country. As soon as this Texan nation ceases to exist, however, I am not entitled to spend another cent. Who has done so much for the country, who is ready to do as much as the Verein—but only for a free Texas; for the state of Texas, not a cent."[3]

Still stewing over Fisher's performance and that of the Congress, Solms called a meeting of the colonial council for the next day. He presided over the engineer Zink, the accountant von Coll, and Dr. Koester. First on the agenda was formulating articles of war for a border patrol. The choice of the term "border patrol" is interesting. Presumably the border in question was that of the colonial camps, and presumably the patrols were meant to defend against Indians, but the idea has a certain resonance in the context of Solms's letter to Fisher of the day before. Was Solms planning a "government within the government"? Did he imagine forcibly excluding non-Germans?

In other council business, the four council members unanimously concluded that Fisher "neither performed his functions satisfactorily nor accepted his responsibilities." The complaints against Fisher mostly concerned the oxen and carts—matters of importance in the circumstance—and his management of expenses. Then the council censured the Adelsverein's secretary in Bremen, a lawyer named Hill, who had provided so poorly for the colonists on their voyage. It was not just the provisioning. He had lost $100 of the association's funds gambling. And, "two women were sent over as cooks for the Commissioner. They were of loose morals and, if one judges them by their appearance and looks, probably got their jobs in return for services rendered." This, like the rest of the council's minutes, has Solms's fingerprints all over it.[4]

Despite the unanimity of the council on its business affairs, it seems that matters were not working so smoothly on a personal level. Solms's diary for the day after the meeting mentions "duel between von Coll and Dr. Koster, plenty aggravation, plenty spectacle." These duels, and there are many of them in the records of the Adelsverein, were of the type engaged in by German university students: ritual swordfights that risked little more than a manly scar. They were affairs of honor.[5]

Solms called another colonial council meeting on Wednesday. Von Coll, who was an army lieutenant as well as—or perhaps more than—an accountant, was appointed border patrol commander. In addition to the standing border patrol under von Coll, a volunteer militia was formed. One part would be a mobile force, another would be a stationary reserve defense team.

The council accepted the families that had been sent over by Fisher on the *Weser*—those who survived—as colonists. Because they were impoverished, they were employed as laborers. Some former Castro colonists were also employed as laborers; they received $5 per month, plus foodstuffs for themselves (but not their families). Reverend Ervendberg was retained as a pastor and teacher. Until such time as the congregation could afford to pay him, he was allocated £20 and provisions for himself and his family. The most important item was understated: "Notice was given that instructions by the directors in Germany had been that six months' provisions were to be taken along, and that at present the end of these is near." It is uncertain whether the shortage was through waste, bad planning, or Hill's malfeasance; in any event, Solms tightened up oversight of the colonial storeroom, prohibiting withdrawals unless approved by von Coll.[6]

The colonists were not going to starve. Solms had money and the association had credit. They could have supplies shipped from Galveston to Carlshaven. But there was the matter of who was going to pay for the food—not all colonists were in a position to do so—and whether it could be obtained at the low prices promised by the Adelsverein. There would be unanticipated expenses. Prince Solms was determined to see colonization succeed. Though organizational capital was somewhat limited (at $80,000), he considered his duty to be defined by the project at hand, not by a budget. He would execute his responsibilities, then account for how much it had cost. He blamed Fisher, who had duped the Adelsverein into believing that colonization could be accomplished for the miniscule sum of $35,000 and who, to Solms's way of thinking, had wasted and misappropriated money. Solms lamented that "as a result of the original delays, seemingly endless costs have accrued to the verein, and I am afraid that more are yet to come because it is hardly possible that this year's harvest, if there is any, will be adequate." Solms asked the association "for considerable further credit since the verein very likely must make many advances from its storehouses because the upkeep of so many families is very high." Making matters worse, the Adelsverein had given independent financial authority to each of the colonial council members, so that they might perform their duties. Zink, von Coll, and Koester each had an expense account drawn on the Adelsverein's credit and, in the confusion of putting the colony together, much went unaccounted for.[7]

Solms was not a trained accountant, and—given the independence of Fisher, Zink, Coll, and Koester—he had a formidable management challenge: "The responsibility of administering the funds and establishing an accounting system, plus the worry that there would always be sufficient funds available so that I would not be left high and dry with so many people, has caused me more anxiety and distress and worry, and has wrung more beads of sweat out of me than the July sun and all the Indian tribes in Texas together." These are not the words of someone who has matters under control; Solms foresaw financial chaos and was building his defense in advance.[8]

The prince was concerned about Fisher's work in Washington. He decided to travel to the capital himself. He returned from Chocolate Bayou to Carlshaven and, after some routine business with Burchard Miller and Samuel White's wife, boarded the sloop *Sarah Foyle*.

He did not get far; that night, the *Sarah Foyle* ran aground in Pass Cavallo. It was refloated quickly, but the captain decided to drop anchor until daylight. In the morning, the wind from the Gulf was contrary, and high rollers crashed at the entrance to the pass. The captain decided not to attempt passage, so he returned to Decros Point. As the sloop approached the dock, Solms stood on the deck and sang a serenade for Mary Maverick on shore. The Mavericks provided dinner and a room. Solms found the couple refined and considered Samuel Maverick tough; consistent with his prior opinion, Solms pronounced Alexander Somervell "a scoundrel."[9]

The next morning Solms sailed back to Carlshaven to wait for a turn in the weather. He lingered almost a week before saddling up with five escorts and riding to Victoria. They reached Louise Ernst's inn at Industry four days later, on January 23. Solms pressed on, passing through Brenham and Jacksonville and stopping at Farquhart's inn just beyond. He was only a few miles outside of Washington, but he decided to summon Fisher from there rather than make the trip himself. Fisher appeared on the morning of January 25 and briefed Solms on matters before the Congress. Solms found Fisher to be "very calm about everything." Fisher's bill had passed on first reading in the House and was working its way through the legislative process. The difficult-to-please Solms complained that the bill did not contain all the elements he wanted.[10]

Then a confounding moment arrived. Solms reported to the Adelsverein that "Mr. Fisher declared that he could do nothing further and asked that I come to Washington, since he would not stay there. His request was so urgent that I could not do otherwise but also travel to Houston and Galveston to permit him no excuse for failure to get his requests approved." But Solms, only a few miles from Washington, did not travel there. It is not at all clear that he ever meant to travel there; after all, why did he summon Fisher to the inn rather than ride into Washington? What Solms did, what he likely meant to do all along, was head for Galveston, stopping for a single day in Houston. If Solms allowed Fisher no excuse for failing to get the bill passed, then he did so by leaving Fisher to sink or swim on his own. And Fisher did not refuse to stay at Washington, as Solms said. He remained in the capital until February 3, when he joined Solms in Galveston. His bill had passed on January 29, giving him until March 1, 1846—more than a year away—to land one-third of his colonists.[11]

Solms misunderstood that one-third requirement. He believed that the contract required six hundred heads of families or single men to colonize, thus one-third would be two hundred. But in January 1844, Fisher and Miller had exercised a clause in their contract that increased the total to six thousand families. The initial requirement was two thousand, not two hundred. Solms was unaware of that fact, and more than once he calculated his obligations based on two hundred initial colonists. Perhaps Fisher did not want to draw attention to that detail, but it was well known in Mainz and it was obvious on the face of the joint resolution that extended Fisher's deadline.[12]

Maybe it was a sign of Solms's disinterest in Fisher's contract. He had made no effort to gain an extension. He had passed up the chance to make a personal appearance before the Congress. The colonial commissioner, who should have been looking after the colonists, was tending to politics; the general commissioner, who should have been tending to politics, had been looking after colonists and now was heading for Galveston. Why? Fisher put renewal of his contract first, above all else. And Solms had decided that Fisher's land grant was too far north into Comanche territory to be of any use. It was too far from the coast and too far from other settlements. He did not intend to move his colonists there. Fisher and his contract were surplusage, but Solms lacked the authority to fire him or to divert the colony. He could only disparage Fisher to his directors, marginalize him in Texas, and wait for the right moment to convert the Adelsverein to his vision.

In Galveston, as in both Washingtons, the talk was of statehood. When James Polk won the presidency in November 1844, incumbent John Tyler realized that the national mood had shifted toward annexation. Tyler wanted to reap the rewards for himself rather than allow them to Polk, who would not be sworn in until March 4, 1845. One of Tyler's first moves was to send Andrew Jackson Donelson, a nephew of Andrew Jackson, to Texas as the chargé d'affaires for the United States. Donelson arrived in November, during the last few days of the Houston presidency, and worked with the Texas executive and the Congress to push annexation to its conclusion.[13]

Tyler delivered his annual message to Congress on December 3, 1844, saying that "a controlling majority of the people and a large majority of the States have declared in favor of immediate annexation. Instructions have thus come up to both branches of Congress from their respective constituents in terms the most emphatic. It is the will of both the people and the States that Texas shall be annexed to the Union promptly and immediately."[14]

Six days later Anson Jones was sworn in as the new president of Texas. Those who heard his inaugural address waited impatiently to learn his position on annexation. Surprisingly, the address did not even contain the word. Commenting on the silence, Saligny wrote that "the partisans of annexation try in vain to conceal their surprise and anger at this omission. The better to cover their confusion, they maintain that only in the next message will the President make known his true views on this great political act, and according to them, he will come out in no uncertain terms in favor of it." But when Jones delivered his first annual message to the Texas Congress a week later, the subject was again untouched.[15]

When Solms reached Galveston, annexation was still before the U.S. Congress. This is why Solms was there instead of at Chocolate Bayou. He had not left the colonists to assist Fisher; he had come to Galveston, where the latest news of annexation could be found and where representatives of England, France, and Texas plotted and gossiped endlessly.

On his first day he conducted some business at Klaener's, the forwarding agent he favored and Fisher opposed, and of course he met with William Kennedy, the British consul. That night he enjoyed dinner at the home of prominent merchant Samuel Maas, who had married opera singer Isabella Offenbach. The ensuing days were filled with meetings with Saligny, Elliot, Bishop Odin, and other local potentates. Fisher and Miller arrived six days after Solms. With them was Friedrich Schubert, a business acquaintance of Fisher who had joined up with the Adelsverein and been at Lavaca when the colonists arrived. Schubert claimed to be a physician; it is not clear that he was. It is, however, clear that his real name was Friedrich Armand Strubberg and that he was a German pulp novelist collecting material for books about Texas. Strubberg would prove problematic for the Adelsverein.[16]

A commotion arose in Galveston upon the arrival of Gen. José Antonio Navarro aboard the 175-foot steamship *John McKim*. Navarro was one of the four Mexican signatories to the Texas Declaration of Independence, a survivor of the Texian Santa Fe expedition, a Lamar supporter, and an advocate of annexation. Upon his arrival, all of Galveston's military companies turned out; Navarro was honored by a cannon salute, and a mob of admirers escorted him to the Tremont House.[17]

Except for that brief moment of excitement, most of Solms's time in Galveston was spent on mundane matters. He played a lot of whist. He dined and met and mingled. He wrote letters and reports. He received a letter from Sophie ("Oh, what joy!"). He had an argument with Charles Fordtran. He dealt with Fisher, who was still in Galveston: "After all these days of correspondence with Fisher my first impression of him has proven correct (he is a scoundrel)." Actually, Solms's first impression had been that Fisher was "a calm, thoughtful man, one who is not a schemer," but that view seems to have faded.[18]

Another shipload of Castro colonists arrived, 204 in all, "and these are already in distress. I do not have the means to help them, although without exception all want to join the Verein. I could well use them, especially as settlers beyond the Guadalupe, or else in Carlshaven."[19]

Solms did some math and figured that it would cost $2.68 per person per month to feed colonists until they were able to sustain themselves. With some five hundred colonists at Carlshaven and Chocolate Bayou, that added up to $1,300 per month just for board. And, by his calculations, there were only 140 heads of families among the five hundred arrivals, so sixty more heads of families—more than two hundred new colonists—would be needed to meet what Solms mistakenly believed was a two-hundred-family minimum. Expenses were going to be much higher than expected.[20]

The Texas Congress adjourned on February 3, and Solms breathed a sigh of relief that it did so "without having acted on annexation, although many members favored it. The possibility of an extra session should not be discounted, although I doubt if there will be one." Absent a special session, annexation could not move forward until the Congress met again in December.[21]

Solms had arrived in Galveston on January 29. He remained there almost a month, until February 23, while his colonists waited. There is no clear reason for the date of his departure. He had gotten bored, and he seems to have been waiting for Captain Simpton, suggesting that he planned to sail to Carlshaven, but on the twenty-third he departed on horseback.

What was Solms doing in Galveston? He wasn't concerning himself with Fisher's land grant or with moving the colonists inland, that much is certain. He was keeping tabs on annexation, but by February 3 he thought that matter was settled. He was socializing (and earlier he had shown a tendency to enjoy relaxing in Galveston while waiting for Fisher), but Solms was not a man to disregard his duties. His diaries, letters, and reports are circumspect, but it is possible to glean a hint that he was working on a special project. If so, the project required time conferring and dining with Saligny (who had backed the Franco-Texian Bill), Kennedy (to whom Solms had proposed the British-German militarized colony), and Elliot (an abolitionist who was willing to consider any plan that would result in prohibition of slavery in Texas). And there is one cryptic entry in Solms's diary, just a week before leaving Galveston: "Plan for the contract with the English government."[22]

Solms may have been spinning a web, but it would be wrong to conclude that the British and French legations were somehow caught up in it. Their dispatches before, during, and after Solms's month in Galveston were focused on the activities of the Texas Congress, the annexation talks in the United States, and the possibilities of peace between Texas and Mexico. They did not mention Solms or his schemes.

CHAPTER 15

# *The Founders Depart*

Henry Fisher had not been the only supplicant seeking a colonization contract renewal from the Ninth Texas Congress. Castro, Grieve (Kennedy's successor), and Bourgeois had also petitioned for relief. The Congress took a logical approach: Fisher and Castro secured renewals because they had already landed colonists and were proceeding diligently. Grieve and Bourgeois had made no perceptible progress, and their applications were denied. Pirson had never raised a finger to colonize his grant and didn't bother asking for a renewal. Thus, the five 1842 empresarios were diminished to just two: Castro and Fisher.[1]

After leading his colonists onto the McMullen lands, Castro set about building a village. In September 1844, when the work had just begun, he was visited by Abbé Ogé and Bishop Odin. Castro, an epicure, hosted dinner. Guests included overseer Louis Huth, quartermaster Charles DeMontel, Auguste Frételliére, Dr. Cupples, and a community stalwart ironically named Bourgeois. Castro's diary provides the menu: "I was able to offer to my guests, to the great astonishment of Monseigneur, vermicelli soup made with the bones of deer (nothing can be more delicate), fried trout, roasted turkey and partridges, filets of deer fricasseed. For desert a cream made with eggs and milk produced in the colony. Pecans gathered at the door of the dining room, medlars and wild pomegranates. Red wine made from wild grapes by a German."[2]

Of course, it was not all deer consommé and partridge. Another group of colonists—who had sailed from France—arrived two weeks later. Then, "rain *deluvienne,*" said Castro. "A depressed, uncomfortable company of people! And this was Utopia! At the best, living conditions were just tolerable. Now with water dripping through that grass so excellently adapted for roofs, and soaking into the dirt floors, with children sniffling, men swearing, fires smoking, food nearly impossible to get cooked—well, where was that paradise of ease? The men could do nothing, and the women, poor souls, could get nothing done. It is no wonder that there was many a disgruntled spirit among them."[3]

Such were the ups and downs of colonizing. As December approached, Castro prepared for the trip to Washington that would obtain his two-year contract extension. He left Louis Huth and Dr. Cupples in charge of the colony. Once Castro received his extension, he was in a position to expand his colonization from the McMullen tract onto his land grant. That was where profits would lie, for Castro received generous portions of land for every colonist settled. So Castro began an effort to attract more colonists.

Like Fisher, Castro continued from Washington to Galveston, where Solms was making his plans. More shiploads of Castro colonists were arriving, and Solms was eyeing their potential. Castro made sure they continued on to Port Lavaca and San Antonio, and he did some poaching of his own. Discovering that there was a group of disgruntled Adelsverein colonists camped on the Lavaca River, he wrote Huth, suggesting that they be brought to Castroville.[4]

Once the newly arrived colonists had been relayed successfully, and after taking care of a few more business matters, Castro booked passage to Boston. As he traveled, he enrolled recruiting agents in Galveston, Mobile, Charleston, Philadelphia, New York, and Boston. But his destination was France, where he could quiet the rumors and condemnations that were besmirching his name and recruit more colonists. When he arrived, he found that suits had been filed against him in Colmar and Strasbourg and that the courts had declared—in his absence—that further recruitment of colonists was prohibited in those quarters, due to fraud. The existence of the decrees did nothing to burnish his image elsewhere. Castro filed a countersuit and prevailed, but it took months.[5]

Castro spent the spring and summer of 1845 in France, restructuring his management system, recruiting colonists, and working with Ludwig Huth, his principal financial backer. It became clear that Huth was reaching the limits of his investment ability. To make matters worse, Huth's import/export business between France and Texas was not working out. That was partly because his son, Louis Huth, had been absorbed into colonization affairs instead of trading, and partly because Huth's trading agents in Galveston were less than reliable. Castro would have to find new sources of financing.

With Ludwig Huth's support, Castro negotiated an agreement with a group of ten Antwerp investors led by banker Guillaume Dhanis. Castro, Huth, and the investors formed a new company, the Société de Colonisation Europée-Américain au Texas. When the ink was dry, the company owned the colonization contract, the rights to the McMullen tract, and all of Castro's 269 contracts with colonists. Castro's share of the company was

30 percent, Huth held 52.5 percent, and the new investors owned 17.5 percent. The Dhanis group was given control over major decisions, and Castro was made general manager in Texas. Profits were to be divided among the investors in proportion to their ownership until everyone had recovered their investment plus 5 percent per annum interest. After that, profits would go half to Castro, half to the eleven other investors.[6]

When we last saw Solms, he had left Galveston for Carlshaven toward the end of February and turned his attention from annexation back toward colonization. Despite his earlier insistence that the colonists entirely avoid Victoria and Gonzales, the reality was that their offerings were essential. Carlshaven was little more than a stretch of beach, and Chocolate Bayou was a camp. Goods, supplies, tools, wagons, stables, craftsmen, warehouses, and decent housing were available only in the existing towns. As Nicolas Zink moved colonists from Carlshaven to Chocolate Bayou, and then onward to the next layover point at McCoy Creek (which Solms named Castell, but the name never stuck), some went through Victoria. When Solms returned from Galveston, he found Zink at Victoria, where he had established a storehouse.[7]

The usual mini-crises raged. Dr. Koester had displayed a "hard and inhuman manner" and Solms suspended him, letting Dr. Emil Meyer (the Swiss physician whom Solms met at Nassau Farm, and who traveled with him to San Antonio) take over his practice. Solms was full of praise for Zink and von Coll but equally generous with his vitriol for Fisher. Fisher disputed Solms's authority and wanted Burchard Miller to have a spot on the colonial council. Solms called a meeting of the colonial council; the minutes of the meeting read like those of a kangaroo court: "The meeting began with a lecture by His Grace regarding the conduct of Mr. Fischer before he arrived at Camp at La Vaca." There followed a string of complaints about Fisher (wagons, carts, and oxen, as usual); the council decided that "Mr. Miller could receive the seat of Mr. Fischer, but only after Mr. Fischer had died or if the Verein gave its permission."

Solms declared that "a harmonious working relationship was not possible. Furthermore, His Grace had documents in his possession which were not trust-inspiring towards the Director. Thereupon the two documents were read." It is not clear what the documents were—perhaps letters of condemnation or accusation. Fisher protested; he interrupted the meeting to confer with Miller. While he was out of the room (or, more likely, out of the tent), the remaining council members decided that the only workable arrangement was to pay off Fisher and send him packing. When Fisher returned—no doubt angry and frustrated—he agreed.[8]

This was exactly what Solms wanted. Fisher had a one-third interest in the venture, and the Adelsverein was obliged to negotiate a settlement price, but Solms was free. Free to direct colonization as he saw fit. Free to disregard the notion of moving his Germans all the way to Fisher's distant lands. It is hard to criticize Solms's rejection of Fisher's lands. They were, by any objective measure, too far beyond the frontier to be settled successfully.

How distant was the Llano from civilization? Consider the ongoing dialogue between Texas and the Comanches over where the boundary between their lands lay. In March 1844, Comanche chief Mopechucope—one of the most powerful chiefs—had written a cordial letter to Houston through an Indian agent:

> Past times are all forgotten and I will come amongst my friends, all I want now is a line run between our countries which line I want to commence on Brazos river passing over the Comanche Peak from thare direct to the mouth of the first large creek running in the Colorado on the west-side below the mouth of the San Saba; from thence in a direct line to the Rio Grande; all above that line is Comanche Country and ever has been I my self never have left it nor never intends to; at this treaty with the Indians if you wish to designate the line fully the aforesaid line will sattisfy the Comanche.

The "first large creek running in the Colorado on the west-side below the mouth of the San Saba" was the Llano. Comanches, when they were in a conciliatory mood, treated that as the boundary of their lands. Texians who went north of the Llano did so at their own risk.[9]

And Houston did not disagree. In October 1844—less than four months before the Texas Congress reaffirmed and extended Fisher's rights above the Llano, Houston attended a grand council with chiefs of twelve Indian tribes. It was a critical moment in Houston's effort to achieve peace on the frontier, and the resulting treaty is a Texas touchstone. The attendees included Mopechucope and Pochanaquarhip, the Comanche war chief. Houston, then still president of the Republic of Texas, tendered a peace treaty that described the boundary between Indians and Texians as proceeding from Comanche Peak "to the old fort of San Saba, and from thence in a Southwest direction to the Rio Grande." This line—proposed by Houston—put all of Fisher's lands inside Indian territory except for a slice at the southeast. The lead Comanche chief present was Pochanaquarhip. He informed Houston that the boundaries were not acceptable; they must go much farther south, almost to San Antonio. Ultimately, Houston and the

Indians decided to strike the boundaries from the document and agree on everything else.[10]

No one at the council disputed that most of the land included in Fisher's grant belonged to the Comanches; their most polite disagreement was whether it dipped another hundred miles south. It is likely that Houston never mentioned this geographic consensus to Fisher or Solms, but the fact is that Fisher's grant was so remote that Houston was perfectly willing to let the Comanches have it, even though he had already promised it to Fisher.

Once Solms had pushed Fisher aside, he had only to find a suitable place for his colony. He could cast it as a way station on the march to the Llano and beyond, but the truth is that he did not in the least intend that his colonists push that far. He meant to find a select tract, build a town, and move forward with his German settlement on the Texas frontier. He meant to keep nudging Elliot (and, indirectly, Solms's cousin, Queen Victoria) to block the United States from consuming Texas and more. If at some point settlement of Fisher's grant appeared practical, and if the colonization contract did not expire before then, and if it would not undermine Solms's other plans, then perhaps Germans might settle above the Llano. But that was a matter of speculation. The matter at hand was to create a secure and prosperous German settlement in a choice position.

Solms needed to get his project moving. It was March, only nine months before the Texas Congress would meet again. Annexation would surely be on the table, and he wanted his colony firmly planted by then. He inspected his company of border patrolmen, then saddled up and rode for San Antonio on March 8, accompanied by two militiamen, botanist Ferdinand Lindheimer, and others. They spent the night of March 9 there with José Antonio Navarro, the celebrated general who had been given a hero's welcome in Galveston. Navarro introduced Solms to another (and related) long-lineage Tejano, Juan Martín de Veramendi, who had been the brother-in-law of James Bowie until the latter's untimely death at the Alamo.[11]

It turned out that the Fountains—the land that Solms had admired on his previous trip to San Antonio, which he believed was owned by El Colorado, the Texian senator and land broker—was in fact owned by Veramendi's sister, María Antonia Veramendi Garza, and her husband Rafael Garza. It was once part of a Spanish land grant to Felipe Enrique Neri, a Dutch embezzler who had changed his name to Baron de Bastrop and ingratiated himself with the Spanish. The pseudo-baron was supposed to establish a colony on the land but never had, and his title had lapsed. In 1831, during Mexican rule, Juan Martín de Veramendi, the ninth Mexican governor of Texas, had received an eleven-league grant under Mexican law that included the Fountains, which was part of Bastrop's land. The vast holdings had passed down through the family. Solms and Veramendi talked business and agreed to continue their discussion later.[12]

On the tenth, Solms stopped for luncheon at the ranch of Manuel Flores, another old-line Tejano. He had fought for Texian independence in Juan Seguin's company of volunteers and pursued Mexican general Vásquez after his raid on San Antonio. Flores and his wife María owned a ranch on the Guadalupe River, below Seguin. Solms hoped that Veramendi would join him there, but it did not happen. Solms rode on, and by six in the evening he sighted San Antonio. His group settled into an old hotel.

Solms and his entourage spent six days in San Antonio. The purpose was to buy the Fountains, resulting in repeated meetings among Solms, Veramendi, Garza, and their lawyers. Solms naturally took time to pay his respects to all the other local dignitaries. By March 15 the paperwork was complete; Solms had purchased 1,265 acres for $1,111. He withheld most of the purchase price until the Veramendis could successfully clear their title of any claims by the heirs of Baron de Bastrop. Because that seemed to pose no material problem, Solms proceeded with his project.[13]

The next morning Solms and his companions rode through Seguin to the Flores ranch, where they were joined by two men from the McCoy Creek camp. The next morning Nicolas Zink, Jean van Coll, Dr. Emil Meyer, and thirteen militiamen arrived. The company rode along the southern boundary of Solms's new acquisition, almost to the Guadalupe. A norther blew in, bringing cold, blustery weather. On the eighteenth they saddled up and rode into the chill winds; they reached the junction of the Comal River and the Guadalupe, where they made camp. In the morning, they awoke to a rare snowfall. The tawny colors of winter were shrouded in white. Was it a sign?[14]

The new tract was superb. On the south, it bordered the Spanish Camino Real from San Antonio to Nacogdoches, the major east-west route through Texas. It was bounded on the east by the Guadalupe River and embraced Comal Creek and the Comal River. The abundant, surging springs of the Fountains were at the head of the Comal River; the junction of the creek and the two rivers was the *comal,* named after the shallow bowl used to make tortillas. The land was in gentle hills just below the Balcones Escarpment, and it was a mix of highlands, valleys, forests, and fields.

It was, in a way, remarkable that Prince Solms secured such a superior plot of land, for he had only glimpsed it from the Camino Real. He never explored even to the modest extent that he had trekked the McMullen and Cassiano tracts; he was dealing almost entirely from descriptions provided by others. When he did penetrate its boundaries he was ecstatic, but the best description of the land comes from Ferdinand Lindheimer, the botanist in Solms's group. He reported that Solms had

> acquired a beautiful little parcel of land . . . where the streams flow crystal clear over the rocky beds. The fluid element gleams emerald green, and in its greatest depths the fish rush back and forth visibly. Powerful springs cascade down from the rocky hills. They are probably subterranean brooks that have gathered in the caves of the limestone boulders and suddenly come to the surface. Forest, grazing land, and land for cultivated fields of the best quality are available. But what does that matter to me? Palmate yuccas, cactus, and mimosas and the fragrance and blossoms of them all, that's for me. Here I have seen for the first time the total splendor of the prairies. Flower upon flower, richer than the richest Persian carpet. Fragrances that sometimes remind one of violets, often of vanilla, flow around the wanderer. The sea wind breathes with a living freshness over the prairies and streams through the treetops of the forest like the murmur of a distant surf.[15]

The first colonist wagons crossed the Guadalupe and reached Solms's camp on March 21, the spring equinox. "Crossing of the first fifteen wagons, but what toil and what difficulty it was. Finally they are *here!*"[16]

The camp was placed on a bluff above Comal Creek, backed against a ridge. Solms came down with a cold. Dr. Meyer prescribed oak bark with red wine. Zink got in an argument and tried to leave camp. More wagons arrived. The militia patrolled. Lipans visited, making everyone nervous, but they left without disturbance. The colonists went about making a habitable camp. Solms directed Zink to erect a stockade for protection against Indian attack. It was named the Zinkenburg.

This was not a camp of the sort established at Chocolate Bayou or McCoy Creek. It was more, even, than the landing that Solms envisioned at Carlshaven. The prince meant for this land to become a permanent town. Regardless of his personal inclinations, the reality was that it was the season to settle and plant crops. It was not practical to move the colonists any farther until crops were harvested; realistically, this place was home until 1846. Solms was not bothered by that. Reaching Fisher's tract on the Llano was something that he was duty-bound to honor—at least until he convinced the directors otherwise—but it was not something that he intended to achieve, at least not during his tenure in Texas. The prince wanted to return to Germany (and Sophie) as soon as possible. His replacement, the Baron Otfried Hans von Meusebach, had already been selected and was on his way.

Solms's vision was of a prosperous German colony within a reasonable distance of the coast, in the vicinity of other settlements, and on a road suitable for commerce. He had liked Cassiano's tract for those reasons. He had liked McMullen's tract because it met most of those conditions; it was too far west, but at least it was not as far west as Bourgeois's grant. The Comal tract was the best of any he had considered. It met every requirement. This was the place to settle, not far into Comanche territory.

And so Solms bestowed an honor upon the settlement. He named it New Braunfels, after his family's realm. The princes of Solms-Braunfels reigned from a castle on a hill above the German town of Braunfels, and Solms meant to mirror that in his new hamlet. He chose a hill that rose steeply above the muddy camp and declared that it would be the site of a stone redoubt. He named his castle in the air the Sophienburg. He had a hut built there, marked out on the ground where the stone walls would someday be, and raised the German flag.

Unlike at any other Adelsverein camp, Solms gave land to the colonists. In the fashion of German feudal villages, each family received a half-acre in town for a residence and ten acres outside the town for farming—in addition to the 640 acres each family was to receive within Fisher's grant. Nicolas Zink set about surveying the town and farms.

When a group of colonists arrived on May 6, one of them described the scene: "I rejoiced because of the woods, the soil, and the water, and at a lovely spot I crossed the Comal Creek by way of huge logs. There I found myself right in the middle of the town which was stretched out in front of me. On one hilltop there was the Sophienburg, on another the encampment. Tents, single trees, small corrals, houses under construction are all scattered over the green plain."[17]

Not all was idyllic at New Braunfels. Someone stole a supply of wine and whiskey. The most likely suspect was Nicolas Zink. He was a good engineer, but he was also a scoundrel. He was traveling with his wife and his mistress. He would divorce his wife, marry his mistress, then divorce her and marry again. He would be followed by controversy and litigation wherever he went. Solms, who once considered Zink among his best men, discovered that he had been submitting false invoices for payment, and he ended up making this evaluation of his engineer: "Zink likes intrigue and tries to set the Officials against the Verein. His character traits are falsehood, cowardice and uncouthness. He is subservient to his betters and excessively rough with his employees." Solms was just warming up. He continued: "Despite all his assurances of loyalty to the Verein, he doesn't hesitate to double-cross and cheat it at every opportunity, be it money or property on purchases. Even the dirtiest means are not too low for him; hence, his personal and family situations are of the dirtiest nature and are the worst example for the Colony. His abilities, which I don't deny, are overshadowed by his selfishness and his greed and the improper way he treats people."[18]

Reverend Ervendberg established his ministry and began holding regular services in an oak grove at the base of the Sophienburg. By August he was conducting German-English classes at the same location. Ferdinand Lindheimer obtained a piece of land on the Comal River, built a home there, and spent his time collecting plants and cultivating a botanical garden.

Meanwhile, tension arose between the colonists and the representatives of the Adelsverein. Solms in particular viewed the colonial enterprise as one of noblesse oblige paternalism, in which the parent organization issued orders and directives that the colonists were to follow dutifully. The colonists, understandably, had a different view. They were going to a new land where they would build a new community based on American—more exactly, Texian—notions of freedom and democracy. A colonist gave a personal glimpse of the situation:

> I saw the Prince on Thursday. He inquired about our trip, remarked that I had gained weight, and lit a cigar for one of the Indian women. He did this as graciously as if he were presenting a rose to a princess. It was a scene worth painting! For several weeks there has been a shortage of coffee in the settlement and people are dissatisfied with the leadership. In the town of New Braunfels the Texas flag has been raised in protest against the German colors at the Sophienburg. The administration of the colony has practically been taken out of the hands of the Verein, as the latter is only regarded as an agency for the supply of material support. Most settlers want to receive their 320 acres and the provisions for the rest of the year immediately. Everything taken from the storehouse (a straw shed) is being recorded against one's name. The soldiers receive five, the laborers three to four bits per month plus board. Intrigues overshadowed the election for interim mayor and aldermen.[19]

Solms divided his time between New Braunfels and San Antonio, moving the Adelsverein's affairs forward. The natives took an interest in New Braunfels, becoming frequent visitors. Reverend Ervendberg held services and served communion. On April 28, Solms presided over the laying of a cornerstone for the Sophienburg. "A short speech by me, then a speech and blessing by the pastor. All this during a thunderstorm. Cannon salute and raising of the flag. At 3:30 P.M. dinner under the improvised tent. Thirty settings. Toast to Sophie's health, then mine. For the first, a 21-gun salute." It is not clear what exactly the Sophienburg was at that time, beyond a cornerstone in the rain. It may have been a reed hut, at most a log cabin. As matters turned out, it was never more than that.[20]

Solms had received a letter from Meusebach, his replacement, dated April 6 and posted at New Orleans. Expecting Meusebach to arrive soon, he scheduled his departure for May 15. "I hope to arrive in Boston in a month so that I can depart from America by steam boat on the 15th of June. However, on account of slow traveling conditions here, irregular communication between Galveston and New Orleans, and the long trip up the Mississippi, nothing definite can be planned."[21]

On the evening of the fourteenth, Solms gave a farewell speech to the colonists. He surveyed the audience proudly. He had brought them from Germany and shepherded them to this place, without the plagues and poverty that others had suffered. They were strong and diligent, and already their village was taking shape on the Texas frontier. There were hundreds of colonists, and thousands more would follow. Of all the colonial empresarios in Texas—even the legendary Stephen F. Austin—Solms and the Adelsverein had accomplished the most.

Early the next morning, Solms awoke at the Sophienburg. His militia raised the German flag and fired a cannonade, and the prince rode out of New Braunfels. Lindheimer, von Coll, and a militia escort accompanied him. Zink, who had overslept, caught up outside town. Five miles into the journey, most of the entourage bid their farewells and returned to New Braunfels.

Solms's diary and reports for this period of travel are notably calm, but he must have been excited to be on the return trip to his beloved Sophie of Salm-Salm. And, having accomplished the first step in forming a strong German colony, he must have been eager to reach Galveston and learn the latest political news. When he had left in late February, the question of annexation was entirely up in the air. The Texas Congress had adjourned, and the U.S. Congress was mired in disputes. But just four days after he left Galveston, the U.S. Congress passed the joint resolution for annexation. News of the resolution had reached Texas in March; by now, Solms must have known. But he could not have known—and could not have imagined—the whereabouts of Charles Elliot.

## CHAPTER 16

# *The Tides Turn*

On March 24, 1845, the British corvette *Electra* entered Galveston Bay; it carried instructions for Elliot and Saligny, sent by their superiors from London and Paris in January. They were to propose a vigorous English and French intervention with Mexico. It had been less than a week since Texas had received news of the annexation resolution adopted by the U.S. Congress.[1]

The two diplomats immediately set forth for Washington, Texas, and arrived on the twenty-seventh. The next day they had long meetings with President Jones and Secretary of State Smith. Both assured the European diplomats that they were in favor of independence but that the will of the Texas Congress was strong. Jones thought that "unless he should be very speedily enabled to offer for the decision of the Country a Measure founded upon the acknowledgment of the Republic by Mexico, unaccompanied by any other than the condition to maintain their independence, He should feel that it was in vain to resist the tide, and that it was his duty to carry out the wish of the people whatever it may be." Elliot and Saligny pressed their views. Jones convened the cabinet twice for consultation and once permitted the diplomats to make their case.[2]

That evening Smith, Saligny, and Elliot signed a brief memorandum reflecting the outcome of their discussions. England and France would seek Mexico's approval of the following points: Mexican recognition of the independence of Texas; a Texas pledge to maintain its independence; boundaries and other conditions to be negotiated; and submission of disputed territory to umpires. In return for the effort of France and England, "Texas for a period of ninety days from the date of this Memorandum agrees not to accept any proposals, nor to enter into any Negotiations to annex Herself to any other Country."[3]

Ninety days. In an era when a diplomatic pouch from England, carried on a military corvette, took two months to arrive in Galveston. There was no time to waste. Jones urged Elliot to go to Mexico personally to deliver the proposal, and Saligny concurred. With some misgivings, Elliot agreed.[4]

When Elliot returned to Galveston, he wrote Lord Aberdeen of his plans, adding that "I shall of course take every practicable precaution to keep my visit there strictly secret and shall not remain one day longer than may be necessary for purpose of full explanation." He outlined elaborate plans for traveling incognito, moving by indirect paths and returning to somewhere other than Texas. On April 5, Elliot boarded the British ship *Electra,* bound for Bermuda with a stop in Charleston, South Carolina, ostensibly to drop him off. Once over the horizon, the *Electra* rendezvoused with the British warship *Eurydice.* Elliot transferred from one ship to the other, posing as a diplomatic messenger bound for the British consulate at Mexico City. He landed in Mexico at Vera Cruz; while taking a coach inland, he had the misfortune to be waylaid and robbed by six masked men, but he persisted and delivered his message to Charles Bankhead, the British representative to Mexico. This was Bankhead's territory, and that of French representative Baron Alleye de Cyprey, and Elliot could do no more than assist, but he remained in Mexico City until the end of the month while the Mexican government tossed around the proposal. Frustrated at the delay, Elliot retreated to Jalapa, near Vera Cruz, to await word from Bankhead. On May 20—with fifty-two of the ninety days gone—Bankhead sent a dispatch to Elliot: "I have the honour to transmit to you, for communication to the President of Texas, a Document containing a full acceptance on the part of the President of this Republick, and signed by Don Luis Cuevas, Secretary of State—of the proposals sent from Texas for the acknowledgment of the Independence of the latter Power."[5]

In light of the bad blood between Mexico and Texas, the achievement was astounding. It was what England, and to a lesser extent France, had been working on for years. But it was not so much a conciliatory gesture as an act of realpolitik. The Mexicans finally realized that, if Texas joined the United States, soldiers would soon be crossing their borders and demanding even more territory than Texas claimed. The best way to impede the United States was—as the Europeans had been insisting for years—to plant an independent Texas in its path.[6]

Elliot returned to Galveston, treaty in hand, on the French brig *Lapérouse* and arrived on May 30. He was not pleased by what he found. A Mexican schooner, the *Rempalago,* had docked in New Orleans on the twentieth. It bore only confidential diplomatic correspondence, but the crew leaked that the Mexican government was considering a British peace proposal, and that Elliot was in Vera Cruz waiting to bring the reply to Texas. The next day the New Orleans papers were full of the news. Galveston learned within a few days, and by the time Elliot landed in Texas the rumor had reached the East Coast. The British were getting lambasted for interference.[7]

Elliot had gone to Mexico in the belief that he had a ninety-day window in which to act. Anson Jones had met the strict letter of that commitment, which was "not to accept any proposals, nor to enter into any Negotiations to annex Herself to any other Country," but he had taken two other steps deep into a gray area that must have caused Elliot concern. On April 15, three days after a meeting with Andrew Jackson Donelson, Jones called a special session of the Texas Congress for June 16, to consider the annexation proposal. On May 5, as the clamor for annexation grew, he went a step further and called for an annexation convention to meet on July 4 and prepare a Texas state constitution for submission to the electorate. Elliot had just over two weeks before the Congress would stampede for annexation, unless he could change the republic's mood.[8]

Elliot was annoyed to discover that Saligny was still ensconced in New Orleans. Weeks earlier, Elliot had specifically asked him to come to Galveston. It was not only Elliot who was annoyed: French foreign minister Francois Guizot wanted to know why Saligny kept leaving Texas. "Why all these continuous comings and goings? The rule is that an agent must not leave the country to which he is accredited without authorization." But Saligny would not budge. He liked it in New Orleans, and on the rich plantations of Plaquemines Parish. Despite the importance of events in Texas, he would never return there.[9]

The United States was showing considerably more interest than France. Donelson, who had been in New Orleans for a few weeks, returned a day after Elliot. He had been preceded by four other American representatives: the war steamer *Princeton,* the sloops of war *Saint Mary* and *Saratoga,* and the brig *Porpoise.* Combined, they mounted sixty guns. The *Princeton* was the first screw-propelled steamer in the U.S. Navy; at the helm was Comm. Robert Field Stockton, who carried the official documents offering annexation to Texas. Stockton personally delivered them to Anson Jones in Washington, then returned to Galveston.[10]

Also in the swirl at Galveston was Prince Solms, who arrived a few days before Elliot. He had crossed paths with Meusebach three days outside New Braunfels. Solms was not about to compromise his itinerary back to Germany—and he was a prince, not a mere baron—so Meusebach tagged along with Solms on the journey to Galveston, hoping to gain some degree of orientation. Solms found Meusebach to be "capable, though slightly absent-minded and at first hard to become acquainted with."[11]

Meusebach and Friedrich von Wrede, a frequent member of Solms's entourage, were sent to check in at Beissner's Hotel, which was providing serious competition to the Tremont House. Solms stayed at the British legation. In fact, he "slept heavenly in Elliot's room and bed." Elliot arrived two days later, forcing a change of habitation. Solms met with Elliot, Kennedy, Meusebach, Klaener, and Arcieri (the secretary of the French legation) and pointedly noted that, when the steamer *New York* arrived from New Orleans, Saligny was not on board.

Elliot left Galveston for Washington. There, on the evening of June 2, he tendered the preliminary agreement with Mexico to President Jones, who professed a continuing dedication to its pursuit. He even went so far as to say that because he had "no firm belief in the final completion of [annexation] (for the difficulties appeared to be very great, if not insuperable, both here and in the United States,) he cordially hoped that the Ministers of the two Powers [France and England] would be able to induce the Government of Mexico peacefully to wait the turn of events." But Jones knew that public sentiment was against independence. He promised to issue a proclamation in a few days, announcing the new developments with Mexico, but he declined to send commissioners to negotiate the details. It was too soon and too delicate. Jones "described the state of feeling here to be that of fever, and like all fevers he said it must run its course for good or for evil."[12]

When Jones announced the agreement with Mexico on June 4, Charles Wickliffe—a newly arrived special envoy from President Polk—called it "a peal of Thunder in a clear skie," proof of a conspiracy between Jones and England to defeat annexation. The New Orleans *Courier* reported "that the feelings of the whole population are roused to the highest pitch by the treacherous conduct of Jones, and his intention, if left to itself, to throw the republic into the arms of England." The annexationists had painted England and France as meddling foreigners, and the Europeans had done nothing to counter that charge.[13]

The Texas Congress met in June as scheduled. It rejected negotiations with Mexico and unanimously voted for annexation. After that, the annexation convention met in July. Its deliberations were more lengthy, for it was charged with drafting a constitution for the state, but on the first day it ignored the Mexican peace proposal and adopted an ordinance accepting the offer of annexation. The delegates worked diligently to craft a constitution that would be acceptable to the United States, and they carefully stayed within the terms of annexation offered to them.

Under the deal from the United States, Texas was to retain its debt and—unlike any other state—retain its public lands. The delegates expected that the land, as had always been the case, would provide the funds to service the debt. On August 27—the day before the convention adjourned—a select committee issued a report on the balance of lands owned by Texas. It concluded that there were 397,319 square miles in Texas. After subtracting all of the land grants, land scrip, colonization contracts, and other encumbrances, the committee concluded that only 160,516 square miles of unappropriated public domain remained.

That meant that, surprisingly, "there is left to Texas an unappropriated country not sufficiently large to subsist the various tribes of Indians now inhabiting this country." The good news was that "Texas will, doubtless, despoil the Indians of this country, whenever it shall be needed for the occupancy of civilized man," but it would be decades before Texas pushed that far west. And when it did, half of the land ("if the accounts of traders and travelers are entitled to credit") was "sterile wastes and mountain ranges." Putting a price of $1.25 on each acre and running the numbers, the committee ascertained that "the present worth of this fund, at 6 per cent., will not meet the public debt of Texas." The nascent state was, in other words, bankrupt.

It is entirely possible that the committee overstated the gravity of the situation. The report has the air of trumped-up justification, concluding by citing "the imperious duty of the Convention to reclaim from the unjust and fraudulent possession of the contractor, and unprincipled speculator, those large districts and tracts of country." After all the committee's careful study, it turned out that the speculative nature of colonial contractors was the problem.[14]

The committee's report was not rendered in a vacuum. The committee members were considering an ordinance that had been proposed earlier; that ordinance—separate from the ordinance approving the new constitution—passed the same day that the report issued. It attacked colonization contracts: "It is believed that said contracts are unconstitutional, and therefore, void from the beginning, and if carried out would operate as a monopoly of upwards of seven millions of acres of the public domain of Texas, in the hands of a few individuals—when, in truth, the citizen soldiers and creditors of the Republic had, by the laws and Constitution of said Republic, a clear and indisputable previously subsisting right to locate upon the public domain thus attempted to be assigned to said contractors."[15]

The ordinance, which would be put before the voters in October, directed the attorney general to file suit against colonial empresarios, seeking to void their contracts. The holdings of the individual colonists, however, were not to be disturbed. (The seven million acres referred to in the committee report was the empresarios' share of the land; the total embraced by all of the colonization contracts, including expired contracts, was over twenty-nine million acres.)

There were only three extant colonization contracts. The Peters Colony, formed in 1841, and upon which Sam Houston's colonization contracts of 1842 were modeled, still had a claim to over ten million acres of land. Its operators were mired in legal disputes about who owned what, and as of July 1844 the colonial population consisted of only 197 families and 184 single men. The contract was not due to expire until 1848. The other two colonial contracts were those belonging to Castro's consortium and the Adelsverein. Both of these colonies were performing better than the Peters Colony, and both had been renewed just seven months earlier. But they were owned by foreign interests; foreign interests were not popular at the convention. And there was no longer any pressing need for colonists; Uncle Sam would fill the void.

The irony—or perhaps the hypocrisy—of the measure is marked. A prominent reason for Texas seceding from Mexico in 1836 was the tendency of the Mexican government to change the rules of colonization and land ownership when they became inconvenient. Now Texas wanted to order the attorney general to renege on contracts blessed by the president and the legislature, contracts held by organizations that had invested substantial sums of money in reliance upon the good faith of the republic.

The ordinance for annexation, along with the new constitution and the ordinance for cancellation of colonization contracts, passed by an overwhelming margin at an October 13 plebiscite. Whether the colonization contracts were unconstitutional or not, whether the attorney general ever moved to cancel them or not, they were under a dark cloud. No informed person would invest in the colonies or rely upon the ability of the empresarios to meet their promises. Meeting the one-third requirement, much less the total requirement for colonists, seemed impossible.[16]

It was a death knell to the colonies. Yet it was not.

CHAPTER 17

# *The Outcome*

John Meusebach was unlike Prince Solms. Meusebach had no grand schemes. He followed a straightforward path to settling the land grant. That the path never quite reached its destination is not entirely his fault. Solms made it clear before his departure that Adelsverein funds and credit in Texas were severely strained. Some historians have given Solms the blame for that, but there is no evidence of mismanagement on his part. Bringing the first year's colonists to New Braunfels was simply more expensive than had been planned for.[1]

To the extent that there was waste, it appears to have been mostly at the hands of Nicolas Zink and Dr. Koester. Some blame must go to Jean von Coll, who was supposed to keep the accounts, and to the Adelsverein itself, which created a flat organization in which each of the colonial council members had independent spending authority without local supervision. At the bottom of it, though, it was the Adelsverein's failure to grasp the cost of colonization that caused the financial shortage. After Solms's departure, the colonial administration was never properly funded.

In 1845 and 1846, Meusebach shepherded five thousand pilgrims from Carlshaven to New Braunfels and beyond. It was an emigration that changed Texas forever. The five thousand Germans more than doubled the population of West Texas. They were more settlers than could be found at Washington, Houston, and Galveston combined. Depending on how one defines the size of a colony (how many people over how many years?), it may well have been the largest organized colonization in today's United States, and it was certainly the last of any significant size.[2]

The fate of Meusebach's colonists compared poorly to the experience of those under Solms. He had practically no funds to manage ten times the number of colonists that Solms had overseen. The facilities at Carlshaven were still almost nonexistent. Colonists built huts out of sod and mud, only to see them dissolve in the rain. Meusebach did not get the colonists off the coast quickly, in part because President Polk trumped up a war against

Mexico and the U.S. Army commandeered most of the available wagons. The winter and spring were especially wet, making it difficult—often impossible—to cross the coastal plains. People suffered on the coast until July, enduring conditions easily as bad as any Henri Castro's people had experienced. Disease raged through the camp at Carlshaven and haunted colonists on the trek inland. Hundreds perished on the trail from the coast to New Braunfels. Many were left by the side of the road to die.

Meusebach stabilized New Braunfels and led the colonists to their next settlement, Fredericksburg. But Fredericksburg was still far short of the Llano River, far short of the Fisher-Miller grant. It was built on land purchased by the Adelsverein.

In 1847, Meusebach directed the establishment of four small settlements just north of the Llano River, a few dozen yards into the Fisher-Miller grant. But the colonization contract had expired the year before, and the settlements were no more than a gesture, or perhaps an attempt to gain the sympathy of the legislature. Of the four—Castell, Leiningen, Meerholz, and Schoenburg—only Castell survives today, and it has been relocated to the south of the Llano, off the Fisher-Miller grant. Henry Fisher's lands were simply too remote for settlement.[3]

In the last days of 1847, the Adelsverein announced that it would curtail its activities. The capitalization of the society was, as it always had been, absurdly inadequate. Surveying expenses had mounted to $80,000. The cost of founding and supporting New Braunfels and Fredericksburg was substantial. Repeated delays and difficulties had strained the treasury. The association was incapacitated. Its offices at Fredericksburg and Carlshaven were shuttered. Its livestock and wagons were auctioned to raise money. Surveying of homesites and ten-acre farms for colonists continued in Fredericksburg and New Braunfels, but further efforts to expand into the land grant were abandoned. Bankruptcy loomed, then arrived. Though it struggled to stay alive through the bankruptcy, in practical terms the Adelsverein ceased to exist. The colonists were left to their own devices.

Prince Solms returned to Germany once he finished his stint in Texas. John Meusebach and most of the other Adelsverein representatives in Texas did not; they remained and participated in the future of the republic and the state.

Henry Castro settled in Texas, though he had little other choice: unlike Solms, his colonization scheme was a personal project undertaken with his own funds. He could not afford to turn his back on Texas.

Castro returned to Texas by steamer in July 1846; his family followed behind by sailing ship. He had departed Europe owing Ludwig Huth more than $3,000. He had drawn $6,000 from the Antwerp society and another $1,000 directly from Guillaume Dhanis. When he arrived in Galveston, he found hundreds of colonists there without means to pay for passage to Castroville. Castro obtained another $3,000 to cover their expenses, submitting a draft for that amount to the Antwerp society's Galveston representative, John H. Illies.[4]

Castro's personal funds were gone, and he depended upon money from Antwerp to develop and operate the colony. He went about that task, founding the town of D'Hanis in February 1847, the same month in which his colonization contract expired. But D'Hanis, like Castroville, was on privately owned land outside the boundaries of Castro's land grant. Only Quihi and Vandenburg, two other small villages established by Louis Huth in Castro's absence, qualified as colonial settlements. They had been established before the expiration date of Castro's contract, but they lacked the population required to meet the contract's terms. Worse, Texas had annulled all colonization contracts upon annexation. Castro's colonists, like the Adelsverein's, were in limbo.[5]

Then the Antwerp society soured on Castro and his colony. They refused to pay the $3,000 in drafts submitted by John Illies. In response, Castro sued the society to void their agreement. The suit was brought in Texas, and the society was given notice of its commencement by publication in a Texas newspaper. Needless to say, the society defaulted in the lawsuit and Castro obtained a judgment nullifying any obligation to the Antwerp investors.[6]

Whatever elation Castro may have felt was short-lived. The contract between Castro and John McMullen was contingent upon McMullen quieting title to his tract, for there were questions about the validity of the underlying Spanish land grant. In 1849 the Texas Supreme Court ruled against McMullen. McMullen's title was void, as was Castro's claim to the McMullen tract.[7]

Castro had known from the outset that there was risk involved in the McMullen title, and he had taken extra steps to protect the land where his initial group of colonists settled, and where Castroville was situated. In 1842, Castro had purchased land scrip from John "El Colorado" Smith, entitling him to survey and claim a league and a labor (about 4,500 acres) of land. When John James surveyed the Castroville townsite, Castro used the scrip to obtain a patent to the land, even though he had also contracted for the tract with McMullen. This suspenders-and-belt approach protected the league and labor from loss.[8]

In the meantime, Castro had somehow managed to wrangle an additional loan of $16,000 from Illies, mortgaging his interest in the colony and in Castroville as security. That loan went unpaid, and by 1852 Illies and Castro were in litigation. Illies prevailed for the most part, the Illies mortgage was foreclosed, and many of Castro's colonists found that they had to repurchase their lands from Illies.[9]

In short, Castro's land grant was lost for failure to perform, Castro's McMullen lands were lost through failed title, and much of Castro's league and labor of land was lost to foreclosure by Illies. Castro still held title to some tracts of land that were not subject to the mortgage, but most of his holdings—and those of his colonists—were gone.

The situation was not entirely different from that faced by the Adelsverein colonists. They failed to settle the Fisher-Miller grant, thus lost their rights to that vast tract above the Llano River. More favorably, their title to lands in Fredericksburg was good, and the Garzas—from whom Solms purchased the Fountains—had successfully defended their title against others who claimed under Baron de Bastrop. But, having done so, the Garzas turned on the German colonists, claiming that the now-bankrupt Adelsverein had failed to pay in full for the land. It wasn't until 1873 that that dispute was settled by the Texas Supreme Court, which favored the equitable rights of the colonists over the legal claims of the Garzas.[10]

Five sets of empresarios—Kennedy, Castro, Pirson, Fisher, Bourgeois, and their respective partners—had been given colonization contracts on eleven tracts of land, strung from the southern tip of Texas along the Rio Grande and deep into the unsettled frontier west and north of San Antonio. Nine of the tracts never received a single colonist. The remaining two had drawn a handful of colonists, too few and too late to meet the terms of the contracts. And the annexation convention had quashed any hope that the contracts might somehow be resuscitated.

But as the years passed, the State of Texas came to recognize the difficulty of the colonists' challenge and faced the reality that families had moved onto the lands even though they lacked legal right. Gradually, more Germans moved north of the Llano and more Alsatians settled on Castro's grant, despite the extinction of their colonization contracts. Political winds changed. John Meusebach became a senator in the Texas legislature. The forces that favored distribution of land scrip to individuals stirred anew.

In March 1848 the State of Texas passed laws for the relief of Castro's colonists and the Adelsverein's. Each called for issuance of land scrip to colonists who came to Texas with the expectation of settling on the land grants, whether or not they actually did so. The scrip applied only to land within the appropriate land grant boundaries and entitled settler families to 640 acres and unmarried settlers to 320 acres. The colonial empresarios—Henry Castro and a reconstituted German Immigration Company—were entitled to bonus lands as provided in their original contracts.[11]

Since the empresarios' rights to scrip were related to the number of colonists settled, it behooved them to locate and invigorate as many of their former colonists as possible. The state appointed commissioners to determine land claims and dispatched them to Castroville and New Braunfels. The commissioners eventually issued certificates to Castro colonists for 277,760 acres of land. Castro himself received 38,400 acres of bonus lands. John Meusebach was appointed the first commissioner to determine the Adelsverein colonists' claims, and he proved sympathetic, as did his three successors. They issued scrip for more than 1.7 million acres of land within the Fisher-Miller grant.

True to Texas tradition, most of this scrip ended up in the hands of speculators. Few colonists actually settled inside the grants' boundaries. Despite the annexation convention's condemnation of speculators, it was another epic Texas land giveaway.[12]

But Henry Castro was not satisfied. His colonists had each agreed to deed half of their lands to him, and he wanted his due. Once more he submerged into litigation. The Texas Supreme Court ruled that the scrip issued by Texas was a separate and gratuitous act by the legislature, free from the terms of the original land grant or Castro's original contracts with the colonists. Castro got lands only from those colonists who were generous enough to volunteer it to him.[13]

Henri Castro did not end up as wealthy as he hoped, but neither did he end up impoverished. His life was an arc, from affluence to influence to an inconsequential ending. He managed and sold his lands and conducted business in Castroville. At one point he opened a border trading post in Eagle Pass. When the Civil War came, Castroville was choked off and virtually abandoned; Castro, like many Texans from Europe, fled to Mexico. He died in Monterrey on November 3, 1863, and is buried there.[14]

CHAPTER 18

# *Aftermath*

Solms had lingered in Galveston only until the *New York* was ready to return to New Orleans. On June 4 he boarded and bid Texas *auf Wiedersehen.* Annexation was on his mind but far beyond his influence. It was time to return to Sophie's arms.[1]

William Kennedy, the British consul at Galveston, reported Solms's departure to his friend Henry Addington, the British undersecretary of state for foreign affairs:

> The Prince has succeeded (though not without a considerable outlay, owing, as I conceive, in a great degree, to a defect in the original arrangements of the German Association) in planting a Colony, numbering six hundred Souls, on a beautiful and productive tract of land, situated about fifteen Miles above Seguin, a village on the Guadalupe river of Western Texas. The name given to this German Settlement is New Braunfels. Provided with farming implements and having a sufficient quantity of land under cultivation to furnish subsistence for the ensuing year, the future progress of the Colony may be considered easy and certain.
>
> The Settlers have neither been molested by Indians, nor visited by sickness, which may fairly be ascribed to the judicious arrangements of the Prince of Solms, who has encountered the difficulties of his arduous undertaking with a measure of patience, perseverance, and foresight which I believe but few Europeans would have been prepared to manifest, under the same circumstances.[2]

We can imagine Prince Solms boarding the *New York* for New Orleans, his head high, his handlebar moustache impeccably groomed. Unquestionably, he would have worn his tight pants and high boots, donned with the assistance of his valet. Over that, a short jacket with a high collar, and his feathered cap. Would he have gone so far as to strap on his sword and pin his medals to his bosom? He might have. He enjoyed making an impression.

Solms, as much as anyone, had completed a pilgrimage. Across the Atlantic, through forests and across mountains by train, carriage, and boat. Down the mightiest river in North America on a thudding, churning sternwheeler, to a city of contrasts and contradictions, a swirling mélange of colors and flavors and trades and passions. Thence to a land of brash men in rough surroundings. He had shot alligators and breakfasted with Indian chiefs. He had seen the ruins of Spain's American empire and the beginnings of the Texians' new one. He had communed with personages as diverse as Sam Houston and Alphonse Dubois de Saligny, Anson Jones and James Hamilton, Charles Elliot and Duff Green. He had sailed and surveyed the remote shores of Matagorda Bay and ridden the vast plains of Texas. He had penetrated the wilds with Jack Hays and serenaded Mary Maverick. He had remained true to his German heritage, remained intent upon his task, formed a company of German soldiers, and shepherded hundreds of families inland. He had exposed scoundrels, leaving Alexander Bourgeois d'Orvanne and Henry Fisher incensed and disgraced. He had founded a town and laid the cornerstone of a great citadel, the gateway to a grand experiment in German colonization.

There was much to be proud of. But looking back at Solms, looking at his adventure and the changes he wrought in Texas—for commencing the flood of German colonization to the Texas Hill Country was no mean feat—the most remarkable aspect of the man is how little he was changed by his experience. He departed as he arrived, a noble German in the service of his country, committed to ideals and principles, certain of his righteousness, intolerant of mediocrity, simultaneously militant, charming, demanding, courtly, impatient, and romantic.

Solms did not return to Germany with a new vision for Texas or a new opinion of Texians. His original notions had only intensified. Texas was crude but surfeit of opportunity. Texians were boorish, base, and unprincipled. The United States was aggressive and obsessive and must be blocked. Mexico was weak, populated by an inferior race. Britain and France were enlightened and sophisticated but inexplicably hesitant. The possibilities for Germans to colonize and capitalize in Texas, to benefit by trade with Mexico, to open commerce with the fatherland, were immense—but annexation would ruin all that. Most unchanged of all was Solms's belief that Texas was not for him. He was German. He was noble. He had spent enough time mingling with the rabble. He had executed his mission. Germany was his home.

In December 1845, Prince Solms sat down in his study behind the high walls of the family castle that loomed above the dark Lahn River. A fire crackled in the massive stone fireplace, warding off the icy German winter that pressed at the windowpanes. He had married his beloved Sophie on the third of the month, in a ceremony appropriate to his stature. His life was settled now and entirely satisfactory. Looking around the sumptuous surroundings, he reflected on the hardships of Texas and on what he had learned there. He adjusted the lamp, took pen in hand, and began composing a long memorandum to his cousin, Queen Victoria of England: "For some time now the eyes of the world have been directed at the mutual interests of England and the United States. . . . In my opinion, only a person who has lived with Americans for a while, studied their character, traveled through the country, become well acquainted with their various institutions, estimated their resources, followed their politics, is, I feel, in the position to make an appropriate judgment about the current situation and offer the appropriate deductions about the future."[3]

His conclusions about Americans were unforgiving: "The so-called American nation is composed of the worst element of all European nations, from the north to the south, from Sweden to Russia, down to Sicily, Spain and Portugal. Immigrants from all of these nations have passed on part of their makeup to their descendants, so that it can easily be said that the United States possesses the vices of all of the European nations without having inherited any of their good qualities."

"The American is cold and calculating," he continued. "From his father who emigrated to the promised land in the New World to become rich, he inherited the characteristic of needing to accrue, of needing to make money. To achieve this, nothing is forbidden."

"In passing I will mention how deeply the ownership of slaves and the trade in these unfortunate ones who are looked on and treated as animals corrupts a person's character. Avarice turns the American into a speculator, by extension frequently into a swindler. So when he turns to politics, his desire being to become a member of Congress, he paves the road to a government position by courting the electorate's favor. He criss-crosses the country on horseback, cleverly hears out the people's opinion and then tells them what they want to hear."

Turning to the question of Texas and Oregon, Solms ventured that, "For years now it has been the policy of the United States to extend its control over the North American continent. This is based on the belief that no European nation has a right to get involved in the affairs of the New World. Although this belief has no basis in our thinking, it suits the American purpose very well."

"Texas makes the United States a neighbor of Mexico, the weak Mexico that consists of immense sparsely populated areas and a land for years torn apart by internal strife. It consequently becomes an easy prey for the United States, which finally can dominate the entire commerce also in the Gulf of Mexico. In a similar way the Oregon Territory with its Columbia River brings the United States to the coast of the Pacific Ocean and on its way to California."

"Of course it has been maintained that Great Britain would not declare war on the United States simply on account of the incorporation of Texas as well as that of the Oregon Territory. . . . If the problem were limited to just these two areas of land, there would be no reason or excuse for a war over them. But Texas is the road to Mexico and the Oregon territory is the road to California and the Pacific Ocean. And through both lies the road to world trade."

"Even if England looks indifferently upon Texas and the Oregon Territory, can it also look indifferently at the control of the oceans? The Atlantic Ocean, the Gulf of Mexico—but especially the Pacific Ocean and the trade with China and East India are questions that intimately affect England. It cannot look at this situation with indifference; it needs to assert its right with all its power."

Solms continued with a factual survey of the U.S. population, growth, navy, army, and fortifications: "Based on this, as well as on my personal opinion, and ignoring all other factors, it appears that at this moment Great Britain holds a significant predominance over the United States. I say now—for who can tell what it will be a few years hence, considering the rapid population increase."

What should be done? Although the immense span of the United States meant that "defending these borders against invasion presents not only endless difficulties, but also some impossibilities," Solms discounted an invasion. Most of the land, particularly in the West, was vacant. What settlements existed were easily evacuated. An army on land would find itself far from support, and often far from the enemy. No, "the Americans' riches are primarily the merchant ships that sail the world's oceans and the riches held in the warehouses located in big cities, which in many cases are also ports. They cannot be left and put to the flame like the cheap wooden huts of the country. Here, then, is where the attention needs to be directed. Confiscation of the merchant ships, destruction of the navy, occupation, and if necessary partial or total bombardment of Boston, New York, Baltimore, Philadelphia, Harlington, Charleston, Mobile, New Orleans and Galveston. This is the means of obtaining a quick and favorable peace settlement."[4]

It was a modest proposal. Attack the United States, hitting its shipping and harbors first. To constrain the ability of the United States to counterattack, Solms recommended putting forces on the ground along the Canadian border. Based on his experience, the best approach was to construct militarized colonies to repulse the United States.

It would be easy at this point to conclude that Solms had lost his wits, but the fact is that the contest for the West had come to this. What could once have been done through diplomacy and finance could now be obtained only by war. If Queen Victoria wasn't willing to go to war, then she was ceding the West to the United States. It was that simple. Solms was simply giving her some suggestions on how best to avoid that loss.

The most interesting part of his proposal to the queen was how he would approach the matter of Texas and Mexico. He noted that Texas had declared the Rio Grande as its border, despite the historical practice of treating the Nueces as the boundary:

"The justification usually given is that mountains make natural borders, but never rivers. This principle is certainly true [he said, perhaps longing for the west bank of the Rhine] but every rule has its exception. Such an exception is found in Texas, where the Guadalupe River is the boundary between the American and the Mexican population. On the left [east] side of the river the American language, customs, and architecture dominate. As soon as the river is crossed, beginning right on its shore, a person has the impression of being suddenly transformed into a different country. The Mexican people, the dark skin color, Mexican costumes, building style, customs and language are spontaneously noted by the traveler. . . . Thus, the Guadalupe River, which rises in the higher mountains of Texas and empties through the Espíritu Santo Bay into the Gulf of Mexico, becomes the factual border of Mexico."

Why would Solms propose an entirely new border between Texas and Mexico? Because New Braunfels was being built immediately to the west of the Guadalupe. The Adelsverein's lands, according to Solms, "extend from here westward into the high mountains and south and southwesterly to the Nueces and Rio Frio and even to the Rio Grande. The Society began its colonization in September 1844 and, as of December 1845, the records show between five thousand and six thousand immigrants." It was true that a second wave of colonists was coming ashore at Carlshaven, and they would amount to more than five thousand, but the prince's geographic claims were entirely prevarications.

Solms told Queen Victoria of his vision for a Mexico returned to monarchy under the helpful assistance of England. "How wonderfully and easily the previously mentioned principle of military colonization could be applied here, either when this land would be returned to the monarchy established in Mexico or if Great Britain should take control of the strip of land between the Gulf of Mexico and the high mountains, the Guadalupe River serving as the northeastern border. With the Guadalupe as a demarcation line, fortifications could be established at appropriate distances on the right side and away from the river. They would be the frontier defense."

Solms's plans would certainly resolve any challenges to the Adelsverein's colonization contract. He would, with the help of the English side of his family, take West Texas for England and Germany. This sounds preposterous, but was it really out of character for Solms? Was it more aggressive than the Franco-Texian Bill, or General Hockley's ambitions for Cozumel, or Solms's attempt to cut San Antonio off from trade with Mexico, or his suggestion to Kennedy that England and Germany send thousands of armed men into the Adelsverein colony? For that matter, was it any more aggressive than the United States' determination to invade Mexico and seize everything between the Louisiana Purchase and the Pacific Ocean? These were times when the prize sometimes went to the audacious.

Solms was not quite done: "There remains one other avenue in which Great Britain can give the United States an awful, indeed a terrifying, jolt. This would be invading and occupying the harbors in the slave-holding states, emancipating the slaves, and thereby bringing slavery to an end. The more that a person is acquainted with this institution, the deeper he despises it." This was meant to be the clincher. No subject brought greater resolve to the British spirit than abolition of slavery.

Apparently Queen Victoria decided not to conquer the West. She did not share the prince's speculative bent. Once that avenue closed, Solms continued in other occupations. He had time to spend with Sophie. He wrote a guide to Texas and remained active in the Adelsverein until it sputtered out. In 1850 the prince rejoined the Austrian army, becoming a brigadier commanding dragoons. He participated in an unsuccessful war by Austria against Prussia, drawing the Hanovers into the conflict in the process. He retired in 1868 with the rank of field marshal and died seven years later at the age of sixty-three. Sophie died the next year, survived by four of their five children.[5]

# Conclusion

In the introduction, I posited that the history of Sam Houston's colonization contracts can be conceived as being seen through a zoom lens: it begins with broad geopolitical issues, then focuses more narrowly on Texas, the contracts and annexation, and finally boils down to the efforts and experiences of two very different men. Summing up, it may be a good idea to progress in the opposite direction, and it may be a good idea to limit conclusions to the immediate field of battle—Texas.

Solms and Castro are a study in contrasts. Readers can draw their own conclusions on that score and can savor the peculiarities of the two men.

At the same time, their colonists, their colonists' dreams, and the outcomes of their enterprises were almost identical. The immigrants founded towns and changed the makeup of swaths of Texas land within and beyond the land grants, but neither colonial venture managed to occupy the land itself in timely fashion.

It is worth taking a moment to consider why Sam Houston's intended colonies never took root as planned. Solms has been excoriated for exhausting the finances of the Adelsverein, but that is patently wrong. He left Meusebach in a financial bind, but the bind was not entirely of his making. And, to the extent there were financial difficulties, the nobles of the Adelsverein were capable of resolving them. The fact is that once annexation came to pass, once the realities of colonization in Texas became clear, the nobles decided not to invest any more in the venture. They purposely abandoned the colonists to their own devices. Solms was almost certainly among those who voted to stem funding.

Castro lacked the muscle of a nobles' organization behind him, but he was not without finances. First Ludwig Huth lent his support, then the Antwerp society bought into the enterprise. They could have handled Castro's expenses, but for whatever reason—distrust of Castro, or perhaps a cold splash of reality—they decided to cut off funding, crippling Castro.

The Adelsverein management style was oppressively paternalistic and disciplined, and it quickly rubbed the colonists the wrong way. Did that contribute to failure? Castro's loose style, at the other end of the spectrum, was just as ineffective. Was there a happy medium that would have worked? Or were management and administration not at the heart of the colonial failures?

Castro was undeniably negligent in caring for his colonists. In contrast, during Solms's tenure the Adelsverein intended meticulous care, though Fisher fell short on wagons and Solms failed to build facilities at Carlshaven. Despite those lapses, the Adelsverein colonists reached New Braunfels in a reasonable time and in reasonably good condition. Negligent or meticulous, both approaches failed to advance the colonists into their land grants.

It could be said that the colonists—or at least many of the colonists—were unsuited to life on the frontier, unaccustomed to building and farming. That unquestionably limited their ability to succeed, but they were neither the first nor the last impecunious, inexperienced Europeans to take a giant leap into the frontier, betting everything on the unknown. People starved at Jamestown, and they starved at Plymouth. The immigrants under Castro and Solms managed to build shelters and raise crops at Castroville and New Braunfels. They survived and eventually flourished, demonstrating that it was not a lack of skills that prevented them from meeting the terms of the colonization contracts.

The Texas Congress and annexation convention must take a share of the blame. Their hostility to European interference manifested itself in legislation that crippled the colonization effort. Houston sought European colonists, but the opposing faction in the legislature undermined him at critical junctures. The colonizers were given no slack.

Still, would it have helped if the Texas Congress had been more liberal in granting extensions to Kennedy, Bourgeois, Fisher, and Castro? As it turned out, the extensions would have had to reach beyond 1848, when the lands became free of Mexican claims. On Fisher's grant, north of the Llano River, it was another two or three decades before settlement was realistic. Only generous and repeated legislative extensions of contract deadlines would have helped.

Again and again, it becomes apparent that the decisive element in the colonial failures was the remoteness of the colonial lands. They were far beyond the reasonable limits of settlement. Where does that blame lie? Certainly part of it could be allocated to Solms and Castro, who never undertook to view their tracts before landing settlers. Given that basic omission, both colonial schemes could be categorized as wild speculation.

But Solms decided early not to settle either the Bourgeois tract or the Fisher-Miller lands, precisely because they were too remote. He meant to find and purchase a suitable site that could nurture his strategic plans. He did just that: the Fountains was an ideal location. Consider this: Solms's settlement at the Fountains did not fail. It struggled, as every frontier town struggles, but it eventually thrived despite the collapse of the Adelsverein. It is hard to saddle Solms with misjudging the settlement potential of the colonization grants.

And Castro quickly realized the preferability of the McMullen tract to his colonial grant. He focused first on his league and labor surrounding Castroville and secondarily on the McMullen tract. Castro consciously deemphasized colonization within the boundaries of his grant.

Criticizing Castro and Solms for reaching too far overlooks that they quickly recognized the problem, then adapted.

The blame for attempting to push too far into the frontier belongs with Houston and the Texas Congress, who best understood the territory. They knew that any group of European colonists, short of a massively funded group of thousands, would serve no greater purpose than target practice for Mexicans and Indians. Houston could have found land—not vast stretches of land, but land—much closer to the settled areas of Texas, in areas that could be successfully settled and farmed. He chose not to. He chose to draw lines on a map of little-explored domain. He invited failure when he dearly needed success.

As a ploy to induce influential Europeans to support the republic financially and diplomatically, colonization contracts weren't particularly successful. England and France sought peace with Mexico for their own reasons, entirely apart from colonization contracts—in fact, despite slights such as rejection of the Franco-Texian Bill, reimposition of the wine tariff, and the Texian blockade of Mexico. No European government lifted a finger to aid the republic's search for financing; thanks to the insulted Alexander Dubois de Saligny, the French foreign ministry actually impeded the effort. Castro and Bourgeois were involved in seeking loans, but they did so because securing a loan would earn a grand commission, not because colonization contracts had been dangled before their eyes. At the bottom of it all, if Houston meant to influence Europeans, he would have been better served by offering high-quality land—land that might have been worth fighting for.

In the short term, Texas was ill served by the colonization scheme. The enterprise eventually brought more than five thousand Germans to the Hill Country, and perhaps two thousand to the vicinity of Castroville, but at a tremendous cost in terms of land, speculation, fraud, and suffering. In its time, colonization was an open sore, and the balm chosen by the legislature only extended a long history of squandering land for the benefit of speculators.

On the other hand, Castro, Solms, and their colonists contributed greatly to the long-term success and character of the state of Texas. The Germans and French were as industrious as their reputations promised. They furthered Texan governance, growth, industry, and society. They created a pool of German Texan culture that remains notable to this day. And they left us some fascinating history.

# *Acknowledgments*

Mostly I work alone. It suits me, but it has disadvantages. One is that I do not benefit from collegial discussion and collaborative labor. That creates a greater risk of an error, oversight, or profoundly stupid theory. Another disadvantage is that I usually don't have many people to thank for their help. This time is a little different.

First I must thank Bjorn Freitag, an outstanding research assistant and translator who also landed a Ph.D. from the University of Texas in the midst of this project. I know few German words other than my last name and could not have completed this book without Bjorn. His ability to discern what was important and what was not, and his obvious intellectual investment in the project, made my task much easier. I also want to recognize Kathryn Sweeney, who did a great job of translating the French scribblings of Henri Castro.

In England, Robert W. O'Hara dug through the archives of the foreign office, spending many hours chasing down a couple of leads for me. In my business, you can't survive without independent researchers in remote places.

I absolutely cannot imagine the amount of dedication and effort that it took for Wolfram Von-Maszewski to translate the diary and letters of Prince Solms, and I marvel over the even greater achievement of Nancy Nichols Barker, who translated the diplomatic correspondence of France. Their projects were pure selfless service to other students of their subjects. Minetta Altgelt Goyne blessed us all with her interest in Ferdinand Lindheimer, as Oswald Mueller did with his pursuit of Ferdinand Roemer. The local historians, compilers, and translators—Don Biggers, Frans Dohmen, Everett Fey, Chester Geue, Ethel Geue, Oscar Haas, and all the others—bestow small gems that are indispensable in understanding the larger picture. For those of us who choose to spin narrative from primary source material, these historical archaeologists are a blessing.

My primary-source research on Henri Castro was almost entirely superfluous, thanks to the excellent work already done by Julia Nott Waugh, Bobby D. Weaver, and Cornelia English Crook. Taken together, their work is an exhaustive exploration of Castro and Castroville; I do not claim to have broken a great deal of new ground on Castro, though I did sort out a few tangled details of land transactions and litigation. For the most part, my Castro work consisted of taking a fresh look and integrating his story into a larger context.

I am not about to finish thanking these people whom I have never met—many of whom have left us diminished by their passing—without tipping my hat to Rudolph Biesele and Moritz Tiling, the granddaddies of German Texan history.

My research took place in many locations, but I want to extend particular thanks to the folks at the Center for American History at the University of Texas, Austin, and those at the Sophienburg Museum in New Braunfels.

Good editors, like Mary Lenn Dixon and Thom Lemmons, possess immense patience and durability. I'm thankful for both, who have both. Good copy editors can humble a writer even when they're being polite. John Thomas was unwaveringly polite, and I am humbled in a grateful sort of way.

Finally, I want to mention what a tremendous service the Texas State Historical Association does by publishing and maintaining the *New Handbook of Texas* and the *Southwestern Historical Quarterly.* The former—six thick volumes on my shelf—is now entirely online and text-searchable; the latter is partially online and growing. When I need a quick factoid—say, a biographical nugget—there is no substitute for the *Handbook.* And when I need comprehensive, deep thinking on some piece of obscure Texana, the *Quarterly* is the first place I look.

My fabulous wife, Jeanne Buchanan, understands why I write books when I should be doing something remunerative. Or at least she puts on a damn fine act. I love that woman.

# Notes

## CHAPTER 1

1. Solms-Braunfels, *Texas,* 7; Biesele, *History of the German Settlements,* 66–67 and n. 1; *New Handbook of Texas,* s.v. "Solms-Braunfels, Prince Carl of"; Hecke, *Reise;* quotation of Hecke edited from Tiling, *History of the German Element,* 7.

2. Some argue that "manifest destiny" was actually coined by Jane Cazneau, crediting her with authorship of the editorial traditionally ascribed to O'Sullivan. See Linda S. Hudson, *Mistress of Manifest Destiny: A Biography of Jane McManus Storm Cazneau, 1807–1878* (Austin: Texas State Historical Association, 2001).

3. Guerrero/Presidio is neither the Guerrero that is best known today (Guerrero Viejo, partially flooded by Falcon Reservoir and to a lesser extent its 1953 replacement, Guerrero Nuevo), nor is it the Presidio that is best known today (in Presidio County, Texas, opposite Ojinaga, Chihuahua). The Guerrero that was the important crossing point from Coahuila into Texas is between Piedras Negras and Nuevo Laredo, on Mexican Highway 2. Because the Presidio del Rio Grande was located there, it was known as Presidio before a road opened from San Antonio to today's Presidio (named for Presidio del Norte in Ojinaga). Guerrero was also the location of the Mission San Juan Bautista and, to make matters more complicated, was sometimes known by that name.

4. See Williams, *Animating Pursuits.*

5. "An Act Granting Land to Emigrants," Feb. 4, 1841, in Gammel, *Laws,* 2:554 (note that date of Jan. 4, 1841, in Gammel is in error and corrected in errata). See Connor, *Peters Colony.*

6. "An Act to incorporate the Texas Trading, Mining, and Emigrating Company," Jan. 30, 1841, in Gammel, *Laws,* 2:542; Saligny to Dalmatia, Feb. 27, 1840, in Barker, *French Legation,* 127; *New Handbook of Texas,* s.v. "Woodward, John."

7. Regarding rampant individualism in the Republic of Texas, see Hogan, *Texas Republic,* 267–290. Hogan, at 271, notes that "at least five

fights disturbed the dubious dignity of the Congress of the Republic, and many others were threatened."

8. For discussions of German political and social evolution during the age of Metternich (1815–1840), see Holborn, *History of Modern Germany, 1648–1840,* 450–471, and Simms, *Struggle for Mastery,* 105–156.

9. Simms, *Struggle for Mastery,* 36.

## CHAPTER 2

1. Saligny to Dalmatia, May 4, 1840, in Barker, *French Legation,*136. This chapter addresses the Franco-Texian Bill, parts of Hamilton's efforts to secure European financing for Texas, and the Pig War. Principal resources regarding the Franco-Texian Bill are diplomatic correspondence found in Barker, *French Legation,* 136–142, 193–194, 196–203, 272–278. The documents regarding financing that are relevant to this discussion (only a small sample of the total) are in Barker, 61–62, 178, and in Garrison, *Texan Diplomatic Correspondence,* 2:1276–1288 and 1336–1359. The Pig War and the financing are addressed in Barker, 209–303; the Pig War is covered in Garrison, 1290–1359. Financing threads through many pieces of diplomatic correspondence in these two sources, and in Adams, *British Diplomatic Correspondence.*

2. Saligny to Mole, Mar. 8, 1839, in Barker, *French Legation,* 61.

3. Saligny to Dalmatia, May 4, 1840, in Barker, *French Legation,* 137.

4. Saligny to Dalmatia, May 4, 1840, in Barker, *French Legation,* 138; to Mole, Mar. 26, 1839, ibid., 721; to Dalmatia, Jun. 24, 1839, ibid., 99; to Guizot, Dec. 8, 1841, ibid., 270, and Dec. 15, 1841, ibid., 271.

5. Saligny to Mole, Mar. 26, 1839, in Barker, *French Legation,* 70; to Dalmatia, Jan. 19, 1840, ibid., 116; Saligny to Thiers, Oct. 30, 1840, ibid., 168.

6. Treat to Lipscomb, Oct. 25, 1840, in Garrison, *Texan Diplomatic Correspondence,* 2:711; Vitalba to Lamar, Dec. 8, 1840, ibid., 720; Hamilton to Lipscomb, Feb. 1, 1841, ibid., 2:1282.

7. Hamilton to Castro, Feb. 11, 1841, in Garrison, *Texan Diplomatic Correspondence,* 2:1288.

8. Saligny to Thiers, Nov. 6, 1840, in Barker, *French Legation,* 170.

9. Theirs to Saligny, Sep. 6, 1840, in Barker, *French Legation,* 162.

10. The French forts were also planned for the Red River, but that was patently of less interest to France. It was Santa Fe that the French coveted. See Nance, *After San Jacinto,* 499–500.

11. Saligny to Guizot, Feb. 16, 1841, in Barker, *French Legation,* 199.

12. I call Dubois de Saligny "Saligny" because that was the name his

contemporaries used for him; I do the same with Bourgeois d'Orvanne, who was usually called "Bourgeois." I cannot explain the differing treatments. This choice of style also explains why Prince Solms-Braunfels is "Prince Solms" but Count Boos-Waldeck is "Boos-Waldeck."

13. Mayfield to Saligny, Mar. 29, 1841, in Garrison, *Texan Diplomatic Correspondence,* 2:1312.

14. Yoakum, *History of Texas,* 316–317; Hamilton to Castro, Feb. 11, 1841, in Garrison, *Texan Diplomatic Correspondence,* 2:1288; Hamilton to Lipscomb, Mar. 3, 1841, ibid., 1302.

15. Nance, *After San Jacinto,* 505–506; "An Act to repeal the Five Million Loan and for other purposes," Jan. 12, 1842, in Gammel, *Laws,* 2:703.

## CHAPTER 3

1. *New Handbook of Texas,* s.v. "Castro, Henri"; Weaver, *Castro's Colony,* 13; Waugh, *Castro-Ville,* 59–60; Wayne M. Ahr, "Henri Castro and Castroville: Alsatian History and Heritage," in Lagarde, *French in Texas,* 129.

2. Saligny to Guizot, Feb. 17, 1842, in Barker, *French Legation,* 287.

3. *New Handbook of Texas,* s.v. "Kennedy, William"; Kennedy to Aberdeen, Oct. 12, 1841 et seq., in Adams, *British Diplomatic Correspondence,* 43–50.

4. Hamilton to Aberdeen, Feb. 20, 1842, and Mar. 25, 1842, in Adams, *British Diplomatic Correspondence,* 58–61.

5. Hamilton to Aberdeen, Mar. 25, 1842, in Adams, *British Diplomatic Correspondence,* 59; Houston to Kennedy and Castro, Feb. 5, 1842, in Houston, *Writings,* 2:472, 3:73, and 4:73; Weaver, *Castro's Colony,* 12–17; "Amendatory of 'An Act granting Land to Emigrants' approved January fourth, one thousand eight hundred and forty-one," Feb. 5, 1842, in Gammel, *Laws,* 2:785.

6. Contracts dated Feb. 15, 1842, Colonization Contracts, files 14 (Castro) and 24 (Kennedy).

7. "An Act Granting Land to Emigrants," Jan. 4, 1841, in Gammel, *Laws,* 2:554; "An Act Amendatory of 'An Act granting Land to Emigrants,'" Feb. 5, 1842, ibid., 785.

8. Saligny to Guizot, Feb. 26, 1842, in Barker, *French Legation,* 290.

9. Saligny to Guizot, Feb. 26, 1842, in Barker, *French Legation,* 290.

10. Saligny to Guizot, Feb. 26, 1842, in Barker, *French Legation,* 290–291.

11. Jones to Saligny, Mar. 2, 1842, in Garrison, *Texan Diplomatic Correspondence,* 2:1357.

12. Smith to Jones, Mar. 15, 1842, in Garrison, *Texan Diplomatic Correspondence,* 2:1358; Saligny to Guizot, Mar. 16, 1842, in Barker, *French Legation,* 293.

13. Francaviglia, *From Sail to Steam,* 122; Guizot to Duperre, Jul. 4, 1842, in Barker, *French Legation,* 342–343; Guizot to the Minister of Commerce, Jul. 4, 1842, ibid., 343–344.

14. Weaver, *Castro's Colony,* 12–18; contract dated Mar. 9, 1842, Colonization Contracts, file 26.

15. Saligny to Guizot, Apr. 11, 1842, in Barker, *French Legation,* 300.

16. Saligny to Guizot, Apr. 11, 1842, in Barker, *French Legation,* 301–303.

17. See Barker, *French Legation,* 332, 336; Jones, *Memoranda,* 25 (Jones is mistaken; Bourgeois negotiated for the $1 million loan, not the $5 million loan, in 1842); Garrison, *Texan Diplomatic Correspondence,* 3:1390.

18. Saligny's return is covered in his letters appearing in Barker, *French Legation,* 307–327.

19. We cannot be certain of the point at which Bourgeois and Ducos first crossed paths. Given Ducos's purpose in Texas, Houston seems the likely place.

20. There is no overt statement that Bourgeois and Ducos were in the group of Frenchmen that Saligny escorted, but Bourgeois wrote from Austin at precisely the right moment for that to have happened, and Saligny talks as if Ducos and Bourgeois were traveling together. See Saligny to Guizot, May 26, 1842, in Barker, *French Legation,* 332; Bourgeois to Minister of Commerce, May 26, 1842, ibid.; Saligny to Guizot, Jun. 1, 1842, ibid., 334.

21. Bourgeois and Ducos's Austin visit is covered by letters from Bourgeois and Saligny appearing in Barker, *French Legation,* 332–338; the quote is from Bourgeois to Minister of Commerce, May 26, 1842, ibid., 332.

22. Saligny to Guizot, Jun. 8, 1842, in Barker, *French Legation,* 336; Biesele, *History of the German Settlements,* 70–73; contract dated Jun. 3, 1842, Colonization Contracts, file 27.

23. Contract dated Jun. 7, 1842, Colonization Contracts, file 2.

24. The colonization contracts inked by Houston are commonly referred to as "land grants," even though they were not grants in the sense of prior Spanish, Mexican, or Texas land grants. They were contracts laden with conditions.

25. Saligny to Guizot, Jun. 8, 1842, in Barker, *French Legation,* 336; Weaver, *Castro's Colony,* 19.

26. "An Act to authorize the President to negotiate a loan of one million of dollars," Jan. 22, 1839, in Gammel, *Laws,* 2:64; Saligny to Guizot, Jun. 8, 1842, in Barker, *French Legation,* 337; Weaver, *Castro's Colony,* 19; Houston

to Jones, Jun. 5, 1842, in Houston, *Writings,* 3:63; ibid., Jun. 10, 1842, at 3:66; also see Houston to Daingerfield, May 17, 1842, ibid., 54.

27. The conversation, slightly paraphrased, is from Saligny to Guizot, May 16, 1842, in Barker, *French Legation,* 325–326.

28. Saligny to Guizot, May 21, 1842, in Barker, *French Legation,* 327–331.

29. Guizot to Saligny, Jul. [1842], in Barker, *French Legation,* 351.

30. Jones, *Memoranda,* 25; Houston to Jones, Jun. 10, 1842, ibid., 203; Bourgeois to Minister of Commerce, Jul. 4, 1842, in Barker, *French Legation,* 347–348.

31. Bourgeois to Minister of Commerce, Jul. 4, 1842, in Barker, *French Legation,* 348.

## CHAPTER 4

1. Smith to Jones, Mar. 16, 1842, in Garrison, *Texan Diplomatic Correspondence,* 2:1359; Smith to McIntosh, May 12, 1842, ibid., 1374; McIntosh to Smith, May 18, 1842, ibid., 1375.

2. Smith to Jones, Jul. 3, 1842, in Garrison, *Texan Diplomatic Correspondence,* 2:971; Aberdeen to Elliot, Jul. 1, 1842, in Adams, *British Diplomatic Correspondence,* 78.

3. *New Handbook of Texas,* s.v. "Elliot, Charles."

4. Elliot was first appointed consul general, then upgraded to chargé d'affaires when the treaties between England and Texas were ratified. Aberdeen to Elliot, May 27, 1842, in Adams, *British Diplomatic Correspondence,* 64; ibid., Jul. 1, 1842, at 78; ibid., Jul. 15, 1842, at 90.

5. See Adams, *British Interests,* 106–108.

6. Kennedy to Bidwell, Jun. 7, 1842, in Adams, *British Diplomatic Correspondence,* 66; Kennedy to Aberdeen, Jun. 8, 1842, ibid., 67; Kennedy to Aberdeen, Jun. 15, 1842, ibid., 69; ibid., Jul. 2, 1842, at 86; ibid., Jul 7, 1842, at 88.

7. Kennedy to Aberdeen, Aug. 25, 1842, in Adams, *British Diplomatic Correspondence,* 95; Aberdeen to Kennedy, Sep. 29, 1842, ibid., 109; Kennedy to Aberdeen, Oct. 24, 1842, ibid., 120; ibid., Aug. 1, 1842, at 93.

8. McIntosh to Smith, May 18, 1842, in Garrison, *Texan Diplomatic Correspondence,* 2:1375; Castro to Smith, May 23, 1842, ibid.; Barbey to Smith, Jun. 28, 1842, ibid., 1379; McIntosh to Smith, Jun. 29, 1842, ibid., 1380.

9. Smith to Jones, Jun. 7, 1842, in Garrison, *Texan Diplomatic Correspondence,* 2:963.

10. Smith to Jones, Aug. 15, 1842, in Garrison, *Texan Diplomatic Correspondence,* 2:1383; Smith to Jones, Aug. 31, 1842, ibid., 1385.

11. Smith to Jones, Aug. 15, 1842, in Garrison, *Texan Diplomatic Correspondence,* 2:1383; ibid., Aug. 31, 1842, at 1385; Smith to Guizot, Aug. 15, 1842, ibid., 1387.

12. The steamship affair is the subject of repeated correspondence, such as Smith to Jones, Sep. 19, 1842, in Garrison, *Texan Diplomatic Correspondence,* 2:1015, and ibid., Oct. 19, 1842, at 1029; Adams, *British Interests,* 102–105.

13. Elliot to Terrell, Sep. 10, 1842, in Garrison, *Texan Diplomatic Correspondence,* 2:1012; Smith to Aberdeen, Aug. (15?), 1842, ibid., 1011; Aberdeen to Smith, Sep. 21, 1842, ibid., 1034; Waples to Eve, Sep. 14, 1842, ibid., 608; Elliot to Terrell, Oct. 31, 1842, ibid., 1043; "Revocation of the Blockade," in Houston, *Writings,* 3:156.

14. Smith to Jones, Aug. 31, 1842, in Garrison, *Texan Diplomatic Correspondence,* 2:1385; ibid., Nov. 13, 1842, at 1395; Adams, *British Interests,* 118; Guizot to Cramayel, Nov. 10, 1842, in Barker, *French Legation,* 381; Elliot to Addington, Dec. 16, 1842, in Adams, *British Diplomatic Correspondence,* 142.

15. Frétellière, "Adventures of a Castrovillian," in Waugh, *Castro-Ville,* 80.

16. Smith to Jones, Oct. 31, 1842, in Garrison, *Texan Diplomatic Correspondence,* 2:1390; ibid., Nov. 2, 1842, at 1392.

17. Castro, *Papers,* Box 3S167; Waugh, *Castro-Ville,* 9; Weaver, *Castro's Colony,* 26–28. Weaver says 144 colonists on the *Ebro.* This is a typo.

18. Smith to Jones, Nov. 13, 1842, in Garrison, *Texan Diplomatic Correspondence,* 2:1395; ibid., Nov. 30, 1842, at 1399; ibid., Dec. 30, 1842, at 31; Weaver, *Castro's Colony,* 26–27.

19. Weaver, *Castro's Colony,* 28–29; Houston to Daingerfield, Apr. 9, 1842, in Houston, *Writings,* 3:20.

20. Smith to Jones, Nov. 12, 1842, in Garrison, *Texan Diplomatic Correspondence,* 2:1394.

21. Jones to Smith, Dec. 26, 1842, in Garrison, *Texan Diplomatic Correspondence,* 2:1407.

22. Bourgeois to Jones, Dec. 28–27, 1842, in Colonization Papers, 2–9/29, folder 9; Smith to Jones, Dec. 30, 1842, in Garrison, *Texan Diplomatic Correspondence,* 2:1410.

23. Jones to Smith, Feb. 26, 1843, in Garrison, *Texan Diplomatic Correspondence,* 2:1422.

24. Proclamation dated Dec. 21, 1842, in Gammel, *Laws,* 2:876; Elliot to Aberdeen, Sep. 13, 1842, in Adams, *British Diplomatic Correspondence,* 105; Jones to Smith, Feb. 26, 1843, in Garrison, *Texan Diplomatic Correspondence,* 2:1422.

## CHAPTER 5

1. We cannot be certain that the meeting was at the palace. We know that it was at Biebrich and that the first member listed by Solms was the Duke of Nassau, who was the society's protector. Prince Moritz of Nassau was another member of the association. It is possible that the duke "hosted" the meeting in absentia, given that the attendees were peers of the prince, not the duke.

2. Solms-Braunfels, *Texas,* 1–2.

3. Boos-Waldeck, *General Report,* Dec. (?), 1842, Solms-Braunfels Archives, 50:150. The report may have been written as late as Feb. 1843, while Boos-Waldeck was in New Orleans with Leiningen. The December date above is derived from language in the report to the effect that it was written four months after his arrival in Texas.

4. Bollaert, *William Bollaert's Texas,* 136; Elliot to Aberdeen, Sep. 22, 1842, in Adams, *British Diplomatic Correspondence,* 108; Elliot to Bidwell, Oct. 10, 1842, at 111.

5. Bollaert, *William Bollaert's Texas,* 132, 136, 137; Boos-Waldeck, *General Report,* Dec. (?), 1842, Solms-Braunfels Archives, 50:150; Elliot to Aberdeen, Aug. 29, 1842, in Adams, *British Diplomatic Correspondence,* 95; Elliot to Aberdeen, Sep. 22, 1842, ibid., 108. Woll crossed the Rio Grande on Aug. 30 and entered San Antonio on Sep. 11; the newspapers did not report the fall of San Antonio until Sep. 20.

6. Boos-Waldeck, *General Report,* Dec. (?), 1842, Solms-Braunfels Archives, 50:150; also see Bollaert, *William Bollaert's Texas,* 135.

7. Biesele, *History of the German Settlements,* 43–52.

8. Boos-Waldeck, *General Report,* Dec. (?), 1842, Solms-Braunfels Archives, 50:153; Houston, *Writings,* 3:199.

9. Strubberg Collection, Box 1, Folder 18; Boos-Waldeck, *General Report,* Dec. (?), 1842, Solms-Braunfels Archives, 50:153–154.

10. Boos-Waldeck, *General Report,* Dec. (?), 1842, Solms-Braunfels Archives, 50:155–159.

11. Frétellière, "Adventures of a Castrovillian," in Waugh, *Castro-Ville,* 81. Frétellière traveled with Castro's second wave of emigrants, in late 1843, but his experience is typical of (or perhaps better than) those who came earlier. Frétellière benefited by the agency of Louis Huth, who was not there for the earlier colonists. His experiences are inserted in this earlier context because you will enjoy reading them here and because the anachronism does no harm. Frétellière sailed on the *Jean Key,* as did Huth. Built in 1829, it was the first transatlantic ship to sail from Antwerp. An artist's ren-

dering of the *Jean Key* is at www.fineartemporium.com/se-Weyts-P2-image.htm (accessed Jul. 11, 2008).

12. Bowen, *Century of Atlantic Travel,* 42–43.

13. Frétellière, "Adventures of a Castrovillian," in Waugh, *Castro-Ville,* 84.

14. Weaver, *Castro's Colony,* 32; Frétellière, "Adventures of a Castrovillian," in Waugh, *Castro-Ville,* 10, 85.

15. Houston to Howard, Jan. 24, 1842, in Houston, *Writings,* 2:440.

16. Lavaca (*la vaca,* the cow) is today's Port Lavaca. Another popular destination on the bay was Matagorda, to the north. Indianola (Carlshaven) did not yet exist.

17. Frétellière, "Adventures of a Castrovillian," in Waugh, *Castro-Ville,* 85.

18. Weaver, *Castro's Colony,* 28.

## CHAPTER 6

1. Barker, *French Legation,* 369–374.

2. Cramayel might have arrived a day or two earlier. Cramayel to Guizot, Dec. 22, 1842, in Barker, *French Legation,* 383; Cramayel to Jones, Jan. 16, 1843, in Garrison, *Texan Diplomatic Correspondence,* 2:1413; Jones to Cramayel, Feb. 9, 1843, ibid., 1418.

3. Cramayel to Guizot, Jan. 2, 1843, in Barker, *French Legation,* 388.

4. Cramayel to Jones, Jan. 16, 1843, in Garrison, *Texan Diplomatic Correspondence,* 2:1413.

5. Cramayel to Guizot, Jan. 20, 1843, in Barker, *French Legation,* 398.

6. Cramayel to Guizot, Jan. 26, 1843, in Barker, *French Legation,* 401.

7. See Houston to Daingerfield, May 17, 1842, in Houston, *Writings,* 3:54, authorizing Daingerfield to place the $1 million loan.

8. Jones to Daingerfield, Jan. 20, 1843, in Garrison, *Texan Diplomatic Correspondence,* 2:1534; Jones to Smith, Feb. 16, 1843, ibid., 1514.

9. Daingerfield to Jones, Feb. 4, 1843, in Jones, *Memoranda,* 207.

10. Cramayel to Guizot, Feb. 5, 1843, in Barker, *French Legation,* 406.

11. This passage and the following discussion from Boos-Waldeck, *Report,* Apr. 1844, Solms-Braunfels Archives, 30:39–69. This report was written a year later than the events discussed in this section, but it refers to that period.

12. Smith to Jones, March 31, 1843, in Garrison, *Texan Diplomatic Correspondence,* 2:1427.

13. Castell to Boos-Waldeck, May 24, 1843, Solms-Braunfels Archives, 49:77.

14. Castell to Boos-Waldeck, May 24, 1843, Solms-Braunfels Archives, 49:80, 81.

15. Smith to Jones, Apr. 11, 1843, in Garrison, *Texan Diplomatic Correspondence,* 2:1431.

16. Smith to Guizot, Apr. 25, 1843, in Garrison, *Texan Diplomatic Correspondence,* 2:1443.

17. Smith to Jones, Jun. 16, 1843, in Garrison, *Texan Diplomatic Correspondence,* 2:1449, and encl.; Jones to Smith, Jun. 21, 1843, ibid., 1452.

18. Cramayel to Guizot, Jun. 25, 1843, in Barker, *French Legation,* 448; ibid., Jul. 17, 1843, at 453.

19. Smith to Jones, Jun. 16, 1843, in Garrison, *Texan Diplomatic Correspondence,* 2:1449.

20. Smith to Jones, Oct. 30, 1843, in Garrison, *Texan Diplomatic Correspondence,* 2:1472.

21. Daingerfield to Jones, Jun. 28, 1843, in Garrison, *Texan Diplomatic Correspondence,* 2:1456; Daingerfield to Smith, Nov. 8, 1843, ibid., 1474; Daingerfield to Jones, Sep. 25, 1843, ibid., 1548; Daingerfield to Castell, Oct. 8, 1843, in Solms-Braunfels Archives, 49:108.

22. Daingerfield to Jones, Sep. 25, 1843, in Garrison, *Texan Diplomatic Correspondence,* 2:1548.

23. Daingerfield to Jones, Sep. 25, 1843, in Garrison, *Texan Diplomatic Correspondence,* 2:1548.

24. Castell to Bourgeois, Sep. 26, 1843, enclosed in Smith to Jones, Oct. 14, 1843, in Garrison, *Texan Diplomatic Correspondence,* 2:1467, 1469. Castell also proposed a method of direct collection of interest on the loan.

25. Smith to Jones, Oct. 14, 1843, in Garrison, *Texan Diplomatic Correspondence,* 2:1467.

26. Daingerfield to Jones, Nov. 12, 1843, in Garrison, *Texan Diplomatic Correspondence,* 2:1537.

27. Castell to Boos-Waldeck, Sep. 16, 1843, in Solms-Braunfels Archives, 49:100.

28. What Fisher had actually obtained was a new contract dated Sep. 1, 1843, giving him eighteen months (one year plus a six-month extension) to settle two hundred families or single men and three years to settle six hundred. This replaced his old one dated Jun. 7, 1842.

29. Boos-Waldeck to (Castell?), Nov. 19, 1843, in Solms-Braunfels Archives, 49:110.

## CHAPTER 7

1. Smith to Jones, Oct. 30, 1843, in Garrison, *Texan Diplomatic Correspondence,* 2:1472; see Connor, *Peters Colony,* 36–45.

2. Daingerfield to Smith, Nov. 8, 1843, in Garrison, *Texan Diplomatic Correspondence,* 2:1474; also see Daingerfield to Jones, Nov. 12, 1843, ibid., 1537.

3. Smith to Jones, Dec. 30, 1843, in Garrison, *Texan Diplomatic Correspondence,* 2:1476; Cramayel to Guizot, Dec. 1, 1843, in Barker, *French Legation,* 488.

4. Cramayel to Guizot, Dec. 1, 1843, in Barker, *French Legation,* 488.

5. Smith to Jones, Jan. 29, 1844, in Garrison, *Texan Diplomatic Correspondence,* 2:1478.

6. Cramayel to Guizot, Nov. 13, 1843, in Barker, *French Legation,* 482; ibid., Aug. 5, 1843, at 460; Houston, Speech Delivered at the Presbyterian Church, Nov. 8, 1843, in Houston, *Writings,* 3:442; Houston to Hatch, Jul. 18, 1847, in Houston, *Writings,* 5:14.

7. Houston to Congress, Jan. 10, 1844, in Houston, *Writings,* 3:508.

8. "Joint Resolution for the relief of Henry F. Fisher and B. Miller," Jan. 29, 1845, in Gammel, *Laws,* 2:1091; Jones to Smith, Sep. 30, 1843, in Garrison, *Texan Diplomatic Correspondence,* 2:1140; Houston to the Texas Senate, Jan. 10, 1844, in Houston, *Writings,* 508.

9. Jones to Smith, Mar. 26, 1844, in Garrison, *Texan Diplomatic Correspondence,* 2:1482.

10. *New Handbook of Texas,* s.v. "Huth, Aug. Ferdinand Louis."

11. Weaver, *Castro's Colony,* 37–38; Huth, Papers, 200.

12. Huth, Papers, 200.

13. *New Handbook of Texas,* s.v. "DeMontel, Charles."

14. Huth, Papers, 200; Weaver, *Castro's Colony,* 37–38.

15. Weaver, *Castro's Colony,* 37–38.

16. Saligny to Guizot, Feb. 6, 1844, in Barker, *French Legation,* 499; Henderson to Jones, Mar. 30, 1844, in Jones, *Memoranda,* 333.

17. Hockley to Jones, Feb. 28, 1844, in Jones, *Memoranda,* 324; Jones to Elliot, Mar. 18, 1844, ibid., 327; Elliot to Jones, Mar. 22, 1844, ibid., 329; Houston to Jones, ibid., 336.

18. Raymond to Jones, Apr. 24, 1844, in Houston, *Writings,* 343; Houston to Van Zandt and Henderson, Apr. 29, 1844, ibid., 309.

19. Boos-Waldeck, *Report,* Apr. 1844, in Solms-Braunfels Archives, 30:40; Solms-Braunfels, *Texas,* 1–3; Biesele, *History of the German Settlements.*

20. Adelsverein Constitution, Art. I, par. 3, in *Gesammelte Aktenstuecke,* 3, as translated in Biesele, *History of the German Settlements,* 86.

21. Announcement in *Mainzer Zeitung,* Jun. 16, 1844, as translated in Biesele, *History of the German Settlements,* 84–85.

22. General Statut fur die Colonial-Niederlassungen des Vereins, Art. 3, in *Gesammelte Akenstuecke,* 29–37, as translated in Biesele, *History of the German Settlements,* 87–88; also see Tiling, *History of the German Element,* 211, for the German.

## CHAPTER 8

1. All details of Solms's journey from London to Texas, except as noted, are from his diary in Solms-Braunfels, *Voyage.*

2. Redman, *House of Hanover,* 219; Holborn, *History of Modern Germany,* 27.

3. Information on Solms's first marriage and his military service are from *New Handbook of Texas,* s.v. "Solms-Braunfels, Prince Carl of."

4. Solms identifies "Albert v. d. Burgh" without elaboration. My conclusion that he is a member of the untitled Dutch noble family of van der Burgh is informed speculation.

5. Edwin Chadwick, *The Sanitary Conditions of the Labouring Population* (London, 1842).

6. Details of Cunard and the *Caledonia* from Bowen, *Century of Atlantic Travel,* 31–41.

7. Solms-Braunfels, *Voyage,* 166–167; Garrison, *Texan Diplomatic Correspondence,* 2:1484; Weaver, *Castro's Colony,* 40. Both Solms and Bourgeois pointedly omitted diary mention of Castro until they reached Galveston.

## CHAPTER 9

1. The story of the journey from Liverpool to Texas is taken from Solms-Braunfels, *Voyage* (which includes the parallel diary of Bourgeois, commencing at Galveston), and from fourteen Solms letters found in the Solms-Braunfels Archives, 49:112–157.

2. Solms to (Castell?), May 18, 1844, in Solms-Braunfels Archives, 49:112. The quote is paraphrased for clarity. The literal translation is "declaration of war by Mexico, which would still be less fearsome than one by England, France and Russia."

3. Solms mentions obtaining land from "Garcia," probably Antonio Garcia, who held a Mexican land grant between the Rio Grande and the

Nueces River. Mexico continued making such grants after Texas claimed independence.

4. Solms-Braunfels, *Voyage,* 18.

5. Solms-Braunfels, *Voyage,* 18–19.

6. Solms to (Castell?), Jun. 4, 1844, in Solms-Braunfels Archives, 49:121.

7. Solms to (Castell?), Jun. 4, 1844, in Solms-Braunfels Archives, 49:118. The last sentence of the quotation is paraphrased for clarity. A more literal translation would be: "If we make proper use of the envy of England and France with regard to commerce with Texas, this must give us the protection that a German fleet should rightfully have to give us."

8. The translator of Solms-Braunfels, *Voyage,* uses the name "Wangen" instead of "Bugs" and wonders whether Wangen might have been a servant of Solms; ibid., 36, 37. In old German script, the letters *g* and *z* are very similar. The correct reading is "Wanzen," Solms's nickname for Bourgeois.

9. Solms to (Castell?), Jun. 10, 1844, in Solms-Braunfels Archives, 49:124.

10. Solms-Braunfels, *Voyage,* 20 (quotation slightly paraphrased); Solms to (Castell?), Jun. 10, 1844, in Solms-Braunfels Archives, 49:124.

11. Solms-Braunfels, *Voyage,* 23.

12. Solms-Braunfels, *Voyage,* 24.

13. Solms to (Castell?), Jun. 19, 1844, in Solms-Braunfels Archives, 49:127.

14. Joseph Conrad, *Heart of Darkness* (New York: Penguin Group, 1999), 60. Of course, Solms could not have been thinking of Marlow or Kurtz, who came after his time.

15. Sinclair, *Port of New Orleans,* 182.

16. Sinclair, *Port of New Orleans,* 187.

17. Solms-Braunfels, *Voyage,* 24; Solms to (Castell?), Jun. 19, 1844, in Solms-Braunfels Archives, 49:127.

18. Castro's Journal, Jun. 14, 1844, in Castro, *Papers.*

19. Castro's Journal, Jul. 3, 1844, in Castro, *Papers.*

20. Castro's Journal, Jun. 14, 1844, in Castro, *Papers.*

21. Solms to (Castell?), Jun. 28, 1844, in Solms-Braunfels Archives, 49:137; Solms-Braunfels, *Voyage,* 26 (change in punctuation).

22. Solms to (Castell?), Jun. 19, 1844, in Solms-Braunfels Archives, 49:127.

23. Solms to (Castell?), Jun. 28, 1844, in Solms-Braunfels Archives, 49:137.

24. Castell to Solms, Jun. 25, 1844, in Solms-Braunfels Archives, 59:147; Solms to (Castell?), Jun. 28 and 29, 1844, ibid., 51:137.

25. Solms-Braunfels, *Voyage,* 27.

26. Solms-Braunfels, *Voyage,* 27.

27. Conrad, *Heart of Darkness,* 20.

## CHAPTER 10

1. The exact location of Malhado has long been debated; it may have been one of the islands or peninsulas south of Galveston Island.

2. Kennedy, *Texas,* 782–783; Bollaert, *William Bollaert's Texas,* 14–20.

3. Bollaert, *William Bollaert's Texas,* 19–20.

4. Natalie Ornish, *Pioneer Jewish Texans* (Dallas: Texas Heritage Press, 1989), 231.

5. The chronicle of Solms, Bourgeois, and Ducos in this chapter is taken in large part from Solms-Braunfels, *Voyage,* 35–96 and 168–191, and the four letters from Solms to (Castell?) found in Solms-Braunfels Archives, 49:150–157.

6. Saligny to Guizot, Jun. 20, 1844, in Barker, *French Legation,* 545; "Count Saligny still remains in New Orleans causado pòr un herida recibido a un desafio General Murphy at Houston. The President and Cabinet at Washington." Bollaert, *William Bollaert's Texas,* 329. A close reading, and a familiarity with the loose punctuation and spelling in Bollaert's diary, suggests that there should be a period between "desafio" and "Murphy."

7. Smith, *Annexation,* 99, 172–173; Adams, *British Interests,* 133, 135, 146–147.

8. Bourgeois's diary, Jun. 1, 1844, in Solms-Braunfels, *Voyage,* 169.

9. Solms reports meeting Grieve on Jul. 2. Grieve and Bollaert were on their way back from inspecting the colonial tract and were bound for England. Bollart's final entry in his journal reports reaching Galveston on Jul. 2. Solms-Braunfels, *Voyage,* 35; Bollaert, *William Bollaert's Texas,* 379. On Kennedy's exit from the contract, see Kennedy to Aberdeen, Oct. 24, 1842, in Adams, *British Diplomatic Correspondence,* 120; Kennedy to Jones, Nov. 9, 1843, in Jones, *Memoranda,* 269.

10. The expedition to the Kennedy grant is described in Bollaert, *William Bollaert's Texas,* 332–379. Solms mentions Stephenson ("Stevenson") in his diary, as does Bollaert. The translator of Solms-Braunfels, *Voyage,* identifies him as Henry Stephenson, but that Texas Methodist preacher died in 1841. Perhaps it was another Henry Stephenson. Solms's diary indicates that Stephenson traveled from Galveston to Houston with Solms, and that Stephenson owned land in the Brazos River drainage. Bollaert spells Jaime as "Jayme," but that seems an unlikely Spanish spelling.

11. Bollaert, *William Bollaert's Texas,* 366, 367.

12. The account of Castro in this chapter is taken from Castro's Journal, in Castro, *Papers;* these quotations are from Jul. 3, 1844.

13. Huth to Castro, Nov. 1, 1844, in Huth, Papers, translation 3k380–04–01, at 200–201.

14. Solms-Braunfels, *Voyage,* 36.

15. Castro's Journal, Jul. 7, 1844, in Castro, *Papers;* Kleberg, "Early Experiences"; Hermann Seele, "Meine Ankunft in Neu-Braunfels," *Kalender der Neu-Braunfelser Zeitung fuer 1914,* 36; Biesele, *History of the German Settlements,* 115–116, n.

16. Solms-Braunfels, *Voyage,* 36; Bourgeois's diary, Jul. 5, 1844, in Solms-Braunfels, *Voyage,* 170; James L. Haley, *Sam Houston* (Norman: University of Oklahoma Press, 2002), 208.

17. Note Bourgeois to Jones, Jul. 7, 1844, in Jones, *Memoranda,* 371.

18. Castro's Journal, July 7, 1844, in Castro, *Papers.*

19. Bourgeois's journal for July 7, 1844, in Solms-Braunfels, *Voyage,* 171.

## CHAPTER 11

1. Bourgeois to Houston, Jul. 8, 1844, in Colonization Papers, 29–2/27, Folder 11.

2. Bourgeois to Jones, Jul. 10, 1844, in Colonization Papers, 29–2/27, Folder 11.

3. Bourgeois to Jones, Jul. 10, 1844, in Colonization Papers, 29–2/27, Folder 11.

4. Solms's First Report to the Directors in Geue and Geue, *New Land Beckoned,* 21; Solms to (Castell?), Jul. 15, 1844, in Solms-Braunfels Archives, 49:153; also see Bourgeois's views in his diary in Solms-Braunfels, *Voyage,* 170–173.

5. Solms, "Evaluation of the Local Officials," in Fey, *New Braunfels,* 1:83; "The Family of Louis Willke," in Fey, *New Braunfels,* 2:277; "The Family of Mathias Sander," ibid., 2:170; Geue and Geue, *New Land Beckoned,* 134, 154; Solms-Braunfels, *Voyage,* 64 n. 10.

6. Geiser, *Naturalists of the Frontier,* 97.

7. On Ervendberg, see Geiser, *Naturalists of the Frontier,* 100–103, 125; and *New Handbook of Texas,* s.v. "Ervendberg, Louis Cachand."

8. On Lindheimer, see Geiser, *Naturalists of the Frontier,* 133–139.

9. Kleberg, "Early Experiences," 172–173.

10. *New Handbook of Texas,* s.v. "Lindheimer, Ferdinand Jacob."

11. Von Hinueber, "Life of German Pioneers," 232.

12. Kleberg, "Early Experiences," 172.

13. Where not otherwise credited, the details of Solms's and Bourgeois's trip to San Antonio and Bourgeois's grant are taken from their diaries in Solms-Braunfels, *Voyage;* from Solms's letter of Jul. 29, 1844, in Solms-Braunfels Archives, 49:157; and from Solms's Second and Third Reports to the Verein, dated Aug. 20 and Aug. 26, 1844, in Geue and Geue, *New Land Beckoned,* 25–39. The presence of Brockhald is extrapolated. He was Bourgeois's servant, at least on the trip from Liverpool. The servants named by Solms, other than "Tory" Torczinsky, are Anton and Pierre. It is not clear whether one of Anton or Pierre is the cook, nor is it clear whether one of them is Jordt. Solms-Braunfels, *Voyage,* 39; Bourgeois's diary in Solms-Braunfels, *Voyage,* 173.

14. Solms to (Castell?), Jul. 15, 1844, in Solms-Braunfels Archives, 49:153.

15. Solms-Braunfels, *Voyage,* 39.

16. Bourgeois's diary in Solms-Braunfels, *Voyage,* 174.

17. Solms-Braunfels, *Voyage,* 40.

18. The account of Castro's and Huth's trip and their experiences in San Antonio is taken from Castro's journal in Castro, *Papers.*

19. Greer, *Colonel Jack Hays,* 109–110.

20. Roemer, *Texas,* 132.

21. Greer, *Colonel Jack Hays,* 41, 58.

22. Castro's Journal for Jul. 31, 1844, in Castro, *Papers.*

23. Solms to (Castell?), Jul. 25, 1844, in Solms-Braunfels Archives, 49:157.

24. Solms-Braunfels, *Voyage,* 41; *New Handbook of Texas,* s.v. "Cassiano, Jose."

25. Solms-Braunfels, *Voyage,* 42; Solms's Second Report, Aug. 20, 1844, in Geue and Geue, *New Land Beckoned,* 33; Solms to (Castell?), Jul. 15, 1844, in Solms-Braunfels Archives 49:153. Oddly, the Jul. 15 request for engraving came from a postscript to a letter written at Nassau Farm, before Solms met Hays or Rahm and before the date of the report requesting the firearms; it must be that the letter was written at the farm but not posted until San Antonio, where the postscript was added. It was not unusual for letters to be composed over a period of several days, or longer.

26. *New Handbook of Texas,* s.v. "Smith, John William."

27. Bourgeois's diary in Solms-Braunfels, *Voyage,* 177.

## CHAPTER 12

1. Solms-Braunfels, *Voyage,* 43.

2. Crook, *Henry Castro,* 66–67.

3. Castro's Journal, Jul. 31, 1844, in Castro, *Papers.* This journal entry appears to have been written over a several-day span.

4. Castro's Journal, Jul. 31, 1844, in Castro, *Papers.*

5. Solms's Second Report, Aug. 20, 1844, in Geue and Geue, *New Land Beckoned,* 26.

6. Castro's Journal, Jul. 31, 1844, in Castro, *Papers.* Agreement dated Aug. 22, 1844, between John McMullen and Henry Castro, recorded in book 2, page 293, Bexar County Clerk. The Castro-McMullen contract was not a conveyance; it was what would today be called a contract for deed. McMullen's title was in litigation, and Castro's obligation to purchase was contingent on the title being cleared in favor of McMullen. Once that happened, Castro had two years and four months to survey the land into 160-acre tracts and to settle one-half of the tracts, in a checkerboard pattern, leaving the remaining tracts to McMullen. If Castro failed to introduce settlers onto half of the lands in timely fashion, then he would receive only 80 acres of each 160-acre tract settled. Castro also had the right to survey townsites within the McMullen lands, treating ownership of the town lots in the same checkerboard pattern of ownership and settlement.

7. Bourgeois's Diary, in Solms-Braunfels, *Voyage,* 183.

8. Castro's Journal, Aug. 12, 1844, in Castro, *Papers.*

9. Bourgeois's Diary, in Solms-Braunfels, *Voyage,* 184.

10. Houston to Solms, Aug. 2, 1844, in Houston, *Writings,* 4:351.

11. Solms-Braunfels, *Voyage,* 54.

12. Bourgeois's Diary, in Solms-Braunfels, *Voyage,* 186–187.

13. In his Aug. 20 report to the Adelsverein directors, Solms suggested buying the McMullen tract too, even though Castro had cemented his deal two days earlier. Surely Castro had made sure that Solms knew of his coup. Solms must have believed that Castro could not carry through, or Solms was in denial, or he altered the facts a bit for his audience at home. The report rambles; Solms was under a great deal of stress.

14. Solms's Second Report, Aug. 20, 1844, in Geue and Geue, *New Land Beckoned,* 29.

15. Solms's Second Report, Aug. 20, 1844, in Geue and Geue, *New Land Beckoned,* 27.

16. Solms's Second Report, Aug. 20, 1844, in Geue and Geue, *New Land Beckoned,* 34; Bourgeois's Diary, in Solms-Braunfels, *Voyage,* 187–188.

17. This would be Friedrich von Wrede Jr. Castell to Solms, Jun. 25, 1844, in Solms-Braunfels Archives, 59:147.

18. Castell to Solms, Jun. 25, 1844, in Solms-Braunfels Archives, 59:147.

19. Solms Third Report, Aug. 26, 1844, in Geue and Geue, *New Land Beckoned,* 36, 38.

20. Solms-Braunfels, *Voyage,* 55. In a report to the Adelsverein, Solms claimed that he "discussed the matter calmly with Bourgeois, as one gentleman would discuss a business matter with another." But his diary makes no mention of meeting and commences the "discussion" with a letter. Solms would have preferred the cold snub of a letter. Solms's Third Report, Aug. 26, 1844, in Geue and Geue, *New Land Beckoned,* 34–35.

21. Solms-Braunfels, *Voyage,* 55.

22. Bourgeois to Jones, Aug. 28, 1844, in Colonization Papers, 2–9/27, folder 11.

23. Fisher to Jones, Jun. 27, 1844, in Jones, *Memoranda,* 367.

24. Castro's Journal, Aug. 26, 1844, in Castro, *Papers;* Weaver, *Castro's Colony,* 48–49.

25. Weaver, *Castro's Colony,* 48–50.

## CHAPTER 13

1. Houston to Jones, Jul. 8, 1844, in Houston, *Writings,* 4:338; Jones to Smith, Jul. 14, 1844, in Garrison, *Texan Diplomatic Correspondence,* 2:1156; Smith to Jones, Jun. 24, 1844, ibid., 1153.

2. Smith to Jones, Jun. 24, 1844, in Garrison, *Texan Diplomatic Correspondence,* 2:1153.

3. Jones to Smith, Aug. 1, 1844, in Garrison, *Texan Diplomatic Correspondence,* 2:1160.

4. Houston to Jones, Sep. 24, 1844, in Houston, *Writings,* 4:371; Jones, Memorandum, Feb. 5, 1849, in Jones, *Memoranda,* 55.

5. Jones, Memorandum, Feb. 5, 1849, in Jones, *Memoranda,* 57.

6. Solms's Diary, Nov. 1 and 2, 1844, in Solms-Braunfels, *Voyage,* 85; ibid., Sep. 8, at 77; ibid., Dec. 12, at 109. Solms's diary reflects repeated meetings and dinners with all the influential players in Galveston during October and November 1844.

7. Solms's Dairy, Oct. 20, 1844, in Solms-Braunfels, *Voyage,* 83; Solms's Fifth Report, Oct. 25, 1844, in Geue and Geue, *New Land Beckoned,* 41, 43.

8. Solms's Fifth Report, Oct. 25, 1844, in Geue and Geue, *New Land Beckoned,* 41.

9. Solms to Jones, Nov. 2, 1844, in Jones, *Memoranda,* 391.

10. Maverick, *Memoirs,* 69.

11. Solms's Diary, Nov. 22–24, in Solms-Braunfels, *Voyage,* 97–98. Solms describes the boat as thirteen tons (displacement), which puts it in the forty-foot range.

12. Solms's Sixth Report, Dec. 23, 1844, in Geue and Geue, *New Land Beckoned,* 46.

13. Solms's Sixth Report, Dec. 23, 1844, in Geue and Geue, *New Land Beckoned,* 46–47; Solms's Diary, Nov. 28–Dec. 2, in Solms-Braunfels, *Voyage,* 98–99.

14. Solms's Diary, Dec. 2, 1844, in Solms-Braunfels, *Voyage,* 99.

15. Solms to Jones, Dec. 3, 1844, in Jones, *Memoranda,* 407.

16. Solms to Kennedy, Dec. 3, 1844, in Adams, *British Diplomatic Correspondence,* 386.

17. Solms's Diary, Dec. 9–10, in Solms-Braunfels, *Voyage,* 109.

18. Maverick, *Memoirs,* 109; Solms's Diary, Dec. 10, 1844, in Solms-Braunfels, *Voyage,* 109. There are date discrepancies between the Solms and Maverick accounts. Maverick, writing after the fact, appears to have combined Solms's Dec. 10 and Jan. 14 visits into one; the serenade seems much more appropriate for Jan. 14 (Solms couldn't have serenaded Mary Maverick before meeting her). The serenade has been changed to that date in this account.

19. Solms's Sixth Report, Dec. 23, 1844, in Geue and Geue, *New Land Beckoned,* 47, 50–51.

20. Solms's Sixth Report, Dec. 23, 1844, in Geue and Geue, *New Land Beckoned,* 47; Solms's Diary, Dec. 14–15, in Solms-Braunfels, *Voyage,* 109–110; also see Lindheimer to Engelmann, Jan. 22, 1845, in Goyne, *Life among the Texas Flora.*

21. *New Handbook of Texas,* s.v. "White, Samuel Addison" and "Chocolate, Texas"; Solms's Sixth Report, Dec. 23, 1844, in Geue and Geue, *New Land Beckoned,* 47; Solms's Diary, Dec. 16–17, 1844, in Solms-Braunfels, *Voyage,* 110 and n. 32. Solms often referred to his camp on Chocolate Bayou as Agua Dulce, but that was the name of the plantation.

22. Solms's Sixth Report, Dec. 23, 1844, in Geue and Geue, *New Land Beckoned,* 48–50.

23. Solms's Sixth Report, Dec. 23, 1844, in Geue and Geue, *New Land Beckoned,* 51–52.

24. Solms's Diary, Dec. 24–26, in Solms, *Voyage,* 111.

## CHAPTER 14

1. Solms's Report, Jul. 28, 1845, in Solms-Braunfels Archives, 30:158; Solms's Seventh Report, Jan. 1, 1845, and postscript, Jan. 5, 1845, in Geue and Geue, *New Land Beckoned,* 53, 54.

2. Fisher to Solms, Dec. 28, 1844, in Solms-Braunfels Archives, 59:91.

3. Solms to Fisher, Jan. 6, 1845, in Solms-Braunfels Archives, 40:99. On the $11,000 figure, see Solms's Eighth Report, Feb. 8, 1845, in Geue and Geue, *New Land Beckoned,* 55, 59.

4. Minutes of First Colonial Council Meeting, Jan. 7, 1845, in Fey, *New Braunfels,* 66.

5. Solms-Braunfels, *Voyage,* 114.

6. Minutes of Second Colonial Council Meeting, Jan. 8 [*sic*], 1845, in Fey, *New Braunfels,* 68. Solms's diary puts the meeting on Jan. 9. The diary was a contemporaneous writing and minutes were prepared after the fact.

7. Minutes of Second Colonial Council Meeting, Jan. 8 [*sic*], 1845, in Fey, *New Braunfels,* 68; Solms's Eighth Report, Feb. 8, 1845, in Geue and Geue, *New Land Beckoned,* 55, 59. See Meusebach to (Castell?), Jun. 3, 1845, in Solms-Braunfels Archive, 51:84, regarding the independent financial rights (and obstinacy) of the other colonial council members.

8. Solms's Eighth Report, Feb. 8, 1845, in Geue and Geue, *New Land Beckoned,* 55, 63.

9. Solms-Braunfels, *Voyage,* Jan. 13–14, 1845, at 114; Maverick, *Memoirs,* 69. Maverick puts the serenade at Solms's first visit, on Dec. 12, but this timing appears far more likely; see chapter 13, note 18.

10. Solms's Eighth Report, Feb. 8, 1845, in Geue and Geue, *New Land Beckoned,* 55–57; Solms-Braunfels, *Voyage,* Jan. 24–26, 1845, at 116; Fisher to Solms, Dec. 28, 1844, in Solms-Braunfels Archives, 59:91.

11. Solms's Eighth Report, Feb. 8, 1845, in Geue and Geue, *New Land Beckoned,* 55, 57; Solms-Braunfels, *Voyage,* Feb. 3, 1845, at 117.

12. Fisher and Miller to Jones, Jan. 6, 1844, in Colonization Papers, 2–9/27, folder 11; Castell to Solms, Jun. 25, 1844, in Solms-Braunfels Archives, 59:147.

13. Middleton, "Donelson's Mission to Texas," at 252 et seq.; Saligny to Guizot, Jan. 8, 1845, in Barker, *French Legation,* 605; ibid., Jan 3, 1845, at 602; ibid., Feb. 1, 1845, at 616. The cabinet demanded that Jones issue to Green a passport out of Texas; Cabinet to Jones, Dec. 30, 1844, in Jones, *Memoranda,* 412.

14. John Tyler, Fourth Annual Message, Dec. 3, 1844, *A Compilation of*

*the Messages and Papers of the Presidents, 1789–1897,* 20 vols., comp. James D. Richardson (Washington, D.C.: GPO, 1897), vol. 4, pt. 2, 334.

15. Saligny to Guizot, Dec. 27, 1844, in Barker, *French Legation,* 599.

16. Barba, *Life and Works of Armand Strubberg,* 40–49; Penniger, *Fredericksburg,* 24–26, 31–33, 36, 78, 80; Biesele, *History of the German Settlements,* 142, 183; King, *John O. Meusebach,* 125–129.

17. Solms-Braunfels, *Voyage,* Feb. 1, 1845, at 117 and n. 62.

18. Solms-Braunfels, *Voyage,* Feb. 7, 1844, at 118; Solms's Fifth Report, Oct. 25, 1844, in Geue and Geue, *New Land Beckoned,* 41, 43.

19. Solms's Eighth Report, Feb. 8, 1845, in Geue and Geue, *New Land Beckoned,* 62.

20. Solms still did not realize that Fisher had increased the number to two thousand, not two hundred, even though the joint resolution extending the contract deadline expressly said so.

21. Solms's Eighth Report, Feb. 8, 1845, in Geue and Geue, *New Land Beckoned,* 55, 62.

22. Solms-Braunfels, *Voyage,* Feb. 17, 1844, at 119.

## CHAPTER 15

1. Fisher to Solms, Dec. 28, 1844, in Solms-Braunfels Archive, 59:91; "Joint Resolution for the relief of Henry Castro and T. Taussaud," Jan. 27, 1845, in Gammel, *Laws,* 2:1078. The Fisher-Miller extension does not appear in Gammel; those familiar with the background of Gammel's work will understand why that might be the case.

2. Castro's Diary, Sep. 11, 1844, in Waugh, *Castro-Ville,* 20–21, lightly edited.

3. Castro's Diary, Sep. 27–28, 1844, in Waugh, *Castro-Ville,* 23–24.

4. Weaver, *Castro's Colony,* 61

5. Weaver, *Castro's Colony,* 62–63; Waugh, *Castro-Ville,* 30–31.

6. Weaver, *Castro's Colony,* 68–69; text of the agreement in Crook, *Henry Castro,* 208.

7. Solms's Ninth Report, Mar. 5, 1845, in Geue and Geue, *New Land Beckoned,* 63.

8. Solms's Ninth Report, Mar. 5, 1845, in Geue and Geue, *New Land Beckoned,* 63; Minutes of the Fourth Colonial Council Meeting, Mar. 4, 1845, in Fey, *New Braunfels,* 75.

9. The letter was actually a transcription of a speech by Mopechucope, styled as a letter, probably transcribed by Daniel Watson or John Conner.

"Letter from Mopechucope, Comanche Chief, to Houston," Mar. 21, 1844, in Winfrey and Day, *Indian Papers,* 2:6

10. "Minutes of the Council at the Falls of the Brazos," Oct. 7, 1844, in Winfrey and Day, *Indian Papers,* 2:103; "A Treaty Signed at Tehuacana Creek," Oct. 9, 1844, ibid., 2:114.

11. Solms-Braunfels, *Voyage,* Mar. 9, 1845, at 135. It would have been Juan Veramendi the younger; his father, born in Bexar in 1778 and once Spanish governor of Coahuila y Texas, had died in 1833, leaving seven children.

12. Solms-Braunfels, *Voyage,* Mar. 9, 1845, at 135; Solms's Tenth Report, Mar. 27, 1845, in Geue and Geue, *New Land Beckoned,* 66; Haas, *History of New Braunfels,* 22; *New Handbook of Texas,* s.v. "Navarro, José Antonio," "Veramendi, Juan Martin de," "Bastrop, Baron de," and "Veramendi Estate."

13. Biesele, *History of the German Settlements,* 116–117; Haas, *History of New Braunfels,* 22. The quiet title suit against the Bastrop heirs was successfully concluded in 1852, but the payment of the balance due was overlooked. The Veramendis' descendants later claimed that they had never been paid in full for their land and, long after New Braunfels had been established, sued to recover their land. The suit was resolved in favor of the citizens of New Braunfels in 1879. See Haas, *History of New Braunfels,* 22; Biesele, *History of the German Settlements,* 117–118 and n. 17.

14. Solms-Braunfels, *Voyage,* Mar. 16–19, 1845, at 137.

15. Lindheimer to Engelmann, Apr. 18, 1845, in Goyne, *Life among the Texas Flora,* 111.

16. Solms-Braunfels, *Voyage,* Mar. 21, 1845, at 137.

17. Seele, *Diary,* May 6, 1845, at 258.

18. Solms's "Evaluation of the Local Officials," in Fey, *New Braunfels,* 82.

19. Seele, *Diary,* May 8, 1845, at 260.

20. Solms-Braunfels, *Voyage,* Apr. 28, 1845, at 141; Solms's Eleventh Report, Apr. 30, 1845, in Geue and Geue, *New Land Beckoned,* 68.

21. Solms's Eleventh Report, Apr. 30, 1845, in Geue and Geue, *New Land Beckoned,* 68.

## CHAPTER 16

1. Saligny to Guizot, Mar. 18, 1845, in Barker, *French Legation,* 636; ibid., Mar. 24, 1845, at 637; Elliot to Aberdeen, Mar. 22, 1845, in Adams, *British Diplomatic Correspondence,* 460; ibid., Apr. 2, 1845, at 462. The letters of Mar. 24 and Apr. 2 are remarkable in their similarity.

2. Saligny to Guizot, Apr. 1, 1845, in Barker, *French Legation,* 638; Elliot to Aberdeen, Apr. 2, 1845, in Adams, *British Diplomatic Correspondence,* 462.

3. "Memorandum of a Conference," dated Mar. 29, 1845, encl. in Elliot to Aberdeen, Apr. 2, 1845, in Adams, *British Diplomatic Correspondence,* 462, 470.

4. Elliot to Aberdeen, Apr. 2, 1845, in Adams, *British Diplomatic Correspondence,* 462; Jones to Aberdeen, Mar. 31, 1845, ibid., 461.

5. Elliot to Aberdeen, Apr. 2, 1845, in Adams, *British Diplomatic Correspondence,* 462; Bankhead to Elliot, May 20, 1845, in Adams, *British Diplomatic Correspondence,* 487; Elliot to Jones, Apr. 5, 1845, in Jones, *Memoranda,* 443.

6. Bankhead to Elliot, May 20, 1845, in Adams, *British Diplomatic Correspondence,* 487. The remarkable document came to be known as the Smith-Cuevas Treaty, after two men who had only marginal roles in its coming to be. But calling it the Aberdeen-Guizot-Elliot-Saligny-Jones-Santa Anna Treaty would have instantly doomed it in Texas.

7. New Orleans *Daily Picayune,* May 21, 1845; New Orleans *Jeffersonian Republican,* May 21, 1845; *Niles National Register,* May 31, 1845.

8. Proclamation by the President of Texas, April 15, 1845, in Proclamations of the Republic of Texas, Texas State Library and Archives; ibid., May 5, 1845; Kennedy to Aberdeen, Apr. 25, 1845, in Adams, *British Diplomatic Correspondence,* 479; Saligny to Guizot, May 2, 1845, in Barker, *French Legation,* 656.

9. Marginal note by Guizot on Saligny to Guizot, Apr. 18, 1845, in Barker, *French Legation,* 652; Saligny to Guizot, May 21, 1845, ibid., 659.

10. Kennedy to Aberdeen, May 21, 1845, in Adams, *British Diplomatic Correspondence,* 490.

11. Solms-Braunfels, *Voyage,* May 19, 1845, at 150.

12. Elliot to Bankhead, Jun. 11, 1845, in Adams, *British Diplomatic Correspondence,* 498; ibid., (private letter), Jun. 11, 1845, at 501.

13. Smith, *Annexation,* 453; Allen to Jones, Jun. 5, 1845, in Jones, *Memoranda,* 466.

14. Select Committee Report, Aug. 27, 1845, in Texas, *Journals of the Convention,* at 329, 331.

15. Ordinance, Aug. 27, 1845, in Texas, *Journals of the Convention,* at 1305.

16. "Statement of the number of votes," Nov. 10, 1845, Texas State Library and Archives, www.tsl.state.tx.us/ref/abouttx/annexation/voters.html#images (accessed Jul. 12, 2008). The annexation ordinance passed by a vote of 4254 to 267, the constitution by 4174 to 312, and the colonization contract ordinance by 3790 to 454.

## CHAPTER 17

1. Meusebach to Leiningen (?), Jun. 3, 1845, in Solms-Braunfels Archives, 51:84.

2. The Mormons, if theirs was a colony, merely relocated in 1847 from their existing colony in Nauvoo; they lacked a state sponsor, which is a fundamental element of colonization. The prizes for both largest and last colonization in North America probably go to the 1922 Mennonite emigration from Canada to Chihuahua, Mexico.

3. A group of idealistic utopians known as "The Forty" were loosely associated with the Adelsverein and established a fifth settlement on the Llano, known as Bettina. Because it was not truly an Adelsverein venture, we consider it as separate from the other four.

4. Crook, *Henry Castro,* 111; Weaver, *Castro's Colony,* 85. The debts were in francs, and the conversion to dollars is approximate.

5. Weaver, *Castro's Colony,* 76–77, 80.

6. *Castro v. Dhanis and Associates,* District Court, Bexar County, Civil Action No. 384. Petition filed Mar. 5, 1848; Decree Spring Term 1849.

7. *McMullen v. Hodge,* 5 Tex. 34 (1849).

8. The scrip in question was Certificate No. 535, issued to Nepomuceno Flores on May 11, 1838. Flores transferred it to land speculator Smith on Jun. 25, 1840. The transaction is addressed in Crook, *Henry Castro,* but that passage misconstrues the nature of the scrip. It was a floating right to survey and patent land, not a deed to a specific parcel. Castro used the scrip to obtain a reliable Texas patent to land that he was also purchasing from McMullen, whose title was questionable.

9. *Castro v. Illies,* 13 Tex. 229 (1854); *Castro v. Illies,* 22 Tex. 479 (1858); Crook, *Henry Castro,* 172–176; Weaver, *Castro's Colony,* 120–121.

10. *Jones v. Garza,* 11 Tex. 186 (1853); *Jones v. Muisbach* [*sic*], 26 Tex. 235 (1862); *Dauchy v. Devilbiss,* 37 Tex. 93 (1873).

11. Re Castro, "An Act to perfect the Land Titles in Castro's Colony," Jan. 21, 1850, in Gammel, *Laws,* 3:497; "An Act extending the time for return of field-notes of Claimants to Land in Fisher and Miller's Colony and Castro's Colony," Feb. 1, 1854, ibid., 3:1469. Regarding the Adelsverein, "An Act to secure to the Colonists of Fisher and Miller's Colony the lands to which they may be entitled," Mar. 20, 1848, ibid., 3:146; repealed and replaced by "An Act to secure to the German Emigration Company and their Colonists the Lands to which they are entitled, and to adjust the liabilities of said company," Jan. 21, 1850, ibid., 3:492; "An Act extending the time for return of field-notes of Claimants to Land in Fisher and

Miller's Colony and Castro's Colony," Feb. 1, 1854, ibid., 3:1469; "An Act to enable Henry F. Fisher and Burchard Miller to perfect titles to the land for which certificates have been issued to them within the limits of Fisher and Miller's Grant," ibid., 1471; "An Act supplemental to 'An Act to secure to the German Emigration Company and their Colonists the lands to which they are entitled, and to adjust the liabilities of said Company,' approved January twenty-first, eighteen hundred and fifty," Feb. 3, 1854, ibid., 3:1479; "An Act ordering the return of certificates in Fisher & Miller's Colony," Feb. 11, 1860, ibid., 4:1443; "An Act to provide for the sale and settlement of the vacant and unappropriated alternate sections of Land in Fisher and Miller's Colony," Jan. 10, 1862, ibid., 5:478; "Joint Resolution concerning the vacant lands in Fisher and Miller's Colony," Feb. 27, 1875, ibid., 8:565.

12. Weaver, *Castro's Colony,* 117–119; King, *John O. Meusebach,* 154.

13. *Causici v. La Coste,* 20 Tex. 269 (1857).

14. Weaver, *Castro's Colony,* 133–135.

## CHAPTER 18

1. Solms-Braunfels, *Voyage,* May 28–Jun. 4, 1845, at 151–152.

2. Kennedy to Addington, Jun. 10, 1845, in Adams, *British Diplomatic Correspondence,* 494.

3. This and all other material from the memorandum are from "Memoir on American Affairs," written Dec. 1845, delivered Jan. 1846, in Solms-Braunfels, *Voyage,* 206–218.

4. "Harlington" (p. 218) must be Arlington, referring to navy yards and docks on the Anacostia and Potomac rivers at Washington, D.C.

5. *New Handbook of Texas,* s.v. "Solms-Braunfels, Prince Carl of."

# *Bibliography*


Adams, Ephraim Douglass, comp. *British Diplomatic Correspondence concerning the Republic of Texas, 1838–1846*. Austin: Texas State Historical Society, 1917.

———. *British Interests and Activities in Texas, 1836–1846*. Gloucester: Peter Smith, 1963.

Adelsverein. *Gesammelte Akenstucke des Vereins zum Schutze Deutsche Einweanderer in Texas*. Mainz: Victor von Zabern, 1845.

Barba, Preston Albert. *The Life and Works of Armand Strubberg*. Philadelphia: University of Pennsylvania, 1913.

Barker, Eugene C. "The Annexation of Texas." *Southwestern Historical Quarterly* 50 (1946): 49.

Barker, Nancy Nichols, trans. and ed. *The French Legation in Texas*. 2 vols. Austin: Texas State Historical Association, 1971, 1973.

Bartlett, John Russell. *Personal Narrative of Explorations and Incidents in Texas, New Mexico, California, Sonora, and Chihuahua*. New York: D. Appleton, 1854.

Benjamin, Gilbert Giddings. *The Germans in Texas*. Austin: Jenkins Publishing, 1974.

Biesele, Rudolph L. *The History of the German Settlements in Texas, 1831–1861*. Reprint. Austin: Eakin Press, [1931] 1987.

———. "Prince Solms's Trip to Texas, 1844–1845." *Southwestern Historical Quarterly* 40 (1936): 1.

Biggers, Don H. *German Pioneers in Texas*. Fredericksburg, Tex.: Fredericksburg Publishing, 1925.

Blanning, T. C. W. *The Nineteenth Century: Europe, 1789–1914*. Oxford: Oxford University Press, 2000.

Bollaert, William. *William Bollaert's Texas*. Edited by W. Eugene Hollon. Norman: University of Oklahoma Press, 1956.

Bowen, Frank C. *A Century of Atlantic Travel, 1830–1930*. Boston: Little, Brown, 1930.

Bracht, Viktor. *Texas in 1848*. Translated by Charles Frank Schmidt. Manchaca, Tex.: German-Texan Heritage Society, 1991.

Castro, Henri. *Papers, 1839–1846, 1884.* Center for American History, University of Texas at Austin.

Colonization Contracts. Texas General Land Office, Austin. Special Collection, box G055, files 2, 14, 24, 26, 27.

Colonization Papers. Texas State Library and Archives Commission, Austin. Boxes 2–9/23 (oversize), 2–9/26, 2–9/27 and 2–9/28.

Connor, Seymour V. *The Peters Colony of Texas.* Reprint. Austin: Texas State Historical Association, [1959] 2005.

Constant, L. *Texas, Das Verderben deutscher Auswanderer in Texas unter dem Schutze des Mainzer Vereins.* Berlin: G. Reimer, 1847.

Crook, Cornelia English. *Henry Castro: A Study of Early Colonization in Texas.* San Antonio, Tex.: St. Mary's University Press, 1988.

De la Teja, Jesus. *San Antonio de Bexar: A Community on New Spain's Northern Frontier.* Albuquerque: University of New Mexico Press, 1995.

Dienst, Alexander. "The Navy of the Republic of Texas." *Southwestern Historical Quarterly* 13 (1910): 85.

Dohmen, Frans J., trans. *Life and Memoirs of Emil Frederick Wurzbach, to Which Is Appended Some Papers of John Meusebach.* San Antonio, Tex.: Yanaguana Society, 1937.

Dresel Family Papers. San Antonio Public Library, San Antonio, Tex.

Edwards, Herbert Rook. "Diplomatic Relations between France and the Republic of Texas." *Southwestern Historical Quarterly* 20 (1917): 341.

Fey, Everett Anthony. *New Braunfels: The First Founders.* Austin: Eakin Press, 1994.

Francaviglia, Richard V. *From Sail to Steam: Four Centuries of Texas Maritime History, 1500–1900.* Austin: University of Texas Press, 1998.

Franz-Willing, Georg. *Die Auswanderung der Deutschen nach Texas, Nordamerica und Ungarn.* Munchen: Georg Granz, 1844.

Fremantle, Arthur James Lyon, Sir. *Three Months in the Southern States, April—June 1863.* Mobile, Ala.: S. H. Goetzel, 1864.

Gammel, Hans Peter Marius, comp. *The Laws of Texas, 1822–1897.* 10 vols. Austin: Gammel Book, 1898.

Garrison, George P., ed. *Texan Diplomatic Correspondence.* 3 vols. Annual Report of the American Historical Association, 1907/8. Washington, D.C.: Government Printing Office, 1908, 1911.

Geiser, Samuel Wood. *Naturalists of the Frontier.* 2d ed. Dallas, Tex.: University Press, 1948.

Geue, Chester W., and H. Ethel Geue, eds. *A New Land Beckoned.* New and enlarged ed. Baltimore: Genealogical Publishing, 1982.

Gish, Theodore. "Carl, Prince of Solms-Braunfels, First Commissioner-

General of the Adelsverein in Texas: Myth, History and Fiction." *Yearbook of German-American Studies* 16 (1981): 79.

———. "Ferdinand Lindheimer's *New Braunfelser Zeitung:* Portrait of a German-Texan Weekly, 1852–1872." *Yearbook of German-American Studies* 17 (1982): 71.

Goyne, Minetta Altgelt. *A Life among the Texas Flora: Ferdinand Lindheimer's Letters to George Engelmann.* College Station: Texas A&M University Press, 1991.

Green, Rena Maverick. *Samuel Maverick, Texan: 1803–1870.* San Antonio: n.p., 1952.

Greer, James Kimmins. *Colonel Jack Hays, Texas Frontier Leader and California Builder.* New York: E. P. Dutton, 1952.

Haas, Oscar. *History of New Braunfels and Comal County, Texas, 1844–1946.* Austin: Steck, 1968.

Hamerow, Theodore S. *Restoration, Revolution, Reaction: Economics and Politics in Germany, 1815–1871.* Princeton, N.J.: Princeton University Press, 1958.

Hecke, J. Valentin. *Reise durch die Vereinigten Staaten von Nord-Amerika in den Jahren 1818 und 1819.* Berlin: In Commission bei H. Ph. Petri, 1821.

Hendricks, Sterling Brown. "The Somervell Expedition to the Rio Grande, 1842." *Southwestern Historical Quarterly* 23 (1919): 112.

Hoffman, August. Papers. Center for American History, University of Texas at Austin.

Hogan, William Ransom. *The Texas Republic: A Social and Economic History.* Reprint. Austin: Texas State Historical Association, [1946] 2007.

Holborn, Hajo. *A History of Modern Germany, 1648–1840.* Princeton, N.J.: Princeton University Press, 1964.

———. *A History of Modern Germany, 1840–1945.* Princeton, N.J.: Princeton University Press, 1969.

Houston, Sam. *The Writings of Sam Houston.* 8 vols. Edited by Amelia W. Williams and Eugene C. Barker. Austin: University of Texas Press, 1940.

Huth, Ferdinand Louis. Papers, 1778–1937. Center for American History, University of Texas at Austin.

Jones, Anson. *Memoranda and Official Correspondence Relating to the Republic of Texas, Its History and Annexation, 1836 to 1846.* Reprint. Chicago: Rio Grande Press, [1859] 1966.

Jordan, Jonathan W. *Lone Star Navy: Texas, the Fight for the Gulf of Mexico, and the Shaping of the American West.* Washington, D.C.: Potomac, 2006.

Jordan, Terry G. *German Seed in Texas Soil: Immigrant Farmers in Nineteenth-Century Texas.* Austin: University of Texas Press, 1966.

Jordan, Terry G., and Marlis Anderson, ed. and trans. "Letters of a German Pioneer in Texas." *Southwestern Historical Quarterly* 69 (1966): 463.

Kaufmann, Wilhelm. *Die Deutschen im der amerikanischen Burgerkriege.* Munich: R. Oldenbourg, 1911.

Kennedy, William. *Texas: The Rise, Progress and Prospects of the Republic of Texas.* Reprint. Clifton, N.J.: Augustus M. Kelley, 1974.

King, Irene Marschall. *John O. Meusebach, German Colonizer in Texas.* Austin: University of Texas Press, 1967.

Kleberg, Rosa. "Early Experiences in Texas II." *Southwestern Historical Quarterly* 2 (1898): 170.

Lagarde, Francois. *The French in Texas.* Austin: University of Texas Press, 2003.

La Vere, David. *The Texas Indians.* College Station: Texas A&M University Press, 2004.

Lich, Glen E. "Archives of the German Adelsverein, Beinecke Rare Book and Manuscript Library, Yale University." *Southwestern Historical Quarterly* 91 (1988): 301.

———. *The German Texans.* San Antonio: University of Texas Institute of Texan Cultures, 1981.

Malsch, Brownson. *Indianola, the Mother of Western Texas.* Abilene, Tex.: State House Press, 1988.

Maverick Family. Papers, 1660–1938. Center for American History, University of Texas at Austin.

Maverick, Mary A. *Memoirs of Mary A. Maverick.* Reprint. San Antonio: Maverick Publishing, [1921] 2005.

Meusebach, John O. "Answers to Interrogatories," *Mary C Paschal et al., v. Theodore Evans,* District Court of McCulloch County Texas, Nov. Term 1893. Austin: Pemberton Press, 1964.

Middleton, Annie. "Donelson's Mission to Texas in Behalf of Annexation." *Southwestern Historical Quarterly* 24 (1920): 247.

Monken, Bernard. "Hardships of a German Family." *Frontier Times,* November 1965: 36.

Morgenthaler, Jefferson. *The German Settlement of the Texas Hill Country.* Boerne, Tex.: Mockingbird Books, 2007.

Nance, Joseph Milton. *After San Jacinto: The Texas-Mexican Frontier, 1836–1841.* Austin: University of Texas Press, 1963.

*New Handbook of Texas.* 6 vols. Austin: Texas State Historical Association, 1996. Online edition, www.tsha.utexas.edu, 1999.

Olmsted, Frederick Law. *Journey through Texas: A Saddle-Trip on the Southwestern Frontier.* Edited by James Howard. Austin: Von Boeckmann-Jones Press, 1962.

Penniger, Robert. *Fredericksburg, Texas: The First Fifty Years.* Translated by C. L. Wisseman. Fredericksburg Publishing, 1971.

Redman, Alvin. *The House of Hanover.* New York: Funk and Wagnalls, 1968.

Roemer, Ferdinand. *Roemer's Texas, 1845 to 1847.* Translated by Oswald Mueller. Austin: Eakin Press, 1995.

Santleben, August. *A Texas Pioneer.* New York: Neale Publishing, 1910.

Schultz, Johann Heinrich Siegfried. *Die deutsche Ansiedelung in Texas besonderer Abdruck einer Reihe das Unternehmen des Vereins zum Schutze deutscher Einwanderer in Texas besprechender.* Bonn: Bei Friedrich Encke, 1845.

Schulze, Hagen. *Germany: A New History.* Translated by Deborah Lucas Schneider. Cambridge, Mass.: Harvard University Press, 1988.

Seele, Hermann. *The Cypress and Other Writings of a German Pioneer in Texas.* Translated by Edward C. Beritenkamp. Austin: University of Texas Press, 1979.

———. *The Diary of Hermann Seele and Seele's Sketches from Texas.* Translated by Theodore Gish. Austin: German-Texan Heritage Society, 1995.

Sheppard, Francis. *London: A History.* Oxford: Oxford University Press, 1998.

Showalter, Dennis. *The Wars of German Unification.* London: Hodder Arnold, 2004.

Siegel, Stanley. *A Political History of the Texas Republic, 1836–1845.* Austin: University of Texas Press, 1956.

Siemering, August. "Texas, Her Past, Her Present, Her Future." *Texas Vorwaerts,* September 21, 1894.

Simms, Brendan. *The Struggle for Mastery in Germany, 1779–1850.* New York: St. Martin's Press, 1998.

Sinclair, Harold. *The Port of New Orleans.* New York: Doubleday, Doran, 1942.

Smith, Justin H. *The Annexation of Texas.* New York: Barnes and Noble, 1941.

Solms-Braunfels Archives. Center for American History, University of Texas at Austin.

Solms-Braunfels, Carl. *Texas, 1844–1845.* Houston: Anson Jones Press, 1936.

———. *Voyage to North America, 1844–1845.* Translated by Wolfram M. Von-Maszewski. Denton: University of North Texas Press, 2000.

Sophienburg Museum and Archives. Records and vertical files. New Braunfels, Tex.

Sörgel, Alwin H. *A Sojourn in Texas.* Translated by W. M. von Maszewski. San Marcos: German-Texan Heritage Society, 1992.

Sowell, A. J. *Early Settlers and Indian Fighters of Southwest Texas.* Reprint. Abilene: State House Press, [1900] 1986.

Strubberg, Freidrich Armand, Collection. Western Americana Collection. Beinecke Rare Book and Manuscript Library, New Haven, Conn.

Tetzlaff, Otto W., trans. and ed. *The Emigrant to Texas: A Handbook and Guide.* Burnet: Eakin, 1979.

Texas. *Journals of the Convention, assembled at the city of Austin on the Fourth of July, 1845, for the purpose of framing a constitution for the State of Texas.* Austin: Miner and Cruger, printers to the Convention, 1845.

Thran, Jakob. *Meine Auswanderung nach Texas unter dem Schutze des Mainzer Vereins.* Berlin: E. Krause, 1848.

Tiling, Moritz. *History of the German Element in Texas from 1820–1850.* Houston: n.p., 1913.

Trease, Geoffrey. *London: A Concise History.* New York: Charles Scribner's Sons, 1975.

United Kingdom, Foreign Office. "General Correspondence before 1906 for Consulates in Baden, Bavaria, Coburg, Frankfurt, Hesse-Darmstadt, Saxony and Wurttemberg. From Mr. Strangeways. 1844 June–Dec." FO 30/86.

Von Hinueber, Caroline. "Life of German Pioneers in Early Texas." *Southwestern Historical Quarterly* 2 (1899): 227.

Wade, Maria F. *The Native Americans of the Texas Edwards Plateau, 1582–1799.* Austin: University of Texas Press, 2003.

Waugh, Julia Nott. *Castro-Ville and Henry Castro.* Reprint. Castroville, Tex.: Castro Colonies Heritage Association, [1934] 1986.

Weaver, Bobby D. *Castro's Colony: Empresario Development in Texas, 1842–1865.* College Station: Texas A&M University Press, 1985.

Williams, Elgin. *The Animating Pursuits of Speculation: Land Traffic in the Annexation of Texas.* Reprint. New York: AMS Press, [1949] 1968.

Winfrey, Dorman H., and James M. Day. *The Indian Papers of Texas and the Southwest, 1825–1916.* 5 vols. Reprint. Austin: Texas State Historical Association, [1966] 1995.

Yoakum, H. *History of Texas from Its First Settlement in 1685 to Its Annexation to the United States in 1846.* 2 vols. Reprint. Austin: Steck-Vaughn, [1855] n.d.

# Index

Note: Page references in *italics* refer to maps and figures. Page references followed by "n" refer to endnotes.

ISBN-13: 978-1-60344-119-3
ISBN-10: 1-60344-119-0

52995

9 781603 441193